Date Due

Jan 30 '5	May 5 67		
Apr 29 '57	Jul 23 '60		
May 14'57			
Jun 2 58	AUG 2 7 1990		
Dec 8 58	OCT 2 6 1992		
Dec 17 59			
Jun 2 60			
Nov 17 60			
Dec 1 60			
Feb 22 61			
Oct 3 61			
Oct 16 67			
Jan 18 62			
Apr 23 65			
Jul 13 66			
Apr 27 67			

Demco 293-5

Understanding Our Behavior

THE PSYCHOLOGY OF PERSONAL AND SOCIAL ADJUSTMENT

Understanding
Our Behavior

THE PSYCHOLOGY OF PERSONAL AND SOCIAL ADJUSTMENT

BY *Lester D. Crow* AND *Alice Crow*

BROOKLYN COLLEGE

NEW YORK *Alfred A. Knopf* 1956

L.C. catalog card number: 56–5892
© *Lester D. Crow and Alice Crow 1956*

THIS IS A BORZOI BOOK
PUBLISHED BY ALFRED A. KNOPF, INC.

FIRST EDITION

Preface

*A*ʟʟ of us, probably, are sometimes surprised by what we ourselves do and say, as well as by the actions and displayed attitudes of our friends and acquaintances. Our behavior appears to be governed by impulse rather than by reason. We cannot always explain the underlying causes of our likes and our dislikes, our motives and our goals, or our reactions to other people and the effect of our behavior upon them. We can observe *what* people do in their relations with one another but we are often unable to understand the *why*.

Human interactions are extremely complex. They reflect the influence upon us of our differing inherited characteristics and the many varying environmental conditions and situations to which we are exposed during our life experiences. We need to recognize the significance of these differences in order to improve our own personal and social adjustments and to help children and adolescents develop constructive life patterns.

In *Understanding Our Behavior: The Psychology of Personal and Social Adjustment*, the authors have attempted to present some of the psychological principles that are fundamental to personal and social adjustment. Beginning with the basic factors of adjustment, they trace the development of personality from birth onward and discuss the dynamic interrelations that exist among the various aspects of adjustment: mental, attitudinal, and emotional. Consideration is then given to the possible thwartings, frustrations, and conflicts that are likely to occur to a greater or lesser degree in the life of an individual, and his attempts to resolve them. The mental and emotional disturbances and disorders that can result from failure to achieve adequate adjustment are treated briefly, and therapeutic measures are described. Since emotional disturbances are too often rooted in sexual maladjustment, some of the adjustment problems associated with sex are considered in the light of their prevention.

Desirable and positive life adjustment is not a general, over-all state of being. Rather, it is specific in terms of a person's particular needs, wants, and desires in relation to the needs and interests of other persons with whom he is associated in his home, in his occupational work, and in his recreational and social activities. Hence suggestions are offered concerning the meeting of problems that are likely to arise as one attempts to adjust to the demands of these various areas of living.

Throughout the book the approach is positive. The prevention of inadequate adjustments and the preservation of personally satisfying and socially acceptable life adjustments are stressed. *Understanding Our Behavior* has a dual purpose. It is aimed (1) at enabling teachers, parents, and other adults interested in young people better to help children and adolescents develop constructive patterns of adjustment, and (2) at assisting adults to gain a greater understanding of the factors that govern human behavior in various life situations.

LESTER D. CROW
ALICE CROW

Contents

Understanding Our Behavior

THE PSYCHOLOGY OF PERSONAL AND SOCIAL ADJUSTMENT

CHAPTER One

The Bases of Human Adjustment

M UCH of our daily activity is concerned with adjusting, fitting, or regulating. Windows, watches, carburetors, microscopes, heating devices, and innumerable other mechanical instruments are adjusted in one or another way to increase their effectiveness. Adjustment refers to the extent to which an object fits the purpose for which it is intended. A door is adjusted or fitted to the space that it is to fill; a watch is adjusted so that it will keep accurate time; the speed of a train is regulated for safe travel over its tracks; the weight of one's clothing is adjusted to the demands of weather conditions. In all these cases the purpose of the adjusting or fitting process is to satisfy the needs or interests of those persons who use them. In a similar way we attempt to adjust situations and conditions in our environment in such ways that our daily program of activities runs smoothly. The housewife organizes her daily routines to meet the needs and interests of the family. Business or industrial management is concerned with the adjustment of worker responsibilities. The student adjusts his daily schedule of activities to include adequate time to be devoted to his studies. Some adjustments are relatively simple; they result from previous experiences in similar situations. The adjustment of a delicate mechanism or of a difficult situation, however, is a job for the specialist.

We are constantly attempting to adjust or fit environmental elements to meet our needs and interests. At the same time we are engaged in the process of adjusting ourselves—our attitudes and behavior—to meet satisfactorily the demands made upon us by our personal problems and our social relationships.

The Process of Human Adjustment

T H E R E are two schools of thought concerning the process of human adjustment. According to one point of view, an individual is personally responsible for his behavior and attitudes in all areas of his life relationships. Emphasis is placed upon the individual's ability to chart his course of action; he is "master of his fate." Contrariwise, an individual's beliefs, attitudes, and general patterns of adjustment at any one time are determined to a great extent by his previous experiences and their effects upon his personality. We recognize the fact that an individual possesses the power to select, and to apply to himself the environmental elements and the experiences that may seem to him to be best suited to satisfactory adjustment. At the same time, however, we cannot disregard the operation in a person's life of scientifically evolved principles of cause and effect.

Basic principles of adjustment. To the lay person, adjustment often represents a relatively vague belief that to achieve a desired condition or situation will result in successful adjustment. The trained person recognizes the fact that human beings of all ages constantly are in the process of adjusting to this or that condition or situation, or to interpersonal relationships. They recognize also that the form of the adjustment may or may not be conducive to the attainment of personal success or of social welfare. An individual's adjustment is adequate, wholesome, or healthful to the extent that he has established a harmonious relationship between himself and the conditions, situations, and persons who comprise his physical and social environment. An individual who is unable to surmount obstacles in his path to achievement or who is rejected by the members of his group is inadequately adjusted. Excessive failure to achieve, or complete rejection is likely to be associated with serious maladjustments.

When we refer to the adjustment status of an individual we generally are considering his habitual patterns of behavior and attitude. One or another characteristic attitude or form of behavior may constitute a significant factor of adjustment, however. For example, serious illness or extreme fatigue may be accompanied by a display of inadequate adjustment. Reaction to failure in a particular experience is closely associated with an individual's general adjustment pattern. Two students take an important examination. Neither one succeeds in passing it. One of the students adjusts to his failure by studying more intensively; he passes a second examination. The other student may have as much ability as the first student, but he is discouraged by the failure; he refuses to take a second examination.

Scientifically interpreted, the term *adjustment* implies a cause-and-effect relationship. The study of human adjustment poses a problem, in that the kind and degree of adjustment achieved by an individual usually are dependent upon a multiplicity of causes. Moreover, human nature is so complex that it is almost impossible to assert didactically that any combination of causes is certain to have a specific effect upon an individual's behavioral pattern. The same environmental factor may become the cause of stress or strain for one individual but have little or no effect upon another person.

Human beings are alike in many ways, but they differ from one another in physical constitution and health status, degree of mental alertness and emotional status. Temperamental differences show themselves in individual likes and dislikes, compelling interests and ambitions, and attitudes and behavior toward other people. Yet, there is one thing that most individuals have in common—the desire to become contented and well-adjusted men and women.

During his entire lifetime every human being is struggling toward the attainment of one or another goal—self-expression, self-realization, adventure, economic and social security. Overt behavior responses are the expressions of inner desires, urges, wants, interests, ambitions, and attitudes. A person's inner compulsion toward activity and its overt manifestation are influenced by the interests, ambitions, and attitudes of other persons. When an individual and the other members of his group are motivated by similar interests and ambitions, their cooperative activities tend to be productive of individual and group satisfaction and interadjustment. It is as a person sets himself to achieve completely ego-satisfying rather than socio-satisfying goals that he is likely to encounter problems of adjustment that seem to defy adequate resolution.

Areas of Adjustment

L I F E consists of many experiences that need to be interwoven or integrated from day to day. A normal adult probably is, or at some time in his life has been, motivated by the desire to marry, rear children, experience a happy home life, and earn success in a chosen vocation. In addition, he desires to enjoy the companionship of friends and associates of his choice, and to spend his leisure time in interesting and relaxing activities. He also strives to achieve a position of respect among his associates, to enjoy democratic rights, and to establish the foundation of an economically and socially secure old age.

Children, adolescents, and adults are faced with the problem of so ordering their attitudes and behavior that they achieve maximum success and satisfaction in their home, school, work, and social activities, without interfering with or limiting the interests, ambitions, and activities of other members of the group. Adjustment to environmental conditions and human interrelationships is a gradually developing process that begins early in childhood and continues throughout life. Moreover, an understanding of what constitutes good adjustment and a willingness to become a well-adjusted person probably can be achieved best through the study and application of the psychological principles that are basic to the development of healthful living and wholesome behavior.

Family adjustment. The family is the basic unit of society. It is generally agreed that as the home is so will be the larger social group. The intimate relations that are inherent in home and family life may build up either closely knit loyalties or disrupting discords.

Bickering, faultfinding, resentments, display of extreme individualism, disregard for the rights of others, and shirking of responsibility in the home are more than likely to be carried over into other group relationships. Through the centuries the home has changed gradually from an independent autocracy dominated by the "head" of the family into a more or less loosely organized social unit. Former rigid parental control of child behavior and more recent child self-assertion can find a meeting ground through a conscious effort to build the home upon a foundation of cooperative family interrelations that are aimed at the healthful development of every member of the family group.

Educational adjustment. A young person's degree of successful adjustment in his learning experiences is affected by many factors: the learner's degree of mental ability; learning readiness; interests and ambitions; appropriateness of curricular offerings; teacher attitudes, and teaching techniques. Problems of adjustment arise in the school life of a young person when or if any one of these factors is inadequate to help him select and engage in the kind of educational experiences that will prepare him for successful participation in his present and future life activities.

To provide proper financial support for education is the responsibility of the nation, state, and local community. The value of education as a means of improved educational adjustment is receiving increased recognition. Better educational facilities are made available for children and adolescents; educational opportunities are being extended to meet adult needs for continued schooling. Adequate financial aid is needed to provide extensive and intensive education. Yet money alone cannot solve all the educational problems of the school community. Educational leaders are faced with the problem of supplying the kind of education that will help young and older learners achieve success in their marital, family, occupational, and social adjustments.

A well-balanced, forward-looking educational program is essential to the development of individual and group adjustment to personal and social demands. The task of organizing and administering such a program is tremendous. Will individual communities be able to meet this responsibility? How much state aid will be needed? Should the federal government give financial assistance when or if a community cannot meet its educational obligations? Are taxpayers willing to support nursery schools and kindergartens? To what extent is the public responsible for maintaining junior colleges, colleges, universities, and special schools? What is to be the content of study? How extensive can be the equipment? What is to be the maximum of educational preparation and of remuneration for teachers? How can community facilities and resources be utilized as learning aids? These are some of the educational problems that are closely related to educational adjustment.

Occupational adjustment.   Job adjustment is dependent upon job conditions, worker attitudes, and degree of efficiency. A worker's chances to perform adequately on the job and to experience personal satisfaction in the work are conditioned by: vocational selection based upon personal interest in the work and ability to meet its demands; appropriate and adequate preparation; available job opportunities; healthful working conditions; intelligent and understanding supervision; pleasant coworker relationships, and adequate financial remuneration. Poor worker adjustment in any one of these areas may give rise to worker inefficiency, discontent, resentment, feelings of frustration, or seriously maladjusted behavior.

This is a critical period of occupational and economic adjustment. High cost of living has brought about disagreement concerning adequacy of remuneration. Technological changes are opening new occupation fields and closing others. Fear of economic security interferes with the occupational adjustment of the worker; uncertainty as to the most effective ways in which human resources and occupational opportunities can be integrated constitutes a serious problem of management adjustment.

Social and community adjustment.   Participation in organized or informal group activity is a test of an individual's power to adjust his own attitudes and interests to the interests, needs, or rights of other people. His interest in community welfare and his cooperative attitude toward community projects are as important as is the exercise of similar interest and attitudes in home and work relationships. In all these associations a person experiences many problems of adjustment that become increasingly serious as group needs and interests change with changing conditions.

Community problems that demand intelligent leadership and citizen cooperation include safety regulations, recreational facilities, health protection, adequate housing, and efficient transportation. Community well-being is dependent not only upon the provision of these environmental conditions, but also upon the displayed attitude and the behavior of community members. Good individual or group adjustment can be hindered by frequent occurrences of asocial acts committed by some of the group members. Accounts of burglaries, muggings, assaults, reckless driving, heavy drinking, fights, and illicit sex relations are featured in the daily newspapers. Apprehension of offenders and prevention of antisocial behavior constitute important areas of community concern.

The Scientific Approach to the Study of Adjustment

A STUDENT of human nature is interested in gaining an intelligent and objective understanding of human behavior and adjustment. Through his study he hopes to improve his own personal and social adjustments and to gain greater ability to help other people effect desirable changes in their attitudes and behavior patterns. The complexity of human nature precludes the possibility to establish simple psychological principles that apply equally well to all phases of human interactions. Psychologists differ among themselves in their explanation of human development and adjustment. Some of these schools of thought represent radical differences from one another. One of the problems of the student is to decide upon the explanation that appears to him to be the most valid. This may involve his ability and willingness to select whatever seems to be pertinent in each of the various points of view, and to achieve thereby his own explanation of the adjustive process.

Another important area of study is concerned with the techniques to be employed in an evaluation of an individual's kind and degree of adjustment, and the basic causes of his adjustment status. In this discussion we review briefly the points of view that are representative of several outstanding schools of psychological thought. This is followed by a consideration of the evaluation of causative factors of adjustment.

Contemporary theories of adjustment through learning. The newborn child possesses certain potentialities of growth and development. The developmental and adjustment patterns that he achieves during his life span are associated closely with the many various learning experiences in which he engages. Viewed broadly, to learn is to change. Since adjusting implies the bringing about of changes within one's self, adjustments can be considered to be the products of learning. What takes place within the individual during the learning or adjusting process is not yet completely understood. Study and research have led to the formulation of various theories of learning, however.

The theory of *connectionism*, propounded by Edward Thorndike, is an attempt to explain learning as bond connection between stimulus and response. Thorndike's well-known laws of exercise and effect apply to the adjustment process, in that an individual tends to adjust to a situation or condition to the extent that he has experience with it. Moreover, a person is likely to adjust satisfactorily to a situation or condition, or to an interpersonal relationship, if he derives pleasure from the experience. Inadequate adjustment is associated with annoying or unsatisfying experience.

Behaviorism and *conditioning* place emphasis upon learning and adjustment as outcomes of the effects upon the learner of environmental learning stimulations. Neither John B. Watson, a proponent of behaviorism, nor Ivan Pavlov, an experimenter in animal conditioning, recognized the significance in the adjustive process of an individual's inner drives, ideas, or attitudes. The kind of adjustment achieved by an individual in any of his life relationships is viewed objectively to be the effect upon his overt behavior of controlled environmental factors of learning.

The *Gestalt* theory stresses the totality of human reaction to stimulation by a whole or entire learning situation. According to the gestaltists, a person adjusts to a situation in the form of a configuration or Gestalt, in terms of his valence (the positive or negative stimulus influence upon him of objects, situations, or conditions). Through insight the individual gains an understanding of his adjustment problems and learns to react to them as an integrated person. The Gestalt theory represents a revolt against Thorndike's theory of specific synaptic connections as the bases of learning and adjustment.

Sigmund Freud's *psychoanalytic* approach to adjustment is diametrically opposed to the behavioristic explanation of learning. Freud emphasized the significance of emotional experiences as determiners of behavior reactions and as adjustment motivators. Psychoanalysts accept Freud's theory that the "unconscious mind" is the seat of maladjustments that are rooted in previous forgotten experiences that had damaged the individual's ego. According to Freud, there is a close relationship between an individual's kind and degree of adjustment and the functioning of his *id, ego,* and *superego.*

The *functional* approach to learning places emphasis upon the value in learning and adjustment of overt activity and breadth of experience. This point of view is gaining considerable attention among educators. John Dewey's interpretation of learning as problem solving is coming to be applied in the solution of personal problems of adjustment. Guidance counselors are achieving commendable facility in the utilization of nondirective techniques to stimulate inadequately adjusted individuals to think through their personal problems toward a possible resolution. Most psychologists do not adhere strictly to any one psychological theory. Their approach is *eclectic,* in that they select from each theory of learning whatever they consider to be pertinent in specific learning or adjustive situations.

Purpose and function of evaluation.   Regardless of the psychological approach that is utilized in the resolution of adjustment problems there is needed a recognition of the nature of a problem, its relation to the client's total personality pattern, and an evaluation of possible or probably causal factors.

The practical and common-sense approach to an evaluation of an individual's adjustment status would seem to be to observe him in action. In his daily activities and in his relationships with his associates an individual is likely to exhibt certain habitual attitudes, interests, and forms of behavior that are either self-satisfying and socially acceptable, or self-disturbing and socially disapproved. To observe or to experience, however, is not synonymous with to understand or to improve. Moreover, good adjustment tends to induce better adjustment; inadequate adjustment is likely to intensify the inadequacy. According to Anderson:

> Desirable behavior also carries an overlay of social consequences. This overlay in many instances makes adaptation easier and simpler than it otherwise would be. When we say that "nothing succeeds like success," we mean that the well-adjusted person to a large extent is continually creat-

ing an environment which makes it easier for him to adjust, and that the poorly adjusted person is continually creating an environment which makes it more difficult for him to adjust.[1]

Through casual observation of a person's behavior may come a recognition of the fact that the individual observed is displaying what is considered to be good or inadequate adjustment. Conclusions that are based upon informal, non-controlled observation are likely to be highly subjective. The observer's own degree of personal adjustment, prejudices, and set of values exercise a potent effect upon the objectivity, accuracy, and adequacy of his observation. Valid observation is controlled in terms of definite purpose and specific area of observation, is conducted by a trained observer, and is free from personal bias or emotional involvement. Moreover, the findings of the observation are reported immediately and accurately.

To observe and to record behavior characteristics do not constitute the whole of evaluation, since good or inadequate behavior is the overt manifestation of inner states. We need to discover, in so far as it is possible to do so, what inner urges, interests, desires, worries, feelings of thwarting, or frustrations motivate the observed behavior. Of equal importance is the analysis of the environmental conditions or situations that are the causes of inner motivation of overt behavior. Hence scientific techniques need to be utilized to obtain pertinent data that can serve as the bases of objective and valid evaluation.

Many measuring instruments have been devised to evaluate various human attributes and their effect upon behavior. These techniques vary in validity (measuring what they are supposed to measure) and reliability (yielding consistent results). The performance of an individual on one or a few of these measuring instruments does not constitute sufficient evidence upon which to evaluate an individual's kind and degree of adjustment or the underlying causes of his adjustment status. A test, scale, or other measuring device can be regarded as *one* tool of evaluation, however. The administration of a measuring instrument may yield some insight into the nature of a client's adjustment problem.

[1] J. E. Anderson, *The Psychology of Development and Personal Adjustment* (New York: Henry Holt and Company, 1949), p. 12.

Scientifically conducted experimentation is an excellent method by which to evaluate the background causes of good adjustment or maladjustment. The experimenter controls or isolates the specific situation, condition, or element to be studied. He then observes, under controlled conditions, the particular factors that he is attempting to study. The validity of the experimenter's conclusions is in direct ratio to the adequacy of his training, to his honesty and accuracy in setting up the conditions of the experiment, to the objectivity of his observations, and to his unbiased interpretation of the findings.

As a result of many carefully controlled and adequately conducted experiments, some excellent principles of behavior causation have been evolved. Those that deal with learner adjustment are extremely helpful to school people. Certain other cause-effect relationships that are associated with worker adjustment have served as the bases of improved working conditions and consequent better worker adjustment. Sociological studies and experiments have yielded data that have been helpful in the improvement of community conditions.

Unfortunately too many people are prone to draw false conclusions from inadequately obtained data, from too small a sampling of cases, or from selected rather than unselected samplings. For example, the untrained person often generalizes in terms of a few instances with which he has happened to have experience. Many superstitions fall into this category; various social phenomena are explained incorrectly.

You probably have heard a layman assert with confidence that the mentally superior are physically weak; the most significant cause of juvenile delinquency is either a broken home or low socioeconomic status; the "only" child is certain to be socially maladjusted; blonds are fickle; short men suffer feelings of inferiority; the number 13 is unlucky; one death in the neighborhood always is followed by two others, or those who can, do—others, teach. The number of these inadequate cause-effect generalizations could be multiplied many times. Put to the test of scientific experimentation, however, such generalizations have been shown to be inaccurate.

Throughout this book attention is directed toward a consideration of those factors of adjustment that have some validity in that they have been subjected to scientific study. Since ability to adjust changes with changing conditions, however, study and experimentation need to be continued as a process of isolating causative elements and relating them to their possible effects.

The dynamics of human adjustment. The term *behavior* implies inner and/or overt activity. At no time is a functioning organism completely passive. For example, a man is sitting in a chair in a relaxed position. He does not speak or change his position. Except for overt signs of breathing, he appears to be in a passive state. Yet he may be daydreaming, thinking through a problem, or creating a bit of poetry or prose which later he will transcribe on paper.

An individual is being stimulated constantly by animate and inanimate factors of this environment. Human behavior is the resultant of interaction between the individual and his environment. Human behavior is dynamic. There is continuous activity that involves the functioning of the various phases of the "self," and is affected by inner purposes and external influences.

Our understanding of the *why* and the *how* of human adjustment is far from complete. Without much more intensive study we cannot expect to obtain all or even most of the answers. One reason for this lies in the complexity of the human organism as well as in the multitudinous array of environmental factors by which the organism is affected. Moreover, existing superstitions or false beliefs concerning the causes of human behavior are deep-seated because of their emotional implications. Hence they cannot be changed or eliminated easily. Progress is being made, however, in that there is evidenced among lay persons as well as among professionals a growing interest in and application of scientifically sound psychological principles. It is generally recognized that the human organism functions as a whole and that the dynamic interaction of all the elements of behavior results either in wholesome, healthy adjustment, or in inadequate adjustment or serious maladjustment.

▶ **Questions and Problems for Discussion**

1. By examples from your own experience, justify the statement that life is a struggle.

2. Explain the connotation of the term *adjustment*. List the adjustments that you make in your daily human interrelations.

3. Trace the story of one of the following: the struggle for political freedom; the industrial revolution; the struggle for economic rights.

4. Name as many as you can of the social, economic, and political world changes that are taking place at present. Show how you, as an individual, are or will be affected by these changes.

5. From personal experiences, describe some of the problems of home adjustment. Present specific ways in which these can be solved.

6. Name some of the basic educational needs of individuals. In what way are you attempting to meet your own educational needs?

7. To what extent should education be a local, state, or federal function?

8. State some of the causes of labor-management disagreements. Show how cooperative action might reduce labor-management difficulties.

9. Enumerate community problems of adjustment other than those discussed in this chapter. Discuss them in terms of your personal relationships with them.

10. Should individual welfare be a personal or a community responsibility? Justify your opinion.

11. How are party politics related to good government?

12. Indicate the extent to which pressure groups known to you have attempted to influence government leaders.

13. Gives examples of present individual interests that may need to be subordinated to public welfare.

14. Outline briefly a workable program for the achievement of intercultural and international understanding and amity. How can the factors of personal bias and prejudice be overcome?

15. How important are you as an individual? What should be your relationship to the group?

16. What are some of the spiritual values that are significant in life adjustment?

17. To what extent have you achieved self-realization and contentment?

CHAPTER Two

Factors of Personality Adjustment

*P*SYCHOLOGISTS and laymen alike recognize the fact that there appears to be a definite relationship between an individual's personal characteristics and his demonstrated degree of success in the various areas of his life experiences. From earliest time onward more or less adequate attempts have been made to find answers to questions such as: What is personality? What causes the personality of one individual to differ from that of another? How can personality be changed?

Exposure of physically unfit infants, use of incantations and charms, astrology, phrenology, and anthropometric measurements are examples of methods that have been employed at successive stages of cultural development in order to explain differences among people in their observable personality patterns. According to some modern media of advertisement there is supposed to be a close relationship between a man's or a woman's personality pattern and matters dealing with dress and grooming; style of clothing; hair do; application of cosmetics; care of teeth; use of deodorants. These approaches to ways of improving personality place emphasis upon the importance of a pleasing appearance, not only as a means of attracting favorable comment from associates, but also as a way of bolstering one's own self-confidence.

If concern about them does not become an all-absorbing interest, good grooming and appropriate dress affect a person's relations with others. They represent, however, personal attitudes and values that constitute only a phase of the total personality; they are not necessarily indicative of the fundamental bases of individual personality, as viewed by the psychologist.

Interpretation of Personality

I T is difficult for anyone to achieve an adjusted life pattern in his relationships with his fellows unless he possesses some understanding of the degree of interdependence that exits between his own personality characteristics and those of other people with whom he associates. Hence it is important that the term *personality* be analyzed carefully so that it may be understood and appreciated.

The ego or self. Expressions such as egocentrism, selfhood, self-realization, and self-assertion are common. Utilization of these terms implies a recognition of one's *self* as different from the selves of other people. The concept of self can be interpreted roughly as the more or less gradually developed and more or less objective awareness of one's own needs, interests, attitudes, and behavior habits. The *ego* concept is related to factors in the physical environment and in relationships with other human beings who comprise an individual's social environment.

The newborn infant apparently has no concept of himself as a member of a world of selves. Self-awareness develops gradually. Self-recognition and self-assertion begin with relatively vague and general recognitions of and urges to fulfill certain physical needs, such as need for food, sleep, warmth, release from discomfort, and activity that is appropriate to the stage of maturation.

As the young child gradually comes to recognize objects and persons in his environment that are associated with his developing feelings of comfort and discomfort, he begins to enlarge his needs to include satisfying relations with these environmental factors and to discover that he is a recipient or a giver of attention. He is developing an awareness of *self*. Also in his own immature fashion, he asserts his *ego* through his attempts to fulfill his increasing needs and wants.

During later childhood and adolescence, and into adulthood the developing individual comes to recognize the impact upon himself, and upon his needs and his urges, of the rules, regulations, customs, and accepted patterns of behavior that are common to the society of which he is a member. To a greater or lesser extent he achieves the ability to evaluate himself in terms of general and specific social modes, standards, and ideals. To the extent that he can measure his own self objectively in his relations with others he experiences an increasingly accurate appreciation of himself. He also develops the ability to adjust himself and his needs and urges in such a way that he can become an accepted member of his group.

Fundamentally, to a greater or lesser extent, everyone is egocentric. The degree of control exercised by an individual over his display of self-regarding behavior depends upon the attitudes toward his personal rights and responsibilities that he has been helped to achieve during his formative years. What is generally referred to as *conscience,* and by the Freudians as the *superego,* is the self-restraining power that is an attribute of an individual's total personality pattern.

Meaning of personality. Any attempt to define *personality* categorically is impossible. There probably is a general agreement, however, that every individual possesses many characteristics that are inherent in his physical appearance, gestures, speech, gait, ideas, knowledge, aptitudes, skills, habits, and emotional reactions. Some of these characteristics are innate; others result from learning and experience, and are more subject to the possibility of change than the inborn. All of these characteristics tend to interact with one another. Hence they function as a more or less integrated whole.

These human characteristics usually are called aspects, components, or traits of personality. Some psychologists prefer to limit the term *trait* to a characteristic that is associated with abilities, powers, attitudes, or behavior rather than indicative of physical structure and appearance, or of physiological function. Moreover, increasing emphasis is being placed upon the totality of personality. An individual's personality pattern is more than the combination of his many characteristics and traits. The continuous interaction of these components results in a general personality pattern that is unique to the individual, and that constitutes his *whole* personality. Temporarily, one trait may so dominate behavior that others may seem to be less significant. The dominance of the one affects not only the functioning of other specific traits but, during that period, alters the entire personality pattern. An example follows.

A successful middle-aged businessman has demonstrated, through his behavior, that he possesses personality characteristics that consistently have gained for him the respect and admiration of his associates. At home, in school, and in his business and social relationships he has given evidence of cheerful, cooperative, sincere, industrious, and ambitious attitudes. As a result, he has achieved a position of leadership, especially in his business dealings. His devotion to his wife and growing family always has motivated him to provide generously for their welfare. Now, he is eager to make available for his adolescent children superior educational and social advantages. He is unable to achieve his aim, as his financial earnings are not sufficient. His ambitions which, to the present, have been kept under intelligent control, now run rampant.

This man is determined to improve his financial status. It has become an obsession. So intense is this urge that all other areas of his life pattern are subordinated to it. Although he has not become definitely dishonest, he has begun to engage in what may be termed "sharp bargains" with his business associates. His constant concern with making money results in the development of harassed, anti-social attitudes. He is becoming an impatient, non-cooperative member of the family for whose benefit he believes he is engaging in his present business activities. His whole personality seems to have undergone an undesirable change. Whether his present drive to accumulate money will continue to dominate his attitude and behavior-motivating traits depends upon factors within and outside himself that may lessen or increase the strength of the ambitious urge of which he now is a victim.

The dynamic aspect of personality. An individual is a living, functioning organism. He usually is sensitive to all the stimulating forces about him, and is more or less able to respond to them in a desirable fashion. The effect upon himself of the degree of success of his reactions aids or hinders the desirable development of all his personality traits. The effect of the overt expression of his personality traits upon other members of his group is in direct ratio to the personality patterns of the others. The adjustment of one's personality, therefore, is an outgrowth of the satisfaction or the lack of satisfaction to himself and to the members of the group that results from the interaction of whatever personality traits dominate individual and group interrelationships.

Personality is not static; it is a dynamic, ever-changing expression of an individual's adjustment to changing factors in his environment. The effects may be far-reaching. Even the satisfaction of his fundamental physical wants cannot be divorced from his relations with other members of his group. He possesses many wants and interests. His social ego as well as his physical self must be satisfied. He craves recognition and approval from his associates. Consequently, he attempts to adjust his behavior in whatever way he considers appropriate to receive self-satisfying social approval.

Attempts to explain personality. Various attempts have been made to associate displayed behavior with the degree of possession of certain physical or other characteristic behavior motivations. In other words, personality supposedly can be classified according to "type."

Hippocrates (400 B.C.) and Galen (A.D. 150) classified personality types and resulting behavior patterns as *sanguine, choleric, melancholic,* and *phlegmatic.* The respective "types" were based upon excess of bile and phlegm, With an increase of knowledge concerning physical constitution, this theory has been outmoded. Emphasis has been placed, however, upon the relationship that exists between degree of balance or imbalance of the hormones of the ductless glands and personality type. For example, a person who suffers from hyperthyroidism tends to be overambitious and domineering; hypothyroidism is associated with laziness and intellectual dullness.

Kretschmer classified personality into four kinds: *athletic, asthenic, pyknic,* and *dysplastic.* Although this classification is not scientifically accepted, some people still assume that asthenics (tall and thin) are difficult to live with and that pyknics (short and stout) are jolly and good-natured.

According to Sheldon's theory, behavior characteristics can be classified on the basis of body types or *somatypes: endomorphic* (body soft and round, and behavior dominated by massive digestive viscera); *mesamorphic* (muscular and bony, hard and heavy physique and thick skin); and *ectomorphic* (fragile and sensitive to exposure.) Elaborate types of behavior patterning and stimulus-response relationships are associated with each of the somatypes. They are believed to be basic to individual adjustment.

One of the most popular theories of personality classification is that of Jung. According to his theory, individuals can be classified as *introvert* (socially shy and interested in their own feelings and emotions) and *extrovert* (socially adaptable and interested in people). Long lists of to-be-expected behavior characteristics have been formulated for each of these two types, respectively. Since most people appear to display both introversion and extroversion in their interrelationships, a third classification, *ambiversion*, was added to the other two types.

These theories place emphasis upon extremes of behavior characteristics. The personality of the average person is affected by many factors both within and outside himself and rarely, if ever, can be classified in terms of any one particular "type." Hence attempts at theoretical classification probably represent academic interest in personality rather than realistic interpretation. As we know, displayed personality characteristics in any situation are dependent not only upon inherited structure and potentialities, but also upon factors inherent in the situation to which an individual is responding.

The Components of Personality

ALTHOUGH personality functions as a generalized whole, the effect upon behavior of its various components is worthy of study. Certain qualities or traits display themselves more or less strongly in an individual's behavior. Hence they may seem to be predictive of expected behavior in various situations. Since the display of a particular trait or characteristic *describes* but does *not explain* behavior, any prediction concerning its functioning in every situation may be inadequate. A businessman, for example, may be extremely cooperative in his business relationships but dictatorial and ungracious in his attitudes toward his family. The underlying causes of the differences in attitude probably lie in the total reaction pattern of the man in his various relationships. Personality traits may be deep-rooted in the personality structure, or their manifestation may depend upon definite environmental situations.

Woodworth and Marquis observed that among the large number of trait names in common use, many come in pairs of opposites. They suggest that the way to utilize the everyday vocabulary of names is to "place a pair of opposites at the ends of a line and regard this line as a dimension of personality, with individuals located at different parts of the line." They prepared a list of 12 of the most clearly established primary traits and placed their opposites alongside of them. A primary trait includes several specific traits which have much in common. The 12 primary traits, however, are relatively independent. The primary traits and their opposites as presented by Woodworth and Marquis are presented here.[1]

Primary Traits	*Opposites*
1. Easygoing, genial, generous, warm	Inflexible, cold, timid, hostile, shy
2. Intelligent, independent, reliable	Foolish, unreflective, frivolous
3. Emotionally stable, realistic, steadfast	Neurotic, evasive, emotionally changeable
4. Dominant, ascendant, self-assertive	Submissive, self-effacing
5. Placid, cheerful, sociable, talkative	Sorrowful, depressed, seclusive, agitated
6. Sensitive, tenderhearted, sympathetic	Hard-boiled, poised, frank, unemotional
7. Trained and cultured mind, esthetic	Boorish, uncultured
8. Conscientious, responsible, painstaking	Emotionally dependent, impulsive, irresponsible
9. Adventurous, carefree, kind	Inhibited, reserved, cautious, withdrawn
10. Vigorous, energetic, persistent, quick	Languid, slack, daydreaming
11. Emotionally hypersensitive, high-strung, excitable	Phlegmatic, tolerant
12. Friendly, trustful	Suspicious, hostile

[1] Robert S. Woodworth and Donald G. Marquis, *Psychology*, 5th ed., pp. 91–92. Copyright, 1947, by Henry Holt and Company and reprinted with their permission.

The evidenced functioning of a personality component is not a matter of accident, but is closely associated with an individual's *established* values in relationship to the satisfaction of his personal and social needs and interests. His educational experiences, formal and informal, exercise a potent influence upon the effectiveness of his total personality pattern.

Socially effective behavior. Certain personality traits as expressed in habitual patterns of overt behavior receive universal approval from society, unless the desirable behavior is colored by the influence upon it of other socially undesirable traits. Among the qualities that tend to earn for the person who possesses them the respect and admiration of his associates can be included neat, well-groomed, and attractive appearance; originality of ideas; punctuality in keeping appointments and in performing assigned tasks; cheerfulness; a sense of humor; good sportsmanship; sincerity; trustworthiness; generosity; kindness and sympathy; cooperation; modesty; loyalty, and ability to keep confidences.

This list of characteristics indicates that, in order to be liked by or popular with his fellows, an individual needs to shift the center of attention from himself and his own wants and desires to the interests of other persons with whom he is associated. The behavior pattern itself is satisfying only to the extent that in its expression may be recognized underlying selfless or social motives. For example, the individual receives disapproval from his group if it is evident that his cooperation or generosity is based upon ulterior motives of personal gain from such behavior; if the sincerity takes the form of an expression of personal feelings or opinions, without regard for their possible effect upon other people; if the sympathetic verges on the sentimental; if the cheerfulness is of the "Pollyanna" type; if the time and effort required to maintain an attractive appearance prevent the individual from participation in other socially approved activities. Successful group living represents intelligently balanced behavior patterns that are the expression of well-integrated, socially directed personality traits. Although certain characteristics appear to have universal significance, specific behavior is conditioned by societal standards of acceptability. For example, modesty is an admired trait. Yet, certain forms of behavior might be regarded by one group to evidence modesty but by another group to indicate lack of self-confidence.

The Developing Personality

THE TOTAL personality is a constantly changing phenomenon, the bases of which lie in the inner and outer factors that direct the various personality components as well as their integrated functioning. Personal and social adjustments are rooted in the effect upon the developing personality of the inner and outer factors of influence. Stresses and strains are aroused by environmental conditions and situations. The degree of success with which the individual's personality meets these stresses and strains depends upon the degree of maturity attained in the various complex phases of personality adjustment and the social demands with which he is confronted. In this way he learns to avoid the development of habits of thought and of action that may earn for him social disapproval and personal unhappiness.

The biological factors of personality may be analyzed into the following four groups, all of which are affected by the environment: (a) physical, (b) mental, (c) emotional, (d) aptitudinal.

Physical factors of adjustment. Through the accident of birth an individual is short or tall, stout or slender; his eyes have one color rather than another, and his hair and skin have a definite shade and texture. He inherits certain body proportions and features. It is a recognized fact that not even between identical twins is there complete identity of all physical characteristics. The most that can be said is that persons bear more or less marked resemblances to other members of their family. In every social group, however, there are traditional attitudes toward the possession of certain physical characteristics. The individual's possession of such traits will receive, aside from any behavior on his part, social approval or disapproval. Unless he understands the basis of the group attitude, he may misinterpret the behavior of his fellows toward him and respond to it in a way that will interfere with his best adjustment to the group.

A few examples may illustrate this point. In America there seem to be generally accepted standards of height relationships. A man should be taller than, or at least the same height as, his wife. Certain boards of education appear to believe that a short man or woman is unable to control the behavior of children. Jokes at the expense of "Shorty" are popular. In school, the small boy feels at a disadvantage among his taller classmates. The unusually tall girl is awkward at dances; she feels that boys avoid her because of her height. The little girl is babied, and boys and men tend to display a protective attitude toward her. Such expressions as "cold blue eye," "large, generous mouth," "curly hair," "long artistic fingers," "flapping ears," "high-brow," "low-brow," "noble-brow," "baldhead row," and "fluffy blond," indicate a rather general and unfortunate tendency to hold a person responsible for characteristics which in themselves are of little importance except as possession of them causes him to receive undeserved approval or disapproval.

A child who possesses a combination of physical traits that are generally admired may be so completely "spoiled" by the praise which he receives that he may develop selfish, self-centered habits of behavior that are conducive of personality maladjustment. In the same way, a child who happens to be the "ugly duckling" of the family may develop definite attitudes of inferiority or of resentment toward the more attractive members of his family. People soon tire of physical beauty if that is all the person has to offer, however. Likewise, they soon forget physical handicaps if the individual has other strong and desirable personality traits.

Mental ability and adjustment.   Mental ability or intelligent behavior may be explained briefly as rooted in the native ability of the organism to adjust to novel situations. Alertness of response to a situation for which there has not been developed a definite habit pattern depends upon the plasticity and permeability of the nervous system. Although the general health state of neurons is important, the original constitution of the nervous system is biologically inherited but is more or less adaptable to environmental stimulation. Even the slow reactor has potentialities that he does not ordinarily exercise, since modern civilization has developed a routine of life that allows for the survival of less able individuals. Adjustments, in order to be permanently satisfying, however, must be within the limits of mental capacity for adjustment.

The demands of the present social order are geared to the abilities of normal and superior individuals—those who have an intelligent quotient between 90 and 150. Other factors being equal, the average group is able to make a fairly satisfactory adjustment to existing life conditions. This adjustment is possible for the normally intelligent person only when he is not forced into fields of activity beyond his mental capacity. Too often parents whose children give evidence of normal or slightly below normal intelligence desire that their children prepare for vocations in which competition with more alert young people may lead to failure, discouragement, and emotional disturbance.

The very bright child may experience difficulties of adjustment in his relations with the less bright, especially if adults place too great emphasis upon his mental superiority. Parents and teachers sometimes are unwise in their laudatory comments to the child that nothing is required of him except to excel in competition with less able children. Since he does not have to exert himself unduly to uphold this slight superiority, he may develop habits of laziness and attitudes of mental snobbishness.

Unless an intellectually superior young person is brought into competition with his peers, there is no opportunity for the proper development of inherent potentialities. Even then the young person needs wise guidance, lest other difficulties of adjustment develop. An active, alert young person may be overstimulated by his elders. Too much may be expected in too short a time. The activities of a bright child may be controlled by his momentary interest to such an extent that no one activity is carried to a logical conclusion; he may become "jack of all trades and master of none" with an accompanying lack of joy in accomplishment.

If a superior individual or a group of superior individuals is kept aloof from less able individuals, there may result a lack of understanding of different types of humans. Such understanding is essential in a world in which no one group can live satisfactorily if it is completely isolated from all other and different groups. Relative values can be learned only through experience.

The problem of the mentally-slow individual is different from that of his brighter brother, but it is equally serious. Disapproval from his family, failure to be accepted socially, and unequal competition in school or on the job may result in antisocial attitudes. An individual's inherited potentiality of intelligent response to his environment is an important factor of his personality adjustment. Just as important is his ability to recognize the adequacy of his adjustment and his ability to initiate desirable changes in those behavior patterns that need improvement. The person who possesses superior intelligence has a decided advantage over the less able person in the adjustment of his personality to social demands.

Emotional factors of adjustment.   The emotions are powerful drives in molding behavior responses. Personality adjustment or maladjustment almost invariably has its roots in the degree of the emotional stability of the individual. We are so much creatures of impulse that many of us require a lifetime of hard knocks in order to develop even slight intellectual control of impulsive tendencies.

An emotion as "a stirred-up state of the organism" results from the interaction of the nervous system and the endocrine glands whenever there arises a situation which is recognized as emotion arousing. One inherits his emotional constitution from his family. At birth he possesses certain potential behavior tendencies that will affect feeling tones that attach themselves to whatever reactions he experiences in the course of his life. An individual's esthetic, social, moral, and religious experiences are outgrowths of his emotional life and are closely linked with an accompanying degree of satisfaction or of annoyance.

It is generally agreed that the well-adjusted person usually is the person whose life is so well organized that his daily program includes proper eating and sleeping schedules, healthful recreation, and interesting and purposeful work. The person who is fortunate enough to have a job for which he is qualified and well trained, and which he enjoys, usually is able to meet most annoying situations objectively. Self-regarding attitudes are satisfying if the individual can recognize himself as a socially productive member of the group.

An individual's degree of personal adjustment reflects his success in his work life. It has been found that mental and emotional disturbances tend to increase during times of economic depression. Job shortage results in the development of an added factor of economic insecurity among workers. Moreover, lack of opportunity to achieve personal satisfaction in successful work activities is a frustrating experience.

Effects of the environment.   The relative effect upon an individual of his biological and his social inheritance, respectively, long has been a subject of experiment and discussion. More than a half century ago Francis Galton made the following statement: "The phrase 'nature and nurture' is a convenient jingle of words, for it separates under two distinct heads the innumerable elements of which personality is composed. Nature is all that a man brings with himself into the world; nurture is every influence from without that affects him after his birth. The distinction is clear: the one produces the infant such as he actually is, including the latent faculties of growth of body and mind; the other affords the environment amid which the growth takes place, by which natural tendencies may be strengthened or thwarted, or new ones implanted. Neither of the terms implies any theory; natural gifts may or may not be hereditary; nurture does not especially consist of food, clothing, education, or tradition, but it includes all these and similar influences whether known or unknown."

Inherited potentialities of an individual, such as physical characteristics, mental alertness, emotional constitution, and special aptitudes develop in specific and definite environments that stimulate an individual toward a multitude of complex and more or less desirable responses. Proper diet, hygienic living conditions, and opportunities for exercise and recreation are potent factors of healthy physical development. Well-organized, comprehensive, and easily available educational facilities bring about—within the limits of an individual's learning readiness—desirable skills, knowledges, and attitudes. Emotional stability is achieved in an environment that is relatively free from stress and strain.

The Adjusting Personality

A PERSON's life consists of a series of physical, mental, and emotional responses that are conditioned by the effect upon him of the people and objects in his environment. Fundamental to every stage of his changing life adjustments is the fulfillment of his needs as these are associated with physical welfare, freedom of activity, and attainment of economic and social security.

Concomitant with the struggle for the achievement of his basic life requirements, an individual experiences many changing but vital desires, urges, and ambitions that take on, at each stage of his development, characteristics which are peculiar to his age level. Successful adjustment to human relationships at any age level is conditioned by the degree of success attained at earlier levels.

Personal habits and adjustment. During the first six years of his life the child, mainly through imitation, acquires a system of habits that are necessary for survival. If he is physically and mentally normal, he learns to walk, eat, talk, and care for his needs according to the patterns of behavior by which he is surrounded and that are accepted by his group. He may acquire a complex of characteristics that show good integration or coordination of habits and impulses. This adjustment will continue just *so long as the child's environment remains relatively fixed.*

As soon as new elements enter the environment, or the child enters a new environment for which his habit patterns are not ready, his former satisfactory adjustment suffers, unless he is able to change some of his existing habits of response or unless new habits are learned. The first day at school may be a bewildering experience to the six-year-old child. The child who enters this larger social group by way of the nursery school and the kindergarten usually is much happier in his adjustment to elementary school life than is the child who goes directly from the sheltered environment of the home into this new and strange world. The experiences of childhood are repeated more or less gradually throughout an individual's life. Learning to adjust to changing stimuli from within and without the organism is a continuous process. Maturing organic functions stimulate the individual in such ways that new responses are needed. An example of this is the adolescent's changed attitude toward his relationships with members of the opposite sex.

More or less frequently during his life the individual meets new social demands: he goes from elementary school to high school and perhaps to college; he enters upon his lifework; he moves from one neighborhood to another; he loses old associates and gains new ones; his economic or social status changes; he is called upon by society to assume new responsibilities; he earns social condemnation or acclaim. All these new and varied experiences require new and varied responses.

Wholesome adjustment. As an individual matures, he retains certain fundamental attitudes and behavior patterns. The developing personality displays a continuous underlying purpose that leads to consistency of behavior, no matter how changed the overt expression of the personality may be. As his experiences increase, the individual develops, in light of his success and failure, certain desirable habits of adaptability. He meets each new situation in terms of responses that are a part of his behavior pattern but that are modified in whatever way may seem necessary. The individual has learned to adjust. He possesses, in consequence, a stable integrated personality that is at all times capable of desirable adaptation.

Healthful adjustment results in effective and socially accepted behavior responses which, in turn, result in satisfaction and mental health for the individual. The fact that a person fits the requirements of a situation makes it easier for him to adjust to another situation that is not too different from the one previously experienced. In this way forward-looking, persistent drives are established. A succession of satisfactory responses stimulated by these drives develops habits which in their strength and effectiveness bring about smoothly running adjustments.

Because of a harmonious interaction of his personality traits, the mentally healthy person is able to adapt a generally stable and persistent series of consistent values to the solution of the specific and varied problems with which he is confronted daily in his associations with other more or less stable individuals, groups, or environmental situations. His behavior is consistent and positive; his personality is wholesome, integrated, and socially valuable.

Inadequate personality adjustment.   Inadequate personality adjustment may limit itself to the inability of one trait to function satisfactorily in any situation by which it is stimulated. For example, the tendency to fear is normal. If, because of unfortunate childhood experiences or as a result of even one such experience, an individual has developed a timid or fearful attitude, he may fail to meet adequately any situation that presents stimuli which for him are fear-arousing. Each such failure reduces his ability to adjust successfully to similar, ensuing situations. In spite of the possession of other very desirable qualities, the fearful individual may become disorganized and unstable.

Maladjustment may result also from a lack of harmony among an individual's various personality traits. In any given situation his behavior may be affected by conflict between two opposing inner drives, both of them desirable. The resulting behavior may be negative or inhibited; it may be vigorous or uncontrolled, and unfitted to the demands of the situation. Because of this conflict, tension develops and the individual does not have the power to adapt himself to the experiences of the situation.

A man who is alert and scientifically trained has developed a general attitude of fair-mindedness, honesty, and objectivity in his relations with others. He is generous and sympathetic. He finds himself, however, in a situation that involves two other persons, both of whom are dear to him and each of whom desires his attention to the exclusion of the other one. The man is torn between his intelligent understanding of the need for objective, fair treatment of the situation, and his urge to refrain from hurting the feelings of either of the two persons. The conflict that arises may drive the man to withdraw completely from the situation. Because of economic or social reasons this action may be impossible. He may engage in a series of behavior responses that alternately favor one and are unfair to the other. In any case, the stress elements of the situation may be so great that the whole pattern of this man's relations with his associates is so colored by his conflict that he becomes socially maladjusted.

Specific personality characteristics are developed by individuals as adjustments to their environments. Although extreme personality disorders are discussed in Chapter 10, we shall present at this point a few of the basic factors involved in individual maladjustment. Personality is the resultant of the interaction of organism and environment. An individual's personality components may take on an exaggerated form. They became fixed to the extent that they interfere seriously with the capacity of the individual to adjust to his immediate environment, to new situations, or to his family or social relationships. For example, daydreaming or fantasy may result in a complete flight from reality. Alcohol, first used as a means of escape from conflict, becomes a mode of life that results in asocial behavior. When these symptoms are severe, the individual is incapable of making new adjustments; he is badly maladjusted or even mentally ill.

Personality adjustment versus maladjustment.   Maladjustments may grow out of constitutional defects, environmental deficiencies, educational inadequacies, or sudden or unexpected shocks or thwartings which themselves may be the result of one or more of the first three. Physical characteristics, degree of capacity for recognition of the significance of stimuli, ambition, emotional drives and excitations—all present possibilities of adjusted or of unadjusted responses. Habits begun in early childhood and persisted in during the lifetime of the individual lead to the development either of good mental health or of mental illness.

The well-adjusted person attacks problems objectively and intelligently. He is able to recognize the significance of his behavior as related to that of other people. His emotional reactions to a problem and its possibility of solution do not interfere with his accustomed habits of meeting difficulties with confidence, born of past experience, in his power to adjust the difficulty with a relative degree of success. If he is not able to achieve complete satisfaction in his solution, he is able to accept the partial failure without undue emotional disturbance. He is prepared to meet other problems which may arise with an equally intelligent and unemotional attitude.

The maladjusted person is a prey to his own emotional instability. If he is confronted by a problem, he becomes so disturbed in its presence that he is unable to organize his thinking processes toward a sane solution. He may attempt to dodge the issue or to resort to tricks or subterfuges, in order to give the impression that he has met the situation adequately. He may attempt to ignore the difficulty and to retreat into a subjective and self-satisfying state of emotionalism. Such behavior causes the solution of subsequent problems to be increasingly difficult. Thus the illusory, irrational dreams of fulfillment cause him gradually to develop habits of irresponsibility and of seeking security in the figments of his own imagination.

Personality is a complex of dynamic, more or less flexible components which are modifiable. At any stage of his development an individual's personality represents a total pattern or *configuration* that is something more than the combination of all the traits that comprise it. Hence it is extremely difficult to isolate, for the purpose of evaluation, the functioning of any one trait or quality. The extent to which and the ways in which psychologists have attempted to devise valid and reliable techniques of personality evaluation are described briefly in the next chapter.

▶ **Questions and Problems for Discussion**

1. Analyze your own personality traits and show specifically to what extent they can be traced to biological and to social inheritance.

2. Indicate specifically the relationship between superior mental ability and personality adjustment and maladjustment.

3. Justify the statement that an individual *has* personality as well as that he *is* a personality.

4. Explain the statement "Personality does not develop in a vacuum."

5. Show by reference to individuals of your acquaintance that no two persons are likely to have identical personalities.

6. In seeking a friend of the same sex, what do you believe to be the important personality qualities?

7. What are the characteristics that you look for in friends of the opposite sex?

8. To what extent do you make friends easily?

9. Describe your typical behavior in the presence of individuals you meet for the first time.

10. What do you consider to be your greatest personality asset?

11. Describe your behavior when you deliberately attempt to impress other persons.

12. Describe the social environment that you believe to be most conducive to the development of mental health.

13. Explain and illustrate the statement that "meager desires produce meager personalities."

14. Show that change of environment affects an individual's personality.

15. Does an individual adjust to the environment or does the environment adjust to the individual? Explain.

CHAPTER Three

Personality Evaluation

*I*F an individual is found to be inadaquately adjusted to normal life situations, any attempt at reconditioning his undesirable attitudes or behavior is dependent upon a thorough understanding of those personal deviations from the normal that are responsible for his maladjusted state. Therefore, any program of personality adjustment or readjustment undertaken by the individual himself or by those interested in his welfare must begin with an analysis of his inherent attitudes and his behavior patterns.

Scope and Methods of Evaluation

F O R a study of human characteristics and qualities to yield reliable data it is (1) inclusive of all phases of personality, (2) based upon the administration of reliable and valid measuring techniques carefully selected and correctly administered, (3) objectively and intelligently interpreted, and (4) followed by practical and effective recommendations for a program of readjustment or rehabilitation.

Scope of evaluation. A study or an evaluation of the various areas of an individual's personality is concerned with such personal characteristics as physical and mental status; special abilities and aptitudes; interests; attitudes; kind and extent of achievement; and emotional reactions. Attention must be directed as well to an evaluation of the total behavior pattern of an individual that commonly is included in the connotation of the term *personality*. Although the physician, the psychiatrist, the psychologist, the teacher, or the employer is interested in an individual's integrated personality pattern, the emphasis upon one or another phase of personality development may seem to be of pre-eminent importance in any given evaluating situation.

Techniques of evaluation.   There are many methods of arriving at an evaluation of an individual's personality pattern. Some of these techniques are used by people in their everyday relations with others. Some techniques should be employed only by trained experts. Since personality and personality traits are subjective and modifiable there probably is no one reliable yardstick by which they can be measured. Evaluating techniques are valuable, however, in that they seem to indicate certain tendencies or trends, the presence of which in some instances appears to be linked with observable forms of behavior disorder. The extent to which such a situation exists for one individual at one specific time is a matter of conjecture to be checked by means of all the obtained data that are available for study.

Various techniques are employed by psychologists, psychiatrists, sociologists, and educators as they attempt to evaluate individual potentialities, achievements, attitudes, and general behavior. These techniques include observation; use of standardized tests, scales, inventories, and projective procedures; interview situations, and the construction of a case history. No matter how carefully any one of these techniques is utilized, its administration represents little more than a time-consuming activity unless the obtained data are interpreted intelligently and the results applied in such a way that the individual thus evaluated profits from the experience.

Evaluation through Observation

U N L E S S an individual is completely self-involved, he is sensitive to the behavior or the displayed attitudes of people whom he encounters in his daily-life activities. Trained persons who, for one or another reason, are especially interested in evaluating an individual's behavior may give careful attention to what that person says and does. Hence observation of other people can be considered to be either *casual* or *controlled*.

Casual observation.   As we sit in a streetcar or a train, or in a lecture hall, or find ourselves in any other group situation, we tend to evaluate the personalities of the people around us. Such casual observations often are wholly or partially inaccurate because of the observer's inability or unwillingness to recognize correct relationships. Prejudice, carelessness in noting details, or lack of experience may invalidate the observation.

Controlled observation.   Effectively controlled observation is definite, specific, and well organized. The subject's behavior is recorded during the period of observation; it then is analyzed without prejudice, and the results of the observation intelligently interpreted. The trained observer begins his observation with a carefully planned list of items to be observed.

Controlled observation may be vertical, i.e., the observer studies an individual over a period of time, with special attention given to developmental changes that may be occurring during the period of observation. The process of observation sometimes is horizontal, i.e., the observer studies the reaction of a particular age or developmental stage group, in order to discover the extent to which and the ways in which the members of the group give indications of similarity and/or difference.

The two methods of approach may be combined. The members of a group are observed, according to a well-planned program of observation, intensively, over a period of time. Not only is each member of the group observed and studied, but group interaction is watched all along the way. The California study of bright children, for example, included observation of the behavior of all the members of the group included in the project from the beginning of the study through the ensuing twenty-five years of their life.

Specifically directed observation is an excellent method of studying behavior patterns of various age, racial, or occupational groups. In order to result in scientifically accepted conclusions, these observations must cover a reasonable number of cases, be reported accurately, and be interpreted unemotionally.

The Utilization of Standardized Testing Materials [1]

T E S T S, scales, and inventories have been devised for the measurement of various areas of human personality. Some of these tests are administered to the subject himself for the purpose of measuring his reactions to the questions or items of the device. Other evaluating techniques are devised for the measurement of an individual's personality characteristics by other persons. Some tests and scales are well standardized as a result of wide application, and are relatively consistent in their measurement of the characteristics that they are designed to measure.

Physical examination. In any study of an individual for the purpose of effecting adjustment or readjustment, first consideration might be given to his physical condition. Lack of interest or of success in work, or emotional or social disturbance often has a physical basis. Furthermore, many vocations demand that the worker possess exceptionally good health and physical strength. For these reasons, complete periodical physical examinations are a necessity for adjusted living.

Although many tests of physical fitness require the administration of techniques by the trained physician, there are available for the layman certain accurate measuring devices. These include comparison charts for height and weight, and performance tests for determining acuity of sight and hearing and extent of muscular control.

Tests of mental ability. At present many schools, colleges, and business houses administer tests of mental ability in order to determine the relative fitness of individuals for meeting specific requirements. Elementary and secondary schools use the results of intelligence tests for class grouping and course selection. Many colleges set up a minimal intelligence quotient as an entrance requirement. Promise of vocational competence in specific areas appears to be in direct ratio to degree of mental acuity.

The results of an intelligence test then are compared with other observable criteria of intelligent behavior, such as demonstrated success in practical situations. Important decisions concerning an

[1] For names and brief descriptions of standardized testing materials, consult the Mental Measurement Yearbooks.

individual's expected behavior ought not to be based upon the results of the administration of only one test. An individual who is emotionally disturbed or who is suffering from fatigue or physical illness may not in one test give evidence of his actual ability. If the subject is physically and emotionally normal, if the utilized tests are valid and reliable, and are properly administered, the results will show little significant fluctuation.

Intelligence tests can be categorized either as (a) group and individual, or as (b) paper-and-pencil, and non-language performance, although some tests include both types of situations. Moreover, regardless of the type of test used, a consideration of general success of performance (expressed in mental age, intelligence quotient, index of brightness or percentile rank) is not enough if the test results are to be used as a means of evaluating an individual's ability as evidenced by his number of correct responses. There is needed, in addition, an item analysis of questions answered correctly and incorrectly, in order that an adequate picture of the individual's strengths and weaknesses may be obtained.

For example, each of two children may complete correctly 50 items of a 90-item test. Unless each child gave correct answers to all of the same questions (which is highly improbable), the interpretation of the test results includes an examination of each item of response. It then may be found that one of the children was relatively consistent in the giving of correct answers to items dealing with mathematical concepts and computation but relatively inaccurate in dealing with items that have to do with the language arts. The other child might have given evidence of superior ability in language arts but displayed weakness in mathematics.

There are on the market many relatively reliable and valid group tests of mental ability that are useful for group classification. To some extent these tests are classified roughly in terms of the age levels for which they are appropriate. In general, these are paper-and-pencil tests. Those designed for young children include much pictorial material to which the child responds by marking or checking certain items, as directed orally by the test administrator. The more advanced intelligence tests may require considerable reading and concentrated thinking in order to arrive at the correct response.

If we wish to make an intensive study of one individual's degree of mental acuity, an individual test of intelligence usually is administered. The testee may be asked to read and respond orally to questions concerning the material read, to manipulate various types of blocks or similar material, or to respond to questions asked by the tester in the areas of general or specific information, problem solving, or accustomed behavior.

Because of the personal elements involved, the scoring and interpretation of individually administered tests are difficult and require considerable training and experience. Otherwise, the conclusions and recommendations resulting from the administering of the tests may not be valid and reliable. The administration of tests, such as the Terman-Merrill Revision of the Stanford-Binet Tests of Intelligence, the Wechsler Intelligence Scales, and others of their kind, therefore, should not be attempted by the untrained classroom teacher or other school person.

Aptitude tests. Satisfactory educational or vocational adjustment by the trial-and-error method is costly and often discouraging. The ideal method would be to discover early the individual's special ability or aptitude and then to expose him to the best training possible in his field so that he may develop expert knowledge and skill.

There are certain general abilities which are conducive to success in various types of vocations and which may be tested in the psychological laboratory. Such testing techniques include tests of speed of reaction time, response to auditory or visual signals, tapping, dynamometer tests of strength, tests of coordination, mechanical assembly tests, tests of color blindness, and sensory tests for aviators and others for whom keen sensory acuity is essential.

Many other tests have been devised and are being used by schools and prospective employers for the measurement of specific aptitudes which, other factors being equal, would predispose toward special success in achievement. Some of the aptitudes that have been measured more or less successfully are musical ability; aptitude for manual occupations; special fitness for clerical occupations, law, medicine, dentistry, surgery, nursing, engineering, or teaching.

Vocational tests serve one of two purposes. Many vocational aptitude tests have been devised for the purposes of prognosis or the discovery of potential ability in a skill, training in which has not yet been given. Other trade tests endeavor to test the successful achievement in a skill as a result of training. These tests include both manipulatory skill and adequate information concerning the techniques required for mastery.

The results of such tests do not guarantee success or failure in a given vocation. The tests may not yet be refined sufficiently for the discovery of the subtle elements of a specific aptitude. Moreover, job analysis has not progressed to the extent of a complete and comprehensive determination of all the characteristics requisite for successful achievement in any one vocational activity. Personality factors other than specific aptitude are influential in determining an individual's eventual vocational accomplishment. Aptitude tests, however, have some value in the adjusting of young people to their occupational life or in the readjusting of failing workers. A few of the more well-known instruments in this area of evaluation are the Thurstone Tests of Primary Mental Abilities; the Differential Aptitude Tests (DAT), developed by the Psychological Corporation, and various classification instruments developed for the Armed Services, such as the Army General Classification Test (AGCT), and the Armed Forces Qualification Test (AFQT).

Achievement tests and scales. One of the most useful means of predicting future achievement is the measurement of past and present accomplishment. An efficient school or business executive does not attempt to place a pupil in a particular grade or a worker in a specific job until he has reliable evidence that the person is fitted for the assignment.

In order to meet the need for an accurate evaluation of an individual's possessed skill or knowledge, numerous scholastic and occupational tests have been devised. For educational adjustment there are available on all levels—elementary, secondary, and college —tests and scales for measuring degree of competence in areas such as reading rate and comprehension; spelling and language usage; mathematics; science; social studies; classical and modern foreign languages; home economics, and commercial subjects. Also included among achievement tests are high-school entrance tests and general culture tests on the college level.

An achievement test may be constructed to serve any one of the following functions: (1) to make a survey of the level of achievement attained by a group or groups of learners; (2) to discover the degree of readiness of a young person for entrance into one or another area of learning (reading readiness tests for young children are among the most popular of these measuring instruments); (3) to diagnose the specific learning difficulties of an individual in a particular field of learning. In general, the survey achievement test still is the type that is most generally used on all school levels. A commendable increase of interest, however, is being evinced by school people in readiness and diagnostic tests. This interest probably parallels a growing concern on the part of educators in regard to individual development and learning progress.

At present there is a trend in achievement testing away from specific tests in isolated areas of learning toward general achievement batteries and comprehensive examinations. A battery of tests, especially on the elementary-school level, includes a series of tests representing pupil achievement in the various subject areas studied. Scoring and interpretive norms or standards follow a general pattern that makes possible an equivalence of performance evaluation of all areas of learning included in the battery. The Metropolitan Achievement Tests (Grades 1 through 9), The Stanford Achievement Tests (Grades 2 through 9), and the California Achievement Tests (Grades 1 through 12) represent three of the most commonly used achievement batteries.

Comprehensive examinations, such as the Cooperative General Achievement Tests (CGAT), the Iowa Tests of Educational Development (ITED), and the Tests of General Educational Development, developed by the United States Armed Forces Institute (USAFI GED) are designed to evaluate general achievement progress on the secondary and higher school levels. The present trend toward the utilization of test batteries and comprehensive examinations gives evidence of an increased emphasis upon the general integrated resultants of learning.

The Utilization of Personality Inventories

A M O N G measuring instruments of personality evaluation may be grouped the various forms of more or less standardized measuring techniques that are designed to evaluate an individual's personal qualities, interests, attitudes, and behavior patterns. These differ from those that can be included among areas such as his physical constitution, general intelligence, specific aptitudes, and knowledge and performance in any special field. Defined broadly, personality tests may be expected to include techniques for measuring degree of possession of such qualities as cooperativeness, perseverance, honesty, sincerity, social adaptability, attitudes toward customs or beliefs, initiative, responsibility, introversion or extroversion, ascendancy or submissiveness, emotional stability or neurotic tendency.

Rating scales and inventories.   Based upon the assumption that it is possible to isolate one or another phase of an individual's total personality, many measuring instruments that deal with trait evaluation have been constructed and still are in the process of construction. Such tests are utilized (1) to enable an individual to rate himself concerning his interests, attitudes, emotional states, temperament, and other aspects of his personality; (2) to help psychologists, teachers, employers, and other interested persons evaluate an individual's status in one or more personality characteristics, provided that the evaluators are qualified to formulate objective and valid judgments concerning the subject of the evaluation.

Among personality inventories that have been widely used, the following deserve attention:

Allport A–S Reaction Study
Bell Adjustment Inventory
Bernreuter Personality Inventory
Cattell-Saunders-Stice Sixteen Personality Factor Questionnaire
Guilford-Zimmerman Temperament Survey
Heston Personal Adjustment Inventory
Minnesota Multiphasic Personality Inventory
Thurstone Temperament Schedule
Woodworth Personal Data Sheet

Interest inventories.   An individual's interests may be recognized in a general way by careful observation of his favorite activities and his recreational sports and hobbies, or by his success or failure in his school subjects. The observation method may be supplemented by the administration of a well-chosen inventory which consists of a systematic series of questions designed to discover the kinds and intensity of an individual's major likes and dislikes among specifically listed activities and attitudes. Although the results of interest inventories are not necessarily indicative of persistent or stable interests, they can be of value in the study of an individual's personality qualities. Strong's Interest Inventories have yielded some worth-while results. Significant interest inventories include:

Allport Study of Values, Revised

Darley and McNamara Minnesota Personality Scale

Kuder Preference Record—Personal

Kuder Preference Record—Vocational

SRA Employee Inventory

Strong Vocational Interest Blank for Women

Strong Vocational Interest Blank for Men

Thurstone Interest Schedule

Validity and reliability of trait measurement. The evaluation of personality traits is difficult because of the complexity of the personality pattern. It probably is impossible to rate a person *entirely satisfactory* or *entirely lacking* in the possession of a characteristic or quality in any situation that may arise. For example, a man may be extremely honest in his home relationships, but his business ethics may be questionable.

It is difficult to divorce completely one phase of personality from another, either in the individual's rating of himself or in an evaluation of himself by another. An evaluator may be influenced by his motives in rating. A school executive who is called upon to submit to another school or to a business house a personality rating for one of his students may be convinced that his students are better than are those of any other school. Hence he is unable to rate this individual objectively and thus admit that the young person possesses any undesirable qualities.

The self-rater may wish to give a good account of himself. Therefore, he responds to individual items of a test or scale as he believes he is expected to respond. Unreliable as the results of various instruments of personality evaluation may be, if an individual portrays certain tendencies as measured by different techniques periodically some trait consistencies may be assumed for the purpose of evaluation. Some constructors of rating scales attempt to check consistency of response by presenting a single concept in two or more differently-worded items.

The Utilization of Projective Techniques [2]

N o matter how carefully the rating of personality traits is done
or how many traits are rated, a total personality evaluation includes
more than the rating of one trait. The subtle interaction and inter-
influence of those traits which make for the integration of personality cannot be discovered through the administration of the paper-
pencil variety of trait measurement. For example, people in general
cannot be catalogued into rigid classifications such as ascendant or
submissive, introvert or extrovert. Consequently, recently there
have been developed certain forms of evaluation that permit the
subject to *project* his habitual attitudes, hopes, ideas, aggressions,
fears, or worries. These evaluating instruments are known as *projective techniques.*

Characteristics of projective techniques. In the administration of a projective technique the subject is presented with more or
less unstructured situations to which he responds freely. He may
give a variety of possible responses. As he describes, explains, or
evaluates the "situation," he supposedly is giving overt expression
to the inner attitudes and ideals that are characteristic of his general
personality pattern.

An increasing number of projective measuring instruments are
being made available. Among the various types that are most
frequently applied are Verbal Techniques; Drawing and Painting; Play and Dramatic Techniques; the Rorschach (Ink Blot)
Technique, and Pictorial Techniques.

Verbal Techniques. Word-association tests, often referred to
as "free association tests," serve as media for discovering an individual's thoughts, associations, and specific emotional states. These
tests were sponsored during the nineteenth century by Francis
Galton and Wilhelm Wundt. In its early form, the word-association
test consisted of a list of words to each of which the subject was
asked to respond with the first word that came to his mind. Each
word reaction was timed. Both the response itself and the length of
time between stimulus and response were considered to be significant.

[2] For an excellent detailed discussion of these techniques consult A. Anastasi,
Psychological Testing (New York: The Macmillan Company, 1954).

This form of verbal technique is used sometimes to discover whether an individual has any knowledge concerning a situation about which he claims to know nothing. It is presumed that a subject will fumble for a response and take more time to respond to a stimulus word that may indicate personal guilt or guilty knowledge.

The presentation to the subject of incomplete sentences which he is expected to complete is another of the verbal techniques. A subject's completion of sentences similar to those presented below would seem to give a clue to his attitudes, opinions, or emotional states.

My job _____.
America's problem is _____.
The place of women in our society _____.
A liberal _____.
Young people today _____.

The way in which a sentence is completed can be indicative of the subject's relations with his associates, his breadth of understanding, or his social philosophy.

At the present time various forms of the verbal technique are being experimented with. The lie-detector technique is relatively well known. Story-completion tests are administered to children as well as to older persons. Their purpose is to discover an individual's creative potentialities, the logical sequence of his ideas, and the extent to which his mental processes respond to realistic continuity or to flights of fancy.

Self-expression through drawing and painting. Emphasis is being placed in early education upon encouraging a child to express his interests, creative abilities, and inner tensions through the media of finger painting, crayon drawing, and easel painting. The child is encouraged to give free expression to his interests and urges. Another form of this technique is to have a child produce a picture of a person or a house as he images it.

The utilization of the drawing and painting techniques has diagnostic value. Through them may be discovered inner motives, ideas, attitudes, or resentments of which the subject himself may be unaware. These techniques also have projective application in dealing with individuals of any age who appear to be suffering an emotional disturbance. Because of the subjective factor inherent in this form of diagnosis, interpretation of the product is difficult and should be attempted only by trained and experienced test administrators. They only are able to apply existing norms to an individual's performance. This caution holds for the administration and interpretation of all types of projective techniques.

Play and dramatic techniques.   Play therapy has received considerable attention among psychologists as a means of releasing tensions among emotionally disturbed young children. A child is allowed freely to handle, play with, and perhaps throw on the floor and stamp upon, one or more members of a doll family. It is supposed that he thereby is giving evidence of his attitude toward, or his feelings of resentment against, the various members of his family. His comments about and to the dolls as he plays with them enable a trained counselor who is listening and watching to diagnose more or less adequately the child's emotional state.

From this beginning has developed the utilization of toys, figures, and similar materials for diagnostic purposes. The World Test consists of one hundred or more toy pieces which the subject is encouraged to arrange according to his interest. Such projective "toy tests" presumably indicate the possession of personal characteristics, such as aggressive rigidity, disorganization, or other symptoms of emotional disorder. Shneidman's Make-a-Picture Story (MAPS) is used as a storytelling device about a scene which the subject has constructed with materials consisting of various backgrounds, people, and animals.

Attitudes displayed by a subject in either of the projective techniques described in the foregoing may offer clues concerning the emotional difficulties suffered by him, and serve as the basis for reconditioning. The behavior of adolescents and adults who participate in *psycho-drama* also may be enlightening. When the subject enacts one or another role on a stage, as he participates in artificially constructed scenes, he is likely to project his inner feelings and attitudes into the role which he is playing. Because of the various factors that may influence the subject's performance, conclusions concerning the emotional state of the subject may or may not be valid.

The Rorschach Technique.   The Ink-Blot test is used widely as a projective technique, especially with adolescents and adults. The subject is asked to look at each of ten cards containing ink blots of various forms. Five of these forms are in shades of black and gray and five others are in two or more colors.

As the subject examines a card he reports to the examiner what he sees in the whole blot or in any one or more segments of it. In a second showing of the cards, the subject points out as exactly as he can the area or areas which represent the various objects or situations that he had seen in the first showing.

The interpretation of a subject's performance is difficult and should be attempted only by a thoroughly trained administrator. Since no two individuals are likely to report similarly, many variations and combinations need to be considered and interpreted in order to achieve some understanding of the subject's performance.

The Thematic Apperception Test. This projective technique (TAT) consists of nineteen cards, each of which represents a situation involving one or more persons against a more or less vague background. One card is blank. The subject is asked to tell a story about each of the pictures, and then to imagine a picture on the blank card and tell a story about it.

The TAT and other pictorial techniques, such as the Children's Apperception Test (CAT) and the Symonds Picture Story Test for adolescents, have not yet been standardized completely. As a subject is motivated to tell story after story concerning the respective pictures, certain attitudes continue to show themselves throughout the test. One boy, for example, to whom this test was administered displayed a combination of fear and aggression as he attempted to interpret the pictures. His comments included statements such as: "The man wants to get into the house." "The girl is trying to run away because she is afraid that someone will hurt her."

Significance of projective techniques. These instruments of evaluation are interesting and challenging. Much more needs to be known, however, concerning their utilization. According to Anastasi,

> It is evident that projective techniques differ widely among themselves. Some appear more promising than others because of more favorable empirical findings, sounder theoretical orientation, or both. Regarding some techniques, such as the Rorschach, voluminous data have been gathered, albeit their interpretation is often uncertain. About others little is known, either because of their

recent origin, or because objective verification is hindered by the intrinsic nature of the instruments or by the attitude of their exponents.

What, then, can be concluded regarding the present status of projective techniques in psychological testing? Today such devices still represent only raw "materials," rather than standardized "tests." As such, they may serve as aids to the trained and experienced clinician. In his hands they may provide effective means for establishing rapport, as well as a rich source of leads to be followed up in the interview. At the same time, current research—such as that of Thurstone and Goodenough—suggests that the projective approach may eventually be utilized in the construction of instruments which can be properly designated as psychological tests.[3]

The Interview as an Evaluating Technique

T H E R E usually are certain personality facts that can be understood and evaluated properly only through the intimate and informal relationship that is possible in a well-planned and sympathetically conducted interview.

Purposes of the interview. The purpose of an interview may be one of the following: to obtain information about the interviewee; to give him information; or to assist him in the resolution of more or less serious problems or conflicts. An information-receiving or information-giving interview generally uses what is referred to as the *direct counseling* approach. When an individual needs and/or seeks assistance in dealing with personal difficulties of adjustment the counselor's or interviewer's approach is indirect. The problem to be solved is the client's; only the client himself can reach a self-satisfying resolution of his problem. The function of the counselor is to keep himself out of the situation as much as is possible, except as he motivates the client to "talk out" the difficulty, evaluate its seriousness, discover possible causes, and finally arrive at a possible resolution of it.

[3] A. Anastasi, *Psychological Testing* (New York: The Macmillan Company, 1954), pp. 621, 629. Used with the permission of The Macmillan Company.

Nondirective counseling may require many sessions between counselor and counselee. The difficulty may be so deep-rooted or so serious that no one but a well-trained analyst or psychiatrist is able to gain an understanding of the client and his problem and his need for assistance. A seriously disturbed person requires more help than can be given him even through intelligently trained non-direction in counseling. The person so afflicted may need the kind of therapy that can be given only in a hospital for the mentally ill.

Effectiveness of the interview. It is the function of the interviewer, by tactful questioning and intelligent listening, to probe beneath the mass of material already obtained by other techniques of evaluation and to discover the fundamental bases of the individual's personality status. In this way, whatever adjustment or readjustment is needed may begin at the core of the difficulty, and not concern itself merely with superficial behavior.

To the extent that the interview or interviews accomplish that which they purport to achieve they are of inestimable value to all persons who are responsible for the guidance of individuals toward the achievement of desirable personal and social goals. The teacher, the social worker, the personnel worker, the employer, the doctor, the psychoanalyst, the psychologist, and the psychiatrist are motivated by different objectives as they conduct interviews. In each case the effectiveness of the interview is dependent upon the spirit in which and the skill with which the interview is conducted.

The individual who needs guidance toward better educational adjustment, the family that needs help in the solution of financial or other family problems, the worker who is experiencing difficulties on the job or with his fellow workers, the applicant who is seeking employment, the patient who is suffering from mental or physical ill health—all come to the interview with a specific need for help. They best can achieve their own self-realization and their own self-direction if the assistance offered them is objective, tactfully and sympathetically given, and based upon a counselor background of thorough training and broad experience. The interview is pre-eminently a medium for wholesome and healthful interaction of human personalities. Regardless of the purpose of an interview, good rapport between the interviewer and the interviewee is needed to accomplish the desired goal.

The Case History

I N the foregoing pages attention was directed toward the value of various measuring or evaluating techniques. Through the utilization of one or more of the instruments of evaluation discussed, significant data can be obtained concerning various phases of an individual's personality pattern. Information obtained from observation, the administration of standardized testing materials, and interview situations usually is adequate for the giving of assistance in cases of minor maladjustments or of relatively unimportant problems.

If, however, an individual is facing a serious problem of adjustment or is suffering from one or another major form of mental or emotional disturbance, a comprehensive study of the client's difficulty is needed. Data concerning him need to be gathered from as many sources as are available and organized into what generally is referred to as a *case history*.

Construction of a case history. Teachers and others interested in human welfare frequently organize their impressions of individual behavior and/or attitudes in the form of anecdotal records or case reports. Such informal accounts, in addition to the material included in a cumulative record, usually provide valuable information concerning individual students.

For more intensive study of seriously disturbed individuals, however, all of the materials included in a personal folder are needed. Important, too, is additional information concerning phases of the individual's life pattern, family history, and environmental conditions. All of these data are organized in the form of a case history. The information contained in the case history of a client usually is compiled by a social worker who gathers data from the home, the school, and other available and pertinent social agencies.

Case histories differ in form, but many or all of the following items are included in a well-organized and comprehensive history:

Identifying data
Present difficulty (reason for referral)
Family background
Birth conditions
Health status and history

Home conditions
Social and economic status
Neighborhood factors of influence
Intelligence
Personal attributes
Study progress in school
Work history
Sexual development and behavior
Social interest and behavior

These data need to be accurate and objectively reported, otherwise they have little if any value. The client can be assisted to effect a readjustment of his existing status only if a clinic staff have sufficient and dependable data to guide their evaluation of the client's difficulties.

Utilization of the case history. When all the data have been assembled, the counselors attempt to interpret them and to offer recommendations for treatment. These recommendations may necessitate cooperation by the home, school, or place of employment. If special therapy is needed, this is administered by a psychiatrist or at a psychological clinic.

No matter how many or what agencies are involved in the readjustive process, progress needs to be reported. Also, after a client has made desirable adjustment, or if maladjustive factors in his environment have been removed or improved, a follow-up of the client's condition is an essential part of the study and therapy.

▶ **Questions and Problems for Discussion**

1. Justify the statement "A psychologist needs to be acquainted with the principles and techniques of personality measurement."
2. Give reasons why the results of personality tests are to be used with discrimination.
3. Study your work habits—either in study or on the job—evaluate them for the attainment of anticipated goals.
4. List any evidence that you have or can recall which will reflect how your parents gave you responsibility during childhood. During adolescence.

5. Explain reasons why personality is difficult to evaluate.

6. What are some limitations of observation as a technique of personality evaluation?

7. In what way may tests of intelligence reflect personality qualities of an individual?

8. Explain what is meant by standardized tests.

9. What are the chief assets of projective techniques as techniques of personality evaluation? The weakness of them?

10. Indicate how projective techniques differ from other standardized testing procedures.

11. What personality qualities can be measured through play and dramatic techniques?

12. How does the Rorschach Technique differ from the TAT?

13. What preparation should be made for an interview by the client? By the interviewer?

14. Illustrate what is meant by direct and nondirective counseling.

15. Discuss the importance of rating scales and inventories in personality evaluation.

CHAPTER Four

The Dynamics of Human Behavior

A H U M A N being, from birth to death, is an active, functioning organism. His activity is purposeful and continuous. An individual strives not only to satisfy his body needs but also to acquire the knowledges, skills, attitudes, ideals, and behavior habits that will enable him to function successfully as a member of each of his various life groups. Social urges have a biological basis, and human drives follow rather definite patterns of behavior adjustment.

Behavior Motivation

M O T I V A T I O N is closely associated with the dynamic aspect of human behavior. To the student of psychology the term *motivation* connotes psychological causation. It refers to sequence or continuity. Every human experience involves a causation factor to the extent that a motive always precedes a particular act. Cause-and-effect relationships in human behavior imply that every motive produces some effect and that every response or effect is preceded by a motive. It is difficult, sometimes impossible, to trace this motive-effect sequence in the thinking or behavior of an individual. The utilization of psychoanalytic techniques of behavior evaluation, however, can help an individual gain some insight concerning deep-seated emotionalized motives that are affecting his behavior.

Meaning and characteristics of motivation. Motivation, as an activating force, affects every area of human behavior. Its field of influence ranges from the directing of a simple act, the motive of which is obvious, to a complex, formal activity pattern, e.g., career behavior, which represents numerous detailed aspects of motivation. There is evidence, however, that human motivation is complex in its functioning, even in apparently simple activities associated with the satisfaction of body requirements such as food, water, and oxygen. Motives may be physiological, biosocial, or political in nature.

Motivated behavior is characterized by *"persistence, exploratory variation, and emotional energizations."* [1] Persistence represents a characteristic of the continuity of behavior. The stronger the desire, the more persistently will the individual pursue the goal. For example, with an increase in hunger goes an increase in food-seeking behavior; with an increase in interest to become a member of the team goes an increased cooperation in practice. Persistence of effort is closely associated with the strength of the motive.

If failure has resulted from an attempt to attain a desired goal, the motivated behavior may take the form of *exploratory variation* that continues until the goal is achieved. During his first day in school, a child, who is a newcomer in the neighborhood may exhibit variations in his behavior as means of earning group acceptance. He displays his possessions; he attempts to demonstrate superior mental or physical ability. If either of these methods fails he turns to another and then another until one works, and he is accepted. By introducing the new pupil to the class members, the teacher can help lessen the child's need to engage in acceptance-seeking activities.

Exploratory variation is seen also in adult behavior, as attempts are made to be accepted by a new group. The degree of variation

[1] By permission from *Psychology of Personality*, 2nd ed., by R. Stagner. Copyright, 1948. McGraw-Hill Book Company, Inc., p. 260.

depends upon the speed with which the stranger is accepted and the extent of his interest in the group. The principle of exploratory variation can be put to greater use by the more able individual than by the dull person.

Emotional tonus gives power to human motives and drives. *Emotional energization* occurs in strongly motivated instances. When there is delay or resistance but the motive is strong, the organism's behavior shows increased energy through emotional tension. The behavior may take the form of anger, anxiety, fear, aggression, or some other emotional expression. If added effort results in successful achievement, great emotional satisfaction is experienced. This reaction is characteristic of the dull as well as of the bright.

Direction and tensions of motivated behavior. Inherent urges, desires, or habitual attitudes are basic to motives that serve as action stimulators. Organized behavior is directed toward goal achievement. Purpose and tensions are aspects of motivated behavior. Tensions may be established by stimuli inside or outside the body. Viewed externally, motivated behavior appears to be purposive; considered internally, motivated behavior represents attempted tension reduction. When it is set off, a tension system runs its course until it is satiated. Hence it is an energy system organized to meet some human need.

The tension systems are unified and dynamic. Their management involves intelligence and motivated behavior. These tensions not only arise from the physiological needs but also from the social culture and habit patterns of the individual. The simplest forms of tension systems are individual appetites. According to Anderson: "Each appetite has its own mode of expressing itself upon the organism, its own cycle, and its own method of satiation." His organization of the appetites is presented in Figure 1.

Motives function continually to fulfill human needs. Some motives may be small or specific and relatively weak; others may influence the continued behavior of an individual over a long period of time. The persistence of motives is based upon human wants and human interests. The energy required sometimes works toward the attainment of a goal; sometimes expenditure of energy acts as a block. Tension systems act as forces in motivation. Anderson concludes that

Figure 1[2] APPETITES

Name	Organic base	Rhythm	Sense or sense organ	Response	Social control	Maladjustment
Thirst	Reduction of fluid in tissues	Few hours	Localized in throat	Swallowing, drinking	Very little	Rare
Hunger	Metabolism	Several times daily: varies with culture	Cells sensitive to stomach contractions; appetite "gnawing"	Swallowing, eating	Foods and habits vary widely	Non-hunger (food refusals) or "gorging"
Elimination	(a) Secretion via kidney and bladder	Few hours	Cells in bladder wall	Urination	Sanitation and modesty	Enuresis (bed-wetting)
	(b) Excretion via intestines	Daily	Cells in intestines and colon; "pressure"	Defecation	Sanitation and modesty	Incontinence or constipation
Rest or sleep	Chemical changes in blood, as result of muscular action	Daily	Fatigue, weariness	Lying down, relaxation, sleep (usually at night)	Time regulated by need and custom	Insomnia, nightmares
Sex	Stimulation of erogenous zones, sex organs, and glands	Glandular secretions have regular period, female has monthly cycle	Localized sensations, general tension	Manipulation, copulation	Marked social control of all aspects	Many disorders

[2] J. E. Anderson, *The Psychology of Development and Personal Adjustment* (New York: Henry Holt and Company, 1949), p. 236.

A tension system involves (1) some impulsion or need within the organism, (2) an object or goal outside toward which energy is directed, and (3) some process of reduction of tension, or satiation, when the goal or object is attained. To describe goals and objects in this reciprocal relation involves the concept of *valence*, which refers to the mutual attractiveness between a need and an object or goal. The organism is within a *field of forces* which is enclosed by a boundary and which may contain both a number of objects with valences and a number of barriers which temporarily block access to them. What the person does depends upon interaction within and with the field of forces. Because he is surrounded by different objects and goals with different valences, *conflict* arises. Out of conflict comes the necessity of choice between alternative lines of action. A characteristic of the person's reactions in a conflict situation is an *oscillation*, or a shifting back and forth from one alternative to another, prior to the decision or action which terminates the disturbance between the tension systems.[3]

Human Drives and Motivation of Behavior

I N order to understand human motives there is needed an understanding of the basic desires that are present in all normal human beings. As an aid to the process of development from birth onward, a human being is equipped by nature with a host of potential desires and cravings that operate as the driving forces of his life activities. The amount of satisfaction or annoyance that he experiences in life situations is determined by the extent to which his interests and urges are gratified or thwarted. These urges are dynamic forces that affect thoughts, emotions, and behavior.

General nature of inner urges. The individual is born with certain potential urges or drives that seek expression. The way in which these inherent desires are satisfied through overt behavior is conditioned by environmental influences and by experience. These experientially modified drives to action become the motivators of human attitudes and actions.

[3] Ibid., p. 256.

The relatively simple behavior drives of early childhood increase in number and complexity as an individual matures and experiences more and differing life relationships. As we are stimulated by varying social values, we attempt so to direct our interests and desires that we may achieve satisfying social recognition. Other less desirable drives may be present within us and become powerful as motivators of our behavior. However, we may refuse to recognize the presence of these drives or we may delude ourselves into thinking that our behavior is motivated by noble impulses.

Importance of motives. Activity-arousing stimuli are supplied by the environment. Human response to these stimuli at any one time is conditioned by the particular urge that is dominant in the individual. For example, a man returns home very tired from a hard day at the office to find that he is invited to join friends in a card game. Normally, he would be delighted to accept an invitation of this kind. This evening, however, his extreme weariness stimulates him to refuse the invitation, in order that he may stay at home and rest. Inner urges determine the nature of responses.

A careful observation of human conduct leads to the conclusion that an understanding of motive is very useful to us in our daily relationships. As we are stimulated by the actions of other persons, we tend to question the motives that give rise to this or that form of behavior. In our search for the underlying motives of our own behavior, or that of other people, we are not always successful in discovering the actual motivating force that stimulates one to act as he does. Our behavior often reflects the functioning of more than one kind of urge at the same time. In general, we are motivated to satisfy bodily needs, to realize a purpose or an ideal, or to achieve personal satisfaction in a socially desirable activity.

Why do humans behave as they do? Do men play baseball because of large audiences? Do pupils conform to school rules because they are expected to do so? Why do people build different types of houses, buy different kinds of clothes, or engage in different kinds of work? In individual urges and desires, as these are modified by experience, can be found the reason for differences in the kind of activity that is personally satisfying.

Just as a child develops functional, positive attitudes of his own, becomes independent of his parents, grows active in self-interest, learns to be self-determining, and eventually outlives his parents, so it is with motives. Each motive originates in whatever inherent tendencies, organic tensions, or diffuse irritabilities man possesses. Adult purposes result from the experiences of infancy and early childhood. However, during the process of maturing, many new neural connections are formed, resulting in a better-functioning human being.

Genetic sequence of motives. During very early childhood our activities are generally self-centered. Later, we are motivated by the wishes of individual members of the family, or playmates. This desire to do for others is further expanded to include relatively small groups, such as the entire family, the school, or the club. As we approach adolescence and then adulthood, our activities and interests are influenced by our desire to cooperate with the large groups in which we are active. These may include religious, political, business, and community affiliations.

Individual motives are always colored by personal desires, likes, and physical urges; social level; economic status, or interest in self or in others. Nevertheless, because of the socializing influences that constantly are present, motives follow an organized pattern in the developing life of the individual as he progresses step by step from infancy to adulthood.

An individual motivated to *pretend* to be a particular kind of person may actually *become* that which he has pretended because of the force and strength of the stimulating drive or motive. Likewise, the genius is forced, through the strength of his own inner drives, toward creation in the exercise of his talents, even though no external stimulus may seem to be active. An individual's active motives may reshape his behavior.

Persistent unconscious motives. A vast number of human irrationalities and maladjustments are due to lack of awareness of motives. There is needed an intelligent understanding of what are the dominant motives operating in the individual, how these are interrelated, how they are affected by continuous experience, and how they organize themselves into beneficial or detrimental patterns of human adjustment. Modern dynamic psychology is gradually revealing the subtle power of unconscious motives and emotional drives to control behavior responses so as to inhibit wholesome personality development. Any effort that will bring the motives to the level of awareness is worthy of careful consideration by those who are responsible for the education of an individual.

When a country is led into war, the people usually are denied the knowledge of the real motives of the leaders that underlie the latters' decisions. Likewise, in advertising, the general public is not told of the motives that have stimulated the writers of the advertisements. More wholesome attitudes are evidenced when underlying motives are expressed and understood by all concerned. Psychiatrists, in treating a neurotic, often need to dig back into past experiences of the patient. He is unaware of his own motives, since these often are buried in an unsatisfied desire, a potent fear, or a difficult life situation.

In dealing with this problem we are in the realm of subjective phenomena. It is difficult to explain the background of a disturbing experience. What does the individual know about the affective value of this stimulus, that experience, or that drive? He needs help in attempted introspection; unaided, his attempts at analyzing his motives for behavior are likely to be affected by his mental set and his physiological condition.

Importance of Inner Urges

A L L of an individual's behavior reflects the functioning of one or another need, want, drive, or urge. Rarely does one of the inner urges act in isolation; seldom can a desire or need be satisfied except in terms of existing environmental conditions. Drive to action can be described as physical or social, but the satisfying of physical needs has social implications.

Urges arising from bodily needs. No matter how well-educated or cultured he is, every human being experiences numerous impulses that arise from body needs. He craves the things that induce feelings of well-being; he strives to avoid those that cause him pain and suffering. The more primitive cravings are closely related to biological conditions in their functioning, but they soon take on social significance in terms of the needs of the situation. For example, we eat three times a day, four times a day, or twice a day;

we like food prepared in this way or that way, depending upon our established eating habits; we accept a certain food as palatable because we have learned to like it. We have eaten it in socially desirable situations. We may eat rabbit and enjoy its taste, yet we hesitate to eat woodchuck.

It can be readily observed that food affects individuals differently as they strive to satisfy their body food requirements. Good, palatable food at one time may become food that cannot be touched at another. For example, a boy had developed a deep affection for a calf that he had fattened for a 4-H Club project and for which he had received a prize in school. For meat, the family rely upon a calf each year. Consequently, they decided to butcher the prize calf as a part of their winter meat supply. While the authors were visiting this home they noticed that the lad was not eating meat. The reason given was that this meat had come from the prize calf. The boy could not forget his warm attachment to the animal during its lifetime. Hence he could not be objective about eating the meat. If we reflect, we probably can recall experiences that we have had that make it difficult for us to enjoy eating a certain food even though it is actually the best that can be purchased.

Not only do we experience the psychological effect of satisfying bodily urges through food, but each of us is sensitive to the value to us of clothing in addition to that of keeping us warm and protected. It may be undesirable to wear a hand-me-down, but less undesirable if the fact is not known to those with whom we associate. Some hand-me-downs may be accepted cheerfully. The owners may tire of wearing articles of clothing more than a few times and pass them on, in excellent condition, to others. As a result, the receivers of the clothing obtain a great deal of comfort and satisfaction from its wear.

The urge to succeed and to achieve. That to succeed encourages continued effort is a fact that has been accepted by most people. During the recent past most educators have learned that success is one of the important factors in child development and effective child living. A child or an adult may strive for long hours to reach a relatively insignificant goal, if it represents a satisfying degree of achievement for him. He experiences great satisfaction from planning an action, overcoming an obstacle, or demonstrating a skill in which he is proficient. The pleasure derived from activities that are accompanied by anticipated success is a most powerful motivating force.

Since individuals differ because of inherited and environmental factors, school people can organize training in terms of the experience and ability level of the individual student so that he may be stimulated by the success drive that is so fruitful of productive activity. Just as the manager succeeds or fails in light of the spirit shown by the members of the baseball team or their belief in the cause for which they are striving, so is the child able to make progress when he is interested in the activity. We can help him keep it there when we provide stimulating and challenging situations for him to meet and solve.

The urge to avoid failure and disappointment. Study the effect upon a child when he fails to do that which he is striving to do. What do you observe in his behavior? Do you find him carrying his head erect or does it droop a little? The learning process can be inhibited or stimulated through teaching techniques. The school that emphasizes failure is not giving the pupil the best chance to get ahead. A teacher who emphasizes success and so individualizes instruction that the learning of the child will be a continuous process rather than a matter of mere promotion from grade to grade is giving attention to individual differences. In the name of good mental hygiene for all concerned—the bright, the average, and the dull—the system of promotions needs to be changed. Teachers then will be prepared to report on the progress of the child at any stage of his school life in terms of accomplishment and not in terms of how many subjects he has not "passed."

Some teachers allow the danger of failure to become a major fear to a learner. Failure is so powerful and so overwhelming that it often inhibits children to the extent that they lose their ability to function effectively. This denies them the success feeling that they normally would have attained had the fear of failure not been instilled.

We are not suggesting that "failure" can be eliminated from life experiences; but we do suggest that more can be done in school life to eliminate the fear effects of failure. A pattern too often has been followed that has helped make educational loafers of the bright and failures and misfits of the dull.

Mastery drives.   It is not enough simply to be doing something. The human being desires to be able to do at least one thing well. Adler believes that the human being desires *to be superior* in some way and that this is the dominant motive underlying basic human behavior. There may be a question about this conclusion. Yet all will agree that "mastery" is fundamental to individual development. The human being seeks to gain attention to and approval of his ideals. When he can socialize his interests, the mastery drive becomes especially wholesome and fruitful.

Attempts by an individual to establish superiority in certain activities very often are responses to a recognition of his weaknesses. If this feeling of inferiority is compensated for through a socially valuable activity, the effect is beneficial. On the other hand, if the individual attempts to achieve superiority through an evasion or another compensating measure, the total effect will be the development of undesirable personality qualities. Or, if this person is trained to make wise use of his abilities, energies, and time, he may extend the greatest possible latitude to the urge of becoming the master of himself, of a certain field of knowledge, or of the situations in which he finds himself from day to day.

Because of the great desire to succeed and to be superior, many persons who fail to earn success through honest effort based upon limited ability turn to unfair tactics. Such behavior may include stealing, lying, or other subterfuge, in order to secure the public approval they crave.

The urge for recognition and approval.   This desire is closely associated with the success urge, but its functioning concerns the attitude of others as well as the inner satisfaction that accompanies achievement through application of one's effort to an individual project. All people experience a feeling of satisfaction in the successful completion of tasks. However, the feeling is magnified and intensified when it is given the approval of the group. Many behavior problems in school are the direct results of the failure on the part of a teacher to give proper recognition or approval to the respective achievements of a child. When a child cannot obtain approval through desirable and acceptable means, he often uses other less desirable techniques.

A boy is careful of his English in a group because he desires approval; a girl dresses as she does because she seeks recognition; a college student conforms or does not conform in order to gain attention for himself. There are great differences among people as to the kind of approval that is desired and as to the form that the approval will take. In our daily life we take too many people for granted. A housewife works many hours preparing an attractive and well-balanced dinner, hoping for an expression of appreciation. A teacher or a student has done a good piece of work for which he desires approval. The giving of deserved praise takes little time and is productive of so much personal satisfaction to the deserving person or persons that the recognition given usually is followed by more and better efforts on the part of the individual praised.

The wise leader appreciates also the effective use of disapproval. It is one of his strongest aids in directing behavior into the channels in which it should go. To be willing to give praise when and if deserved, to be ready to disapprove misbehavior, and to recognize and approve desirable attitudes are basic to the development of socially commendable and effective attitudes that will function in a wholesome way in the life of an individual.

The urge for sympathy and affection. A dominant drive is that of sympathy. We constantly seek the sympathy of others. A child has a difficult problem to solve. If he can talk about it to a sympathetic listener, his ego is helped. The child receives a scolding. There is easing of the sting if he can talk about the incident to someone who appears to be understanding. The child injures himself. If he can suffer in the presence of those who give him sympathy and who show by their actions that they know how badly it hurts, the child is thereby comforted, and tensions are relaxed.

Any problem that requires the sympathetic understanding of a superior or of a group can be handled in the light of all the inherent factors. Sympathy can be given in a wholesome manner. It needs, however, to be given objectively, and continued so long as its effects are of positive value to the person needing it. As much harm can come from its use as can good, if the person learns to withdraw from situations just to get the sympathy of others. It may be better in that case to withhold sympathy and offer an understanding reproof.

Even though sympathy is sought by all of us in varying degrees, at different times and under different circumstances, tactful expressions of it often seem difficult. Have you ever felt helpless in trying to extend your true feelings to another? To sympathize is to experience, with the hope that the other person will appreciate your true feeling toward him in the specific situation under consideration. At a time of great sorrow we try to be sympathetic. We search for words and know that they are inadequate because we realize that we can feel so much more than we can reveal through words. Fortunately, the other person usually is able to recognize the sincerity of our affection, sympathy, or respect even though our overt expression of these attitudes may be inadequate.

The urge for security.   A feeling of insecurity is one of the most serious factors of maladjustment. An individual, in order to be satisfied with his life adjustment, needs to be sure that he has earned the respect and admiration of his coworkers, that he is secure in the affections of his family and of his intimate friends, that he is in no danger of losing his job, and that he and his family may be reasonably certain to enjoy financial security throughout their lives. The child craves the security of his parents' love and protection; the individual at any age desires to be confident that his presence is welcomed in his social group; the worker needs to be sure that his workmanship and his employer's financial stability are such that he is relatively free from the fear of adverse criticism or loss of his job.

Economic security is an important mental and emotional adjuster. An increasing number of persons are seeking affiliation with organizations that offer tenure of job and pension rights. Consequently, the number of civil-service employees has increased tremendously. Workers gradually become interested in stable and permanent though possibly lower incomes rather than in immediately higher but possibly insecure wages. Desire for security against loss of income resulting from death, disease, accident, unemployment and similar factors of economic insecurity has materially advanced the popularity of all forms of public and private insurance plans.

The urge to experience the new and the different.   The craving for adventure inherent in every normal human being is limited in its expression by the many restrictions imposed upon an individual's behavior through the social and environmental restrictions of present-day civilization. Consequently, an individual needs to develop a respect for values.

Children find little difficulty in discovering excellent outlets for their spirit of adventure; but to the extent that the adult's regular work is routinized, he must satisfy this urge in other ways. He may turn, for relief, to gambling or to some other *undesirable* habit. This urge is sometimes satisfied through attendance at a night club, through the frequenting of the "hangout" of the gang where the adventure is largely a matter of tall stories, or through actual exploits that are harmful to the community.

It is normal to want to see a new car, a new face, a new scene, a new picture, a new anything. In some people these drives are spasmodic and completely unplanned. That is, a person does not want to participate in planned activity. He wants to be free to follow his whims of the moment. He decides to do one thing today and another tomorrow. Another person develops some control of his spirit of adventure. Consequently, he eventually gains his desired experiences but is the better for it since he has cultivated the art of living and experiencing in a systematized way. He knows that he will be able to get across the river much more quickly by ferrying than by swimming.

The wise leader constantly provides situations that awaken the spirit of adventure in desirable ways, thereby satisfying the drive through exhilarating and productive activities. Awaken his interest, and a man will have as much enjoyment in working with a new idea as he will with the *new* in other situations.

The sex urge.   This drive is powerful and biologically important. It is so powerful that animals have been known to go through difficult pain stimulations in order to satisfy it. The human often shuts his eyes to disease possibilities or social disapproval in attempts to give unbridled expression to the sex drive. Nature uses this drive to secure the perpetuation of the species. It takes many forms in subhuman organisms, during their mating activities and the production of offspring, and in providing for the latter's growth and development. In humans, energy is produced by the physical organism in order to make possible the satisfaction of this urge.

Physical stimuli are potent motivators of sexual behavior because of the sensitivity of the genital organs and other erogenous zones. The psychological factor is extremely significant, however. Memory and imaginations play their part in associating past experiences and present stimuli with romantic or sexual satisfaction. Much of a person's activity is influenced by interests and attitudes that have their bases in the sexual urge to reproduce but that have been refined and sublimated so that they express themselves in creative productions of literature, music or art, or in activity directed toward the welfare of other persons.

This physical urge or appetite is more constant in the human than it is in animals. He differs from them in his capacity for thought and feeling, his ability to remember and to plan, and his interest in the emotions with which the physical and biological drives of sex are invested. It is the human's capacity for love that, through his work and play, has so utilized his creative abilities as to give much beauty to art and religion and to the many other aspects of his life that he has changed for world betterment.

In an advancing civilization the persistency of the sex drive makes necessary a psychological development. There is a psychosexual development that includes the thoughts, feelings, and emotional attitudes which accompany the physical maturing of the reproductive organs from birth. These mental attitudes are influenced by the inner nature of man and by environmental and educational factors, especially by the incidental sentiments and attitudes of which the child becomes increasingly aware in his enlarging environment. He develops certain mental and emotional patterns or ways of thinking and feeling that give him his social attitudes toward sex, and condition his sex drive to that extent.

It is through his early experiences in his family life that the child develops his basic patterns of love life upon which he builds his later love relationships. Given the example of desirable parental behavior and of other adult life in the home, a child can build strong, wholesome attitudes that are devoid of the "suggestive" which so fill the thinking of those who are shocked to learn that the children are imitating adult behavior. Without their realizing it, adults give children distorted attitudes in the area of sex. Many of these are difficult to outgrow.

▶ **Questions and Problems for Discussion**

1. Discuss the influence of inner drives upon overt behavior.
2. Indicate in what ways stimuli and readiness are important to the arousal of urges.

3. Describe ways in which motives are affected by personal interests.

4. Explain the effect of imitation, suggestion, and integration upon motives.

5. Give examples to indicate that the spirit of adventure is easily satisfied.

6. List and explain reasons why adolescents are rebellious against authority.

7. In what ways may the approval of another become a motivating force in your life?

8. To what extent are you motivated to further activity by praise? by punishment?

9. Name two urges which you have, in the past, satisfied in unwholesome ways. Report behavior changes that might have been made for better adjustment.

10. What can school do to reduce the damaging effect of failure upon learners?

11. Compare the motives of children with those of adolescents; with those of adults. What differences do you find?

12. Explain fully what is meant by motivation.

13. Explain why the urge for security is so important to an individual.

14. What are the individual adjustment problems that arise because of the strength of the sex urge?

CHAPTER Five

Mental Activity and Adjustment

D ESIRABLE adjustment to human relationships is closely associated with an individual's degree of mental growth and development. Throughout his life every human being is challenged constantly by situations in which there is needed an evaluation by him of the factors inherent in the situation, both within and outside himself. To the extent that a person has the mental power to evaluate his own attitudes and behavior in his association with other people he is helped thereby to satisfy his needs, his wants, and his interests, in terms of socially effective patterns of activity.

An individual gradually develops the power to recognize his own inherited potentiality and acquired ability. As these effect changes in his habit patterns, he learns to adjust to whatever situations in which he may find himself. Fortunate is the person who develops early an intelligent and scientific approach to the problems that confront him as he strives toward life adjustment. The young person who is trained in sound techniques of problem solving is being helped to establish thinking habits that can be of great service to him throughout his entire life.

Basic Factors of Mental Activity

A s a person looks at a book, not only is he aware of the book as an object in his environment, but he also is conscious of its significance in his past or present experience. If an individual is stimulated by an emotion-arousing situation, he is aware not only of the situation itself but also of its effect upon himself.

Significance of mental activity. Every activity, be it digging a ditch, making a pie, painting a picture, driving an automobile, or advising another person, requires coordinated bodily function and movement. However, basic to more or less habitual overt behavior there must be well-integrated and specifically trained mental direction of the activity, if the results are to be satisfying. *Thinking* and *doing* go hand in hand. The deed cannot be completely successful unless the thought behind it is well organized and adequate. Mental activity is stimulated and directed by environmental factors. The results of mental activity show themselves in overt behavior.

In order to transmit *ideas* or the material of mental activity from one person to another, certain vocalizations have come to take on specific meaning in the form of words in this or that language. The fact that man has been able to give identity of meaning to words has made possible the transmission of ideas. In so far as an individual, through inherent mental alertness and adequate training, is enabled to understand his relation to the world about him and to give satisfactory expression of this understanding in his words and deeds, he achieves a well-adjusted personality. Moreover, his life is enriched as he responds continuously to all the influences by which he is surrounded.

Mental life as a cumulative process. Mental growth is a continuous process. An individual is never too old to learn something new. In a favorable environment a person gradually acquires knowledge and experience that function as grist to the mental mill. As he lives among people, a person is stimulated by their behavior to build up attitudes toward them and relationships with them. The keener is his mental acuity and the greater his emotional control, the more likely he will be correctly to evaluate existing customs and mores, and the more able he will become to adapt his own thinking and behavior toward personally satisfying and socially desirable ends.

Consider an individual from birth onward and note the changes that gradually take place within him as he attempts to respond to the many situations by which he is stimulated. His attitudes, his needs, and his wants fluctuate as he lives in his environment and interacts with it. If he is helped to build habit patterns of worthwhile thinking and action, his personality will be strengthened by his day-by-day experiences, by his integration and adjustments, and by the energies that he utilizes in order to harmonize his inner drives and desires with the interests of the social order. The cumulative effect of education gives encouragement to those who believe in the possibility of effective mental development through the utilization of the agencies and influences of the environment, as these stimulate the capacities and aptitudes of the individual.

Normal mental activity. The greater part of mental activity falls within the concept of *normal*. Under certain conditions, every person may deviate from the normal in one way or another. So long as an individual does not vary too much in his mental activity from the social norm he is accepted as one whose thinking is acceptable.

An individual lives in a group and is expected to exhibit behavior traits that are in keeping with those of the group. His intelligence, his specific aptitude, his skills, his emotional reactions, and his other personality or character traits must not deviate too far from those of the majority of his associates if he is to be considered normal in his mental responses.

The mores of a group need to be known in order to determine whether the behavior of any member is satisfactory for that group. Since group attitudes may shift their emphases from time to time, the term *abnormal* is a relative one. What is abnormal thinking or behavior at one time later may become normal thinking or behavior. Hence, although the normal person is likely to encounter many difficult problems of social adjustment, he keeps his major personality traits functioning by virtue of established habit patterns of thinking and of dominant drives or motives.

Although mental activity goes on continuously, it may be greatly reduced at one time and greatly accelerated at another time. When one is aware of his mental activity it is regarded as being on the conscious level. Mental activity of which we are unaware at the moment but which we recognize through its functioning is referred to by such terms as subconscious or unconscious activity.

Mental activity, at any one time, is influenced by environmental stimuli. One situation arouses certain mental functionings; another situation encourages another phase of mental activity. At any given moment little of a person's accumulated experience is in the focus of consciousness. Thus it is possible for an individual to show different sides of his personality or his different "selves," at different times and to different people. He may "think" one way in one group and another way in another group. It is only as mental habits become relatively fixed that an individual develops consistency in his relationships with other people.

Development of Positive Mental Habit Patterns

P E O P L E differ in their ability to learn. Differences in the amount and rate of learning are explained partly in terms of ability or capacity. The greater the power of a person to deal with abstract ideas by means of words, the more intelligent he is presumed to be. Although there is disagreement concerning the exact meaning of intelligence, it is commonly thought of as referring to understanding, alertness, capacity to profit by instruction, or ability to adapt to novel situations.

It is known that some persons adjust to life situations better than do others. There appear to be differences among individuals in the ability to understand and to respond to the demands of a given situation. The more intelligent are able to learn more quickly and with greater success than are the less intelligent. A sound educational program not only stimulates the mentally superior toward better use of their inherent abilities, but also encourages the less able to meet their day-by-day responsibilities adequately. Apart from formalized education, every individual (more or less consciously) acquires, within his mental capacity to do so, a host of adaptations to the demands of group living.

The development of intelligent behavior. Education does not begin when a child enters school. From birth to death an individual responds more or less successfully to informal educational influences. Habits are formed almost unconsciously. Many of these habits arise out of the customs of the group and are useful to the individual. However, one must be careful lest he lose the habit of adaptability to changing conditions. When and if a person allows his thinking and behavior to follow fixed patterns, he is admitting to himself that intelligent application of energy no longer is desired and that change or adjustment is to be avoided rather than sought.

At any given time behavior is dominated by impulses that are stimulated by one or more sets of conditions. Impulses arising from stimulation of the eye, the ear, or another sense organ combine to form a pattern of behavior that is adjusted to inner urges as well as to environmental situations. There is present in all intelligent behavior an attempt at inner changes that will conform with environmental demands. This struggle continues as long as there are desirable goals that have not yet been attained.

If a person's behavior is motivated by definite goals and objectives, by desirable interests and ambitions, by a recognition of duty and a sense of justice, and by an urge to achieve, he is likely to possess a high degree of integration in his mental life. His attitudes and activities are consistent. His associates are able to predict with confidence what his probable reactions in any situation will be. Minor or incidental interests or attitudes may influence his responses in a particular situation, but his fundamental thinking patterns will dominate his general behavior.

If a person lacks dominating drives or motives, he is not able to direct his mental activity so effectively as he could through the application of interested effort in the solution of the problems that confront him. A worker who understands the purpose of his job and the steps that are necessary for the achievement of this purpose is in a position to bring to his work his best mental effort. His interest in the project stimulates him toward careful and thoughtful workmanship on his own initiative. Thus he develops self-control and self-direction that will further his own mental development.

As a person achieves desirable habits of diet, elimination, sleep, work, and relaxation, and as his interests, ambitions, and relationships with other people follow satisfying behavior patterns, his energies gradually are directed toward personally and socially accepted roles. Through his highly organized and sensibly functioning behavior patterns the individual achieves a healthy, wholesome, and well-integrated personality. To the extent that a person's habits do not function harmoniously there may arise faulty adjustment and inner conflict, or actual mental disorder may result.

Factors that promote learning.   A learner cannot begin easily with an absolutely new learning situation. The mastering by an American, who has had no previous experience with a foreign language, of the Chinese language begins with the learner's understanding of the function of any language. From this starting point he attempts a mastery of symbols that are very different from those of his own language. Through a constant repetition of these symbols in varying relationships he gains an understanding of the rudiments of Chinese media of communication. The success of this mastery, step by step, brings with it a satisfying effect that, in turn, makes the learner more ready to apply his already-acquired skill toward more complete mastery of Chinese.

An individual interested in learning, willing to give time and effort to it, and possessing a healthy nervous system, can utilize his motives and drives to establish a system of thinking habits that will serve him at all times. The person does not suddenly acquire an education. He achieves whatever degree of mental development he possesses through experiencing, thinking, integrating, and acting. These all function together to make productive thinking possible. Whatever skill one possesses has come to him only through the hard road of application and more application until he establishes relationships.

Values.   In order to become effective citizens we constantly must choose and evaluate. Whatever direction the mental development takes must be based upon ethical and social considerations. We must be responsive to the mores and social codes of our age and community. An active wish may involve more than the individual. Many of us are responsive to the wishes and thoughts of others. What satisfies others should not set the limits of the satisfactions that should be ours, however.

The human attends to the physical and social stimuli of his environment; he is conscious of the values that are emphasized; he learns to discriminate in his selection of situations, places, people, and, eventually, particular stimuli. He not only selects his friends, but is selected by them. His friends have definite traits to which he attends as he seeks their company. He has definite reasons, usually unexpressed, for the choices that he makes. These attitudes of attention and of ability to choose and select are among the important human achievements. They determine the kind of environment that the individual selects for himself. In turn, the stimuli in that selected environment determine the kind and nature of the mental development that he will experience.

Importance of Perception in Mental Activity

M E N T A L activity and development are made possible through the adequate functioning of the sense organs. These sensory experiences or perceptions are meaningful sensations that assume an important role in the life of an individual, in psychological research, and in the clinic.

Figure 2 [1]

Observe the black vase on the white background. Now fixate on the white part of the page. What do you see?

Perception is influenced by the structure of the sense organs, by both present and past experience, and by attitudes of the individual at the moment. If the eyes are unable to discriminate between what is seen and what actually exists, an illusion results. For example, if you drive along the Pulaski Highway at the rate of fifty miles per hour, it is impossible to see the six-inch iron posts that are spaced six inches apart. The eye records only the light, and there is clear vision. However, if the driver slows down to twenty miles per hour it is difficult to see between the posts.

[1] From L. D. Crow, A. Crow, and C. E. Skinner, *Psychology in Nursing Practice* (New York: The Macmillan Company, 1954), revised ed., p. 250. Used with the permission of The Macmillan Company.

Misinterpretations are the causes of false perceptions or of different perceptions in situations. Two distinct perceptions can be experienced from ambiguous figures. An outline of a book, for example, can be seen in two different positions—facing toward you or facing away from you. The picture shifts from one to the other. Another illustration of perceptual shift from one pattern to another is shown in Figure 2. As you look at the figure, new meanings and organizations are brought to bear upon the situation. First look at the black vase; then look at the two faces in the figure. If at one time you fixate on one part of the figure you perceive one picture; at another time a different picture. At one moment you perceive the black vase against a white background, and at another you perceive the two faces as in a frame against a black background. The frequency of these fluctuations depends upon the individual and his attempting to hold one perception in focus as long as possible. In spite of your best efforts to prevent these fluctuations, they will occur in both the book outline and in the above figure.

Mental set, an attitude of expecting an object or situation to be something in particular, affects perception. A child who expects ice cream may believe that a dish of cottage cheese is ice cream until he tastes it. The ringing of the telephone may appear to be the door-

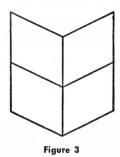

Figure 3

As you fixate on this outline observe how the book reverses its position.

bell, if you expect a visitor. A strange voice on the telephone may be mistaken for the voice of a friend from whom you expected a telephone call. Mental set affects perceptual development in both favorable and unfavorable ways. The magician is an artist at getting the members of his audience to see or hear what he wants them to see or hear. Normally, an individual develops adequate perceptions.

Significant disorders of perception. Although illusions occur as daily experiences they seldom are classified as disorders. Grave perceptual disorders, however, may arise from defective sensory equipment, limited experience, or disordered thinking.

Hallucinations represent significant perceptual disorders. In a hallucination there is no situation present to induce the perception, yet the response appears to emanate from sensory stimulation. However, a hallucination is defined as a perceptual response to the nonexisting sensory pattern of experience. At one time a sharp line of distinction was drawn between an illusion and a hallucination in terms of the need of sensory stimulation. Now, it is believed that there may be present a slight sensory element which is misinterpreted. Thus the victim of delirium tremens seems to perceive "snakes" or "fierce lions."

Hallucinations are uncommon during the waking life of normal individuals. Yet among the mentally ill hallucinations are frequent, either during the day or at night. It is possible, however, for a normal person to experience a hallucination when he is ill or excessively fatigued. A strong mental set during the day may produce a hallucination at night. For example, a person may hear the voice of his or her mother who has recently died. Or a teacher who is especially anxious about the behavior of the members of his class may experience unusual difficulty with them during sleep. This type of hallucinatory experience is connected with night dreams. Extreme hallucinations during waking hours are likely to indicate a serious mental disorder, however.

Importance of Thinking as Mental Activity

I N thinking, the mental process is not confined to the particular object or event as it is in perception or memory. It has to do with what a person experienced yesterday or the day before and the ideas that were associated with them, without regard to time or place. Its nature is general or universal. There is a close association with imagination, although in imagination the emphasis is upon a particular form. There are four kinds of thinking inherent in human development and adjustment. They are (1) free association, (2) daydreaming, (3) autistic thinking, and (4) reasoning. The meaning and significance of each are presented briefly in the following. Thinking occurs as the individual experiences images of former experiences, as he utilizes the necessary symbols (words). There is meaning in this flow of consciousness as the relationships are established between ideas.

Daydreams enable an individual to escape temporarily from unpleasant situations. Through imagination he can reshape reality to conform to his unsatisfied motives, and the goals can be attained without any delay. During a class period, for example, he can turn his thoughts toward more pleasant fields; he can cut short a long journey; he can achieve his highest ambition without coping with the frustrations or disappointments that occur so frequently in real life. When imagination is stimulated, mental activity may proceed without external stimulation; past experiences can be reorganized into weird patterns; reality can be controlled to suit the needs of the person. All this can be completed within the confines of the classroom and the class period.

Reverie or *autistic* thinking is self-directed and engaged in by everyone. It represents mental activity on the level of the present. Through free association of ideas, daydreaming, or night dreams we satisfy our desires without regard for logical principles. Much of an individual's mental activity during the day may be motivated toward self or autistic thinking. There may be an intermingling among free association, daydreams, and, perhaps, motivation toward reasoning.

In their discussion of autistic thinking Asher, Tiffin, and Knight suggest:

> When thought sequences are determined entirely by the desires of the thinker, with complete disregard of logical principles, facts, reality, or social confirmation, we have a kind of thinking known as *autistic thinking*. It might be called wishful thinking. It may go on as fantasy-thinking which serves directly or obscurely the imaginary gratification of unfulfilled desires. In this form it is not unlike the daydream. On the other hand, it may occur on a reality level. Here, however, it is so strongly motivated by deep-seated desires that the desires are represented as already fulfilled. Incompatibilities with reality are ignored.

This type of thinking is more prevalent in childhood than in adulthood, partly because of the immaturity and lack of experience of children and partly because of the treatment accorded them. The household is regulated to meet the infant's every need. Hardly does he cry for food before it is brought to him. If he drops something on the floor, a willing attendant replaces it. When sleepy, he is made comfortable in bed. If he shows interest in an object, it is given him. His every desire is satisfied through no effort of his own. The infant has reason to believe that thought is omnipotent. It takes time for him to learn differently. . . .

Though many things combine to help bring about the needed discipline, autistic thinking is seldom completely outgrown. Many adults do not see a thing as it is because of their desire that it should be different. A man who wishes to become governor of a state may convince himself that he has numerous friends throughout the state who are anxious to make him governor, when, as a matter of fact, he may be poorly qualified for the office and have only a few supporters. Or a woman may seriously argue that she needs a new dress when she already has more dresses than she can afford.[2]

Reasoning as the highest type of thinking is directed toward action in which the individual comes face to face with a problem. The problem may be immediate or deferred. Dewey presented five steps in reasoning; a host of others have organized examples to illustrate these steps. In his discussion of the principal stages in reasoning, Dashiell, however, uses slightly different labels in his explanations of the steps involved. The reader may be interested in this approach because of its clarity.

According to Dewey's famous analysis, a complete act of reasoning would include five steps. Not all five always appear distinctly in everyone's reasoning but they are at least implied.

(*1*) *Maladjustment.* Some crux or difficulty obstructs the motivated person. It may be a practical prob-

[2] Eston Jackson Asher, Joseph Tiffin, and Frederic B. Knight, *Introduction to General Psychology*, pp. 340–341. Copyright, 1953, by D. C. Heath and Company and reprinted with their permission.

lem for him, like a waste-pipe that is stopped up, a distant
city that must be reached by some one of several routes,
an error in the day's balance sheet, the soil of a field that
demands special treatment for raising a certain crop, or a
party that must be given for one's house guests. Again,
the difficulty may be a theoretical question, like the identity of the real murderer in a detective story, or the au-
thorship of the Apocrypha, or the causes of a war, or the
boundaries of the universe.

(2) *Diagnosis.* The difficulty is located and defined
by discrimination and insight. Precisely what is the source
of the trouble? The man who buys the bottle of patent
medicine because he is not feeling well is on much the
same level of diagnosing as the college girl who fails in
chemistry and admits to her counselor that she does not
know whether the trouble lies with her laboratory work,
her notebook, her reading of the text, or her understanding of the lectures. A first requirement in a good reasoner
is an ability to discern and go to the heart of the matter. . . . When one is facing a situation that is urgent he
must face the difficulty in as clear-eyed a manner as possible. He must try to locate the crux of the matter, as precisely and narrowly as he can. The physician calls this
diagnosing; but the lawyer, too, must perform this function for his client, and the businessman for himself and his
partners. Ability to put one's finger on the sore spot, to go
to the root of the matter, is the first intelligent step toward
a solution.

(3) *Hypothesis.* To any but the most stupid people, various suggestions, guesses, conjectures, will occur
in the form of nascent or tentative activities that may
promise to solve the difficulty. Tentative formulations or
concepts appear in the cogitations of a lawyer, an engineer, a physician, a manufacturer, a tradesman, or a chef.
"Is this a case of . . . or a case of . . . ?" Now, this
phase of reasoning is more or less adventurous. The step
is taken not as a directly determined consequent of the
immediately preceding (as when one says "34" after "27
and 7"), but is a trial, a "flyer." This inductive leap, as

the logicians call it, depends not upon a person's logical
consecutiveness in thinking but upon his fertility, his
spontaneous and seemingly irresponsible originality. On
the other hand, simply because the new idea or hunch or
inspiration seems often to pop up uncaused by the immediately preceding train of thought, we are not to assume
that it is uncaused. It is, of course, a function of the particular individual, and arises somehow from the deeper
groundwork of his habits and attitudes which have longer
histories than this particular episode. What controls its
arousal now? . . .

(*4*) *Deductions.* Once a suggestion for solving a
difficulty has occurred to a man, he will examine it carefully—unless he is the snap judgment sort of person who
goes off half-cocked and at any tangent. His inspirations
may come to him best in irresponsible fury, but he must
check them in critical phlegm. He must follow out their
bearings, must deduce their consequences. "*If I* do this,
then what will happen?" "*If* this is the real fact, then what
about *x* and *y* and *z*?"

Here is the point where the formalized logic of the
philosopher has its application. His syllogism is a device
for explicitly setting forth the involved concepts and
their relations so that their cogency may be directly as-
certained. Compare the two following:

(*A*) Bubbles are appearing on this liquid in my test
tube.
When sulphuric acid is poured on copper, bubbles
will appear on the surface.
Therefore, the contents of my test tube are sul-
phuric acid and copper.
(*B*) All animals having jointed dorsal columns are ver-
tebrates.
This specimen has a jointed dorsal column.
Therefore, this specimen is a vertebrate.

For a clear-cut example of deductive reasoning in
which each step is seen to follow clearly upon its pred-

ecessors, the reader should turn to geometry and its succession of propositions.

(5) *Observations or experiments.* The purely subjective check made by deduction often needs the support
of an objective check, either by literally trying the hypothesis out, or by watching for further instances to see
if it will fit them. Does it square with the observed facts?

Finally, at the conclusion of his thinking, the thinker
is ready for action again; and if his interpretation or solution has stood the tests of consistency in step 4, and of
validity in step 5, it will become his cue for further conduct or for further thinking.[3]

Creative thinking involves the same mental processes that are
utilized in other forms of thinking—experience, association, and
expression. As a correlate of reasoning, creative thinking has been
analyzed into four stages: (1) preparation, (2) incubation, (3) inspiration, and (4) verification. A long period of preparation and the
development of insight are needed in creative thinking. It results
from the application of energy to discover new relationships.

In his excellent discussion Johnson presents the following analysis of creative thought.

In spite of all the irregularities and peculiarities of
procedure in creative thinking, several acute observers, of
their own thoughts and others', have agreed in identifying
four phases: *preparation, incubation, illumination,* and *revision.* One psychologist, Catherine Patrick, has been able
to obtain more or less objective evidence for these phases
by asking poets and artists, as well as untrained students,
to write a poem, or draw a picture, or plan a psychological
experiment.

Preparation is the initial phase of organizing the data
at hand, setting up the requirements of the problem, and
the production of pertinent ideas or thoughts. It usually
begins as soon as one brings his thoughts to focus on a
problem and can be identified by looking over the poet's

or artist's shoulder and noting the occurrence of new thoughts or directions of activity.

Incubation, which is often the next phase, consists of "the spontaneous recurrence from time to time of a mood or idea with more or less modification, while the subject is thinking of other topics." Many artists, scientists, and inventors have testified that they often incubate an idea for months—working on it occasionally, then forgetting it temporarily—before it develops into a usable product. Even when a poem is written to order, for an inquisitive psychologist, the basic ideas of the finished poem may be thought of in the first few minutes, then discarded in favor of others, then recalled and reworked, discarded again, and so on. Most creative thought, 60 to 80 per cent of experimental cases, gives evidence of this sort for the phenomenon of incubation.

Illumination is the formulation or organization of the central idea, form, or design on which a poem, picture, experiment, or invention is based. The idea or plan, which has often been incubating for some time, may be accompanied by emotion: "Hurrah! I've got it!" It may come to mind suddenly, in a flash of insight, and mysteriously, as if it had no antecedents, but when the phenomenon of incubation and the suddenness of perceptual reorganization are recalled, much of the mystery dissolves. Nevertheless, illumination is often a dramatic moment, a favorite of the biographers of great thinkers.

Revision is the refining and polishing of the central idea, i.e., putting it into finished form. The thinker's attitude during revision is quite different and certainly less excited than during the earlier phases. He stands back and looks critically at his efforts, recalls his main purpose and his audience, looks at general effects and details. He judges the relative advantages of alternative solutions and may even calculate gains and losses. If the finished product looks good, he is done. Thought ceases. If not, the whole creative process may begin anew, or he may pick out a small part to be adjusted or polished or reworked. Any careful observer, watching an artist, poet, scientist, inventor, or ingenious businessman at work, can differentiate this phase from the others if the thinker will talk about his efforts and disclose his progress to view.[4]

The Affective Side of Mental Development

M A N's mental and emotional nature is such that he strives to become as complete an individual as he can. He needs the stimulation of challenging problems. He desires to know some of the limitations imposed upon him, yet he does not want to be hemmed in on all sides by restrictions. Give him freedom, within limits. When he is adequately stirred, he will create ideas through his insight, experience, and previous learning. Deny him this feeling of personal accomplishment, and the thinking possibilities of which he is capable may be inhibited.

Value of freedom of expression. For fundamental adjustment, a maximum of desirable freedom is necessary. If it is to be wholesome, individual freedom needs to be limited by the rules of the game, by the customs of the group, by social codes, or by the restrictions that respective groups have imposed upon themselves in order to insure efficient and effective group living. The individual can be given a chance to achieve within the limits of the rules, without too close supervision. His training at every step may help him to respect any trust that has been placed in him for the extension of his own self-direction and control.

If adults fail to provide for children the kind of activity that keeps the latter busy and gives them an opportunity to exercise their boundless energy, young people are likely to plan and carry out their own activities with consequent harm to themselves or others. Young children crave activity and need to be given opportunities for engaging in worth-while projects without too severe restrictions upon their activity. To prescribe is to inhibit. A well-trained adult gives guidance in such a way that implicit obedience is expected in fundamental situations, so that the child may make wise use of the freedom that is granted to him from time to time.

A child can be led to understand the difference that exists

[4] By permission from *Essentials of Psychology*, by Donald M. Johnson. Copyright, 1948. McGraw-Hill Book Company, Inc., pp. 206–8.

between freedom to do as one wishes without regard for the rights of others and freedom of activity that respects the welfare and safety of other members of the group. It has been the misuse of freedom that has caused the adult to hesitate to extend it to the growing child. If we guide the child's thinking and direct his behavior within desirable limits, however, the young person is likely to use his freedom in desirable ways. When social freedom and clear understanding go hand in hand, fewer individual and social difficulties arise.

Danger to society often comes from the person who has been closely guarded and not trained, rather than from the person who has been carefully trained and not so closely guarded. Yet, when attempts are made to give added responsibility to an individual so that he can do his work in his own way, opposition to this freedom often arises from unexpected sources. If freedom of activity is to become an accepted ideal, there must be general agreement as to what constitutes freedom of expression and to what extent it is desirable.

If an individual who exhibits a wholesome attitude toward his activity, whether the activity is pursued alone or with others, or a leader who can guide the activities of the individual and of the group is given freedom within reasonable limits, there is encouraged the development of responsibility, initiative, and insight, and a better adjustment of all—individually and socially. These questions are often asked: Can a child be trusted with freedom? How much freedom should be given to a leader? Too much freedom, unintelligently used, is dangerous. If, during their training, both the child and the leader know that they are to be granted extended freedom of action, habits of responsibility can be developed. Consequently, desirable individual and social results can be anticipated.

Character in relation to mental activity. A healthy-minded person tends to respect the truth. The attitude of wanting to tell the truth dominates the life of such an individual. Since character traits are built early in life, parents and other adults are responsible for the development of a child's habits of truthfulness or dishonesty. This is true of all personal attitudes and behavior patterns that can be referred to as character traits. Sometimes we tend toward a self-righteous criticism of a person who is engaging in undesirable overt behavior. Too often, as we criticize, we fail to recognize the fact that we have contributed to the development of the undesirable behavior pattern.

A quantitative description of one's behavior indicates the relative strength or weakness of certain character traits. "Virtues and vices" are important in all social relations. The character of an individual determines for the individual his ultimate success and happiness so far as social values are concerned. The laws of learning and habit formation are of prime importance in the formation of character. Many a person's character qualities are results of imitation, either conscious or unconscious. Suggestion also is powerful and contributes in various ways to the ultimate mental attitudes and character traits that are potently active in the dynamic life of an individual.

Religious experience and mental development. Human beings respond to values which are spiritual in nature. No matter how sordid the social conditions, there is in man a hope that springs eternal. More often than not he is able to view existing conditions in the light of their larger meanings and relationships. When the emphasis in religion is changed from creed or formalized belief to belief or faith in the supernatural, to a faith in the order of things, to a faith in human beings, it is then that the doubter more fully appreciates the significance of religion.

If religion is to function in the lives of people, it must do so through the specific creeds that have been developed and that are being developed. The child acquires an appreciation of spiritual values from the home in his daily living, as well as through his attendance at religious services. Religion is an experience, and one grows in strength in it as he continues attending to and living that experience. Most of these experiences are caught as they are taught.

Sound religious experience has many possibilities. It gives the individual a chance to face his total existence and to adjust his attitude toward the whole life. A healthy state of mind is achieved when a person enlarges his perspective. Among the well-adjusted and happy people are those who are keenly sensitive to the spiritual values about them and who are not overwhelmed by the existence of other forces that are striving to destroy those values.

Most people who achieve wholesome religious attitudes are able to resolve some of their difficulties as they attempt to realize higher values. This amelioration of inner disturbance sometimes comes through a religious experience called *conversion*. True conversion recognizes a reorganization of purposes and enables the individual to develop a greater harmony both within himself and with his environment, upon the basis of spiritual values. The mental attitudes resulting from these religious experiences tend to give strength and poise to the individual. This feeling of confidence that a truly spiritual man possesses is a source of mental stability.

It is possible that inadequate forms of religion develop a narrow emotional and intellectual outlook to which the individual's whole pattern of life must conform. Religion is not lived solely on the emotional level. To be most worth-while in our advancing culture, spiritual adjustment increasingly is becoming a persistent human need. The greatest ethical values will accrue to him who is disciplined in the religious experiences that emphasize righteous, wholesome living.

Our faith should supplement not contradict our reason. We can recognize that there are values which we have been unable to reduce to logical or scientific terms. The faith by which we live should be afforded a place in our rational thinking. It gives us assurance that the idealism to which we hold will help us further to understand the events of life and their relationships.

Power of interest in attempting something new. Many persons grow up under the constant and close supervision of others to the extent that they are not permitted to try anything new or different for fear that the consequences may be undesirable. The result is that, as adults, these persons are timid and are afraid to confront or to meet new or different situations. They have not learned to make decisions for themselves in terms of their own best judgment, but need training in order to become efficient in self-directed activity.

It is difficult for many persons to make decisions completely on their own. How much easier it would be for them if, through the wise assistance of parents and teachers, they had been trained to make their own decisions and to arrive at conclusions on the basis of their own best judgment! A person needs training in taking responsibility in order to strengthen his belief in his own ability to make worth-while decisions.

Children are likely to perform tasks rather crudely at first, but if they are allowed to complete them, in spite of the errors and mistakes that they may make, they gain mental stature. A teacher may think that he is helping his pupils by showing them how much he knows. In this he is mistaken. Children need a chance to express themselves and, through that expression, they may gain facility to present their ideas on respective issues. A parent too often believes that he is assisting his child's learning process by preparing the latter's homework, by repairing his toys, or by doing a hundred and one things for him. Mental growth and development accompany the carrying out of respective activities. If the child performs those activities, he is the one who gains in mental strength.

Too close supervision in the home, in the school, in the shop, or in the office denies to an individual the experiences of success in self-initiated and self-executed activity. If a worker has demonstrated that he is capable and responsible, he can be given an opportunity to grow in his ability. A wise sales manager, after giving his men training in the fundamentals of good salesmanship, allows them freedom in the development of individual techniques.

A successful professional woman has never managed her own money affairs and now realizes that certain mental growth comes from these experiences. Before her marriage, her mother planned the spending of the young woman's monthly check; now her husband manages the family finances. Needed money is always available and she is not extravagant. Although she appreciates the fact that she is spared the task of keeping accounts, she also misses the joy of planning a budget and of effecting economies that would give her a feeling of personal responsibility and achievement.

When an individual is provided with many desirable and stimulating influences and is permitted to use these so that he can gain mental strength, he is bound to emerge the master of his fate and to possess mental powers commensurate with his ability and training. The person who has been fortunate enough to receive advice or guidance that has enabled him to grow in self-direction during his early years and who, as an adult, has ample opportunity for the exercise of desirable freedom in his work and social activities presents a success story that is stimulating reading to anyone interested in hygienic mental development.

▶ **Questions and Problems for Discussion**

1. Show how competition may serve fruitful purposes in mental development.
2. Why are the theory and practice of mental hygiene so closely related to an understanding of the cumulative interpretation of mental concepts?
3. Describe in detail all the essentials that must be actively present during the process of mental development.
4. Explain the statement: Habits cannot be broken.
5. What is the relationship, if any, between mental condition and physical disease?
6. Under what conditions does the "sour grapes" attitude enter into the hostility between social classes of different economic status?
7. Explain fully why it is unwise to keep an employee long on a job that does not challenge his intelligence.
8. How does a daily schedule for a person's work affect his mental life?
9. Why should a teacher dread going to school if he really enjoys teaching?
10. What are the conditions conducive to dishonesty in school?
11. Examine a Weschler-Bellevue Intelligence Scale to discover the areas it attempts to measure.
12. Explain why the average I.Q.'s of high-school graduates usually are higher than the average I.Q. of entering freshman.
13. People who have adjustment difficulties frequently are unaware that other persons have similar problems. Explain.
14. What restrictions should be placed upon an individual's freedom?
15. What values are likely to accrue to the individual who carries out well-laid plans?
16. To what extent, if any, does ability to reason depend upon age?
17. Explain the importance of the environment in relation to mental development.

CHAPTER Six

Attitudes and Adjustment

A N ATTITUDE is personal. It relates to the way a person feels, thinks, or behaves in specific situations. A person is reputed to be kind, tolerant, friendly, or critical, as he displays one or another of these behavior traits in his habitual relationships. An individual's feeling tone or affective experience when he is stimulated by a person, an idea, an activity, or an object is a specific response of approval or disapproval. This acceptance or rejection is aroused within the individual by the total situation and is based upon his previous experiences. Every human experience is accompanied by a feeling tone or affective experience. This affective experience or attitude, in turn, influences an individual's thoughts, interests, and behavior.

Personal Emphasis in the Development of Attitude

ATTITUDES and interests may be quiescent (latent or potential), or active (kinetic). The active attitude or interest may function as a force by itself or as a part of the total dynamic behavior of the person at the time.

The nature of attitude. All daily experiences that become a functional part of life have an affective side. The accompanying sensations possess feeling aspects of pleasantness or unpleasantness, satisfyingness or annoyance. A composite of these qualities that forms a part of every experience constitutes a feeling tone or affective quality.

Attitudes are, in effect, certain kinds of habit patterns. They result from learning and are subject in their formation to the accepted laws of learning. Attitudes operate in behavior patterns, become a part of the rich mental and emotional life of an individual, and give him his joys and his sorrows or both.

Dynamic interrelationships between situations and desires give rise to attitudes that are important in the functional organization of emotional patterns. The attitudes that result from values relating to self are quite subjective. A person is concerned about his problems, his worries, his behavior, or his possessions. The mother is subjective in her attitude toward her own children but evidences a fundamentally different affective response toward the children of another family. Each individual evaluates every situation in terms of his training and experience. The resulting attitudes and affective qualities determine his behavior.

The influence of mental qualities. The development of wholesome attitudes and good habits is important for mental health and efficiency. An attitude gives mental tonus or set to experience —real or anticipated. Personal problems and conflicts are definitely supporting stimuli for attitudes. The more intense is the desire or the conflict, the stronger is the accompanying attitude. Attitudes are closely associated with specific experiences and are difficult to generalize. Thus a person has a habitual attitude toward his work, toward other people, toward authority, toward parents, or toward world conditions.

An individual's conscious attitudes do not always remain consistent toward any of the above-mentioned persons or situations. He may show one attitude at one moment and an entirely different attitude at the next, when or if conditions or an understanding of the situation changes. However, some persons are set in their attitude toward some things. For example, regardless of the existing conditions, they always vote the Republican ticket or the Democratic ticket. Yet the election is carried by one political party this time and by another party next time, by those voters whose attitudes are changed by changing conditions.

Physical constitution and attitudes. The actual attitudes that constitute the affective side of man's nature result from his living in his particular environment. The trend of his established attitudes —his attitude toward others and their attitude toward him—is rooted in his own personal constitution. Such factors as size, physical uniformity, physical disability, health, potent drives, degree of emotional stability, and potential energy, are significant because of their possible effect upon the individual himself and upon other persons. The proper functioning of the nervous, glandular, or circulatory system is conducive to the development of positive attitudes. A malfunctioning of one or all of these systems may result in socially undesirable attitudes and personality traits.

An individual's physical features may become very important as attitude directors, especially if too much attention is given to an apparently undesirable characteristic. A girl may admire small, smooth hands, but her own hands may be large and rough. Consequently, an attitude of shame is developed. During a visit to a friend's home the first thing that an adolescent girl called to the visitor's attention was her chapped hands. Had she not mentioned them the probabilities are that they would not have been noticed. A boy may desire a thick, bushy head of hair, but his hair may be thin and sparse. The physical trait in and of itself may not be important. It is when the person is possessed with a strong wish to be different that undesirable attitudes are strengthened. Consider the possible attitude of the boy who, as a result of a severe case of typhoid fever, lost his hair and returned to college baldheaded. The fact that he could do so was proof that he possessed certain inner attitudes that helped him during that trying time. It is this kind of experience, however, that often is the beginning of attitudes that lead to maladjustment and that are difficult to correct.

It is not the malformation itself that affects attitudes, but the way in which people react to the peculiarity. The girl who is six-feet-three is not aware of her height in the same painful way if her height is near the norm of the group, rather than the exception. To be tall when tallness has value is desirable. It is satisfying to a young woman to be tall and slender if it shows how well she can wear evening dresses; it is quite unsatisfying if she wishes to become an air hostess, since that position usually calls for the small, petite type.

Attitude and age levels. In general, children's attitudes are imitative, and not based on reasoning. A child tends to fall in line with accepted group attitudes. He acts with little understanding of the reason for his behavior; what he does often is divorced from his best interest.

An adolescent's attitudes are more personal and are directed by his own individual drives. Behavior on the part of elders that interferes with his freedom may stimulate adolescent antagonisms. The teen-ager tends to feel that adults are intolerant and non-understanding. He considers himself to be "broadminded," but his attitudes actually are biased in terms of his personal wishes and felt needs. He is interested in trying the new—anything that is considered "taboo" by his elders. His behavior may be motivated by an attitude of self-sufficiency or a belief in his own personal power and rightness.

In general, an adolescent's attitude is hopeful and forward-looking. He is driven by an urge to reform the world. Although his attitude toward an individual child or a particular old person may be one of impatience, he has a kindly attitude toward children as a group, and pity or sympathy for those who are very much older than himself. Toward the members of his own age group his attitude is conditioned by his relationship with them. He may be resentful of those who possess superior advantages or who seem to receive more attention than he does. He may exhibit an attitude of superiority toward those other young people who appear to be less able or less successful than he is.

The attitudes of adults are colored by their own personal whims and selfish interests; by their work and family experiences; by their social status; by the recognized degree of success that they have achieved; by all other factors that affect their life patterns. They want recognition from others; consciously or unconsciously, they give expression to this attitude. If they are thwarted in the realization of their desire for attention, they may develop an attitude of bitterness toward their associates or an attitude of personal futility.

Attitudes offer great possibility for achievement in life. They are important in every activity and affect all human values. Efficiency results when a person is impelled to continue and complete an activity, rather than to avoid an unpleasant task. A child need not be permitted to do completely as he wishes; usually he can be stimulated toward desirable activity through the arousal of interest in worth-while projects. Constructive attitudes, developed during childhood, serve a person well during his adolescence and adulthood.

If a person believes that no one cares for him, he experiences a loss of relationship with other human beings. He needs the sympathetic understanding of others. This desire appears early in life and continues throughout life. The child, the adolescent, or the adult wants to feel that he belongs. He wants to identify himself with a group or with groups in which he recognizes the fact that he is important, that he is well thought of, and that he is a person. This bolsters his ego, since thereby his strong points are emphasized and his shortcomings are discounted.

Attitude affects the entire nature of an individual at any age: his learning, his thinking, his emotions, and his overt behavior. A person's attitude also exerts a powerful influence upon other people who associate with him. Much of the directing and controlling power or influence of one human over another is based upon attitudes.

Influence of unconscious attitudes. Our behavior is influenced by mental states of which we may not be fully aware. We do many things without an understanding of the reasons that prompt our behavior. These unconscious attitudes provide the basis for much of our unexplainable conduct and inner conflict. The effect of these attitudes is not fully appreciated by us because we do not realize the effect of our behavior upon others and, consequently, do not recognize the fact that our actual motives may be very different from those believed to be ours by other persons who observe our behavior.

A person's actions, for example, may exhibit attitudes of selfishness, insincerity, domination, or self-interest; the person himself might be very much surprised if he were accused of possessing any such attitude. A grandmother may believe sincerely that the advice and help given by her are best for a child. A mother-in-law does not always want to interfere, but her unconscious attitudes sometimes affect her behavior. The drive to have things done in the way that she considers best is so strong that she cannot yield to those who have the right to plan their own lives. Parents, in their desire to help their children, often inhibit desirable self-direction. Such parents are not aware of their underlying self-centered attitude. A father may want his son to be a doctor, a teacher, a lawyer, or an accountant. It takes more than the wish of a parent, however, to arouse an interest on the part of his child. If the parent is too persistent in his expressed attitude he may help develop strong antagonism in the child toward parental choice of vocation.

If a person admires another for one outstanding personality trait, he is likely to accept all of the other person's behavior. In the same way, if one personality trait is disapproved of, other desirable traits of the person are not recognized. If a person loses at cards he feels that someone else is at fault. Moreover, if the opponent who has won begins to gloat over his success, a deep-seated attitude may be expressed in the words "I don't mind losing but I don't like to have it rubbed in." Many examples could be cited to illustrate the influence of unconscious attitudes upon our relationships with our associates.

We should strive to keep unsocial attitudes as dormant in the unconscious as possible. Hates, prejudices, and resentments are encouraged by these attitudes as the latter find their way to active consciousness. The real motive for our behavior often is so subtly disguised that we honestly believe that our attitudes are wholesome and aimed at socially desirable goals. What widowed mother who has given much possessive love to her son can see anything of worth in any girl who may take her son away from her? This mother honestly may believe that her attitude is aimed at assuring for her son a happy life. Actually, the woman is motivated by self-interest. Overt expression of felt attitudes often presents a truer picture of underlying motives to those who observe the behavior objectively than it does to the one who is trying unwittingly to satisfy unconscious attitudes.

The skilled and proficient worker builds into his habit pattern many attitudes that become a part of his everyday living. He gains satisfaction from plans well made and work well done. However, as he works from day to day, he dreams of the time when he may retire from active service and enjoy the leisure that will be his. Too often, when this man does retire, he realizes that he has lost not only his work but also the satisfying attitudes that accompany successful achievement. It is in retrospect that we often really appreciate the satisfactions that were ours during former experiences.

Attitudes and values. Direction is given to attitudes in terms of our interests and values. If an obtained object or goal has little value, the effect upon our attitude is negligible; if the article is lost or is easily replaced, attitude changes are slight. If, however, we are emotionally involved with an object, person, or situation, and we hold it in high esteem, we are moved deeply when it is lost or destroyed. The writers recall the emotional turmoil suffered by a young girl who had lost, through fire, her prized possession—her diary. At that moment this girl considered the diary to be extremely important; yet, later, when she no longer was emotionally involved, she remembered little that was written in it. When its replacement or duplication is difficult or impossible, the attitude of an individual toward an object or situation approaches that of an emotional stress.

According to Stagner, the three characteristics of attitude always are (1) an object, (2) a direction, and (3) intensity. In his discussion concerning attitudes and values he suggests that:

> "The object may be considered the intellectual or cognitive aspect of the experience. The direction is given by the predominantly pleasant or unpleasant feeling tone bound up with this intellectual understanding. Intensity may be thought of as related to excitement, or degree of activity which will be released by situations involving the attitude. Thus a stereotype, e.g., "scab," has both a meaning and an effective element. A "pro-fascist" attitude involves both comprehension of certain situations and emotional reactions for or against these conditions.
>
> *Stereotype and Attitude.* Two points of view exist among psychologists with reference to these attitudes. One considers the stereotype, or the intensity of the affective reaction to the stereotype, as the most important aspect. According to this view, the study of prejudice against Jews, for example, would concentrate on determining the presence of this prejudice and its intensity. This task of measurement is met by the Thurstone opinionaire technique. . . . By this method it is possible to describe a person with considerable accuracy as regards his emotional reaction toward war, communism, birth control, and so on.
>
> The other point of view implies that, while the emo-

tional stereotype is significant and its measurement is important, the real question is, what are the specific forms of behavior out of which this generalized attitude developed? We might call this a genetic or an analytical approach. In a great many cases it is important to distinguish between one's attitude toward a verbal label and the attitude toward the psychological object, independently of the stereotyped label. We would suggest, then, that, in considering the total behavior of any individual, we might find specific emotional conditionings (complexes) relating to particular objects—dogs, for example; generalized emotional conditionings (stereotypes) relating to more abstract objects, such as the church; and still more generalized conditionings (traits) in which we can no longer distinguish an object; but only an abstracted relationship to the total situation, as in self-confidence.[1]

Opinion versus attitude.   Language can be used to convey to the listener that which the speaker wishes to transmit, but words often represent opinions rather than deep-seated attitudes. Spoken or written expression may or may not present the actual beliefs or feelings of an individual. Attitudes expressed in behavior are more useful and reliable in determining individual reactions since they function in a more dependable way. Existing circumstances do not affect behavior expressions of deep-seated attitudes as they influence the verbal expression of attitudes.

Too many of our attitudes are of the "lip service" variety. It is more important that a person live his "Excuse me" or his "I am sorry" than it is that he learn to say the words. It is more important that we *live* tolerance than that we *talk* about the desirability of tolerance. The expression of opinion is important, but the opinion must be translated into behavior if the attitude expressed is to have any weight.

In many situations our expressed attitudes and our actual behavior do not agree. For example, we have certain expressed attitudes toward war, yet we exemplify war in the toys that we give to children. Therefore, a child hears about the destructiveness of war and at the same time is given a gun as a play toy. We talk about

[1] By permission from *Psychology of Personality*, 2nd ed., by Ross Stagner. Copyright, 1948. McGraw-Hill Book Company, Inc., pp. 202–3.

our love for mankind, but in our daily life our behavior often is an expression of hatred, resentment, and envy. Proper attitudes toward other people need to be instilled into our behavior habits so that greater understanding of people different from ourselves can be evidenced. From the standpoint of adjustment, behavior attitudes and verbal expression of opinion should harmonize.

An individual may express a specific attitude toward an issue. When action is required, he may respond by behavior that is contrary to his expressed attitude. In a group, a boy may express approval of a member whose activities are praised by other members of the group; when he is alone with one of his friends, he calls attention to the many faults of the person whom he had praised publicly. At one time he expresses the opinion that is expected by others. Later, he shows his real attitude.

It is difficult for us to distinguish an attitude from an opinion; sometimes we are not aware of all of our attitudes. We rationalize our beliefs. Hence our expressed opinions often are at variance with deep-seated attitudes. We may appear to be tolerant toward people when their activities do not affect our lives. Our true attitude shows itself in a situation in which our own interests are at stake.

One of the most difficult things for anyone to do is to state an objective opinion, free from bias. Responses to questions in personality tests indicate that many people answer in terms of what they *think* they should say rather than in terms of their real belief or attitude toward a given question.

Attitudes as directive forces. The direction of our thinking is influenced as our own interests are related to the environment. Our behavior, in turn, is affected by the sensory experiences and perceptual outcomes that make possible the changing relations among ideas and thought processes, as these are experienced and expressed from time to time. The dynamic nature of sensory and perceptual experiences gives rise to a dominance of one idea at this moment and of another at the next. Yet basic to the fluctuation of ideas in terms of existing environmental conditions is the influence of experience-born attitudes that direct our mental pattern. We may not be conscious of the fact that the very dominance of one idea over another is a selective process motivated by our attitude or feeling at the moment.

The directing influence of an attitude or interest is apparent in our responses to any given situation. For example, a person may be reading a manuscript editorially. He is mentally set to evaluate the manuscript in terms of the value and accuracy of content, style of writing, correctness of spelling, and grammatical construction. As he reads, his attitude toward *what the writer says* may so engage his attention that he fails to respond to *the way in which it is said.* Perhaps not until a flagrant typographical error is encountered does he become conscious of the fact that he had directed his attention toward content only. Our mental activity and consequent overt behavior are conditioned by our existing attitudes more definitely than we often realize.

Developing Attitudes toward Certain Life Issues

w e cannot hope here to present a complete treatment of attitudes in their relation to all life experiences, since these run into the thousands. Therefore, for the purpose of giving a few positive suggestions for wholesome attitude development, we have selected six areas of experience. The experience areas selected are those associated with blame, disease, failure, sex, work, physical handicaps, and character.

Blame. It is easy to blame others when things go wrong, but it is not so easy to accept personal responsibility for undesirable behavior. Recently the writers overheard two persons discuss the outcomes of a project in which both had been active. One speaker insisted that he was responsible for the successful outcomes of the project, but he placed the blame for its partial failure upon the other person. As a matter of fact, the speaker was the guiding factor of the entire project. His judgment was responsible for both the successful and the unsuccessful outcomes. The words *credit* and *blame* are generally misused. In their relations with children, teachers, parents, and other leaders are guilty of this practice. Growing children can be helped to develop the trait of honest self-appraisal. Self-deception can be avoided by all persons responsible for the training of children.

A child can be given opportunities to participate in activities in which he may assume responsibility. He then needs to be guided and trained through them to be careful, honest, and forthright in his dealings with everyone who is in any way connected with him in a situation. A child's first opportunities to develop self-reliance are offered by his parents in the home. He experiences here, at first-hand, the values that can be derived from his own efforts and accomplishments. He learns that his pants get on the hanger only when he puts them there, and they stay there only if he places them securely on the hanger. A child's parents provide experiences and training that enable him to emancipate himself from dependence upon them. They provide opportunities for him to make judgments for himself; he learns to depend upon his own judgment, rather than upon external authority, in making decisions.

When a child goes away from home and, with strangers, participates in activities in which he can do well, he learns to evaluate the success of his achievement. In this way he gradually learns to accept blame for lack of accomplishment instead of developing the attitude that his failures are the result of the behavior of others. Through these experiences he is led to recognize the fact that false arguments and excuses do not supply the essentials of lasting success.

The kind of punishment that is experienced by a child determines in part his desire to shift blame. An honest admission of guilt deserves treatment different from that given to an evasion of the truth, even though the situation is one that requires a redirection of behavior. However, honesty of the response is paramount. Often a child may seem to be honest and sincere when, as a matter of record, he has been most untruthful. To accuse without good cause is not conducive to the development of good attitudes, however.

Children usually need training in good sportsmanship. Whenever teams or individuals play, there is a loser. To be a good loser is an art that, if acquired early in life, can be most helpful. The development of this attitude helps the player enjoy the game and stimulates him to play the game according to the rules. The attitude of good sportsmanship removes the temptation of cheating in order to win. One wants to win fairly or not at all. Parents and other adults can help instill this attitude through example.

Disease. It is an accepted fact that a patient's attitude toward his illness is often harder to treat than the disease itself. At home and in school a child becomes acquainted with disease possibilities. He can be helped to develop desirable health attitudes that will strengthen his physical resistance. This teaching can be done carefully so that it results not in an emotional fear of disease but in an intelligent understanding of good health hygiene.

Harmful germs are present by the millions and in varying degrees of virility. Through knowledge of germs and their potentialities a person learns to develop an attitude toward them that enables him to live in their midst and find ways and means of combating them, if necessary. A person's attitude can be that of discovering ways of conquering disease rather than that of allowing himself to become a prey of disease. Physicians are learning that it takes more than medicine to effect cures. Their personal ability to impart confidence is as beneficial as the drugs that they prescribe to destroy germs or to aid in tissue building.

Failure.   Fear of failure as a behavior-directing stimulus is not so potent as some persons consider it to be. The desire to succeed is to be encouraged rather than the attitude of avoiding failure. When fear of failure becomes the dominating attitude, there may result a blocking of ideas and an inhibiting of successful responses. This interferes with one's best production.

A college senior once reported to the writers that he could not do well in true-false tests because, in the past, he had learned to fear them. He said further that he can think effectively in class if he is permitted to volunteer. If he is called upon when he has not volunteered, he experiences mental blocking. In order to help him in his work, confidence is to be restored. The child who accepts the fact that he may experience temporary interruptions in his progress is thereby enabled to utilize an occasional failure as a stimulus toward greater effort to succeed. There is danger in the theory that schoolwork may come to be regarded by the child as play activity. If a child realizes that in his studies he may encounter real but not unsurmountable difficulties he usually is eager to accept the challenge of hard work. In this way he is helped to develop an attitude of willingness to overcome difficulties and to master situations.

Sex.   The psychology of sex has to do with the building of proper *attitudes* toward this very important human urge. There are many teachers today who are well qualified to teach the biology, the hygiene, or the physiology of sex. Few teachers are able to present effectively the attitude phase of the problem. In developing desirable attitudes toward sex, much can be accomplished through the use of indirect methods. Wholesome sex attitudes can be instilled through the intelligent use of literature, nature study, and science.

What will be a young person's eventual attitude toward sex? This will be determined by the attitude taken by his elders. If adults associate undesirable stories with sex, young people are helpless in trying to develop a wholesome attitude. However, if adults associate wholesome attitudes of life and romantic love with sex, saner attitudes toward sex can be strengthened.

There are many adults who have acquired a twisted point of view toward sex. These attitudes are so closely tied up with the emotions that, in order to train them properly, we must concern ourselves with the education of the emotions with which those attitudes are so closely associated. This is discussed more fully in the chapters dealing with behavior drives and emotional adjustment. (See Chapter 12 for a discussion concerning sex adjustment.)

Work. Some work has undesirable attitude values, largely because it is not or has not been dignified in the minds of people. At one time it was not considered socially desirable to teach school, because of the attitude of the public toward it. Today it is an accepted activity with good social standing. Numerous factors have contributed to this change in attitude toward teaching. Nevertheless, there are many types of activities that are "beneath the dignity" of some members of the group. Because of this attitude, some persons would rather be idle than engage in such activities.

One of the results of modern industrial routinization is the fact that to some people work becomes little more than a means to an end. This attitude is quickly caught by a growing child long before he is able to understand or evaluate it. He learns to regard work of any nature as an evil to be avoided. This attitude may persist until he discovers that desired rewards usually come to those persons who have cultivated a more positive and energetic attitude toward work activities.

If an individual worker is interested in his job merely as a means of earning a livelihood, he may develop the attitude of doing as little as possible so that the job may last longer or that others may have work. Personnel departments are attempting, through individual ratings, bonuses, and improved working conditions and wages, to stimulate workers toward pride in their jobs. Thereby, worker attitudes can be changed from indifference to, or actual dislike of, the job to that of interested and energetic participation.

Physical handicaps. In the home every attention and care that can be given usually is extended to members of the family who suffer from physical defects. Until recently the public attitude has been that physical handicap is an individual problem, with the result that little or no public funds were made available for the care of individuals thus afflicted.

At present there is developing in most communities an attitude of responsibility for the care and rehabilitation of their handicapped members. Complete and effective programs are being organized in the public schools of many cities for the purpose of training physically handicapped boys and girls for participation in effective vocational and social activities. This attitude has been strengthened because of the fact that many men suffered handicaps in recent wars. The citizenry recognizes its responsibility for caring for these men. Not only do the handicapped deserve the best possible medical care, but they also can be given training and opportunities for participation in occupational activities within their physical ability so to participate.

Attitudes in relation to character. We usually differentiate between reputation and character by saying that reputation refers to what people think you are but that character is what you really are. One's character traits soon stand out as those that are a part of his consistent behavior. Character education includes the development of right attitudes as well as the acquisition of behavior habits that are socially desirable. Not only can rules and regulations concerning good conduct be taught, but they can be understood and appreciated in the light of their values to the individual and to society. The child can be aided in making deliberate choices of behavior in harmony with his own and social betterment.

Attitudes toward people, events, or things are molded by what is said about them. Truth is often helpless when confronted by convincing misrepresentation. If a person who is known to have a good character is accused falsely of wrongdoing, he can save himself from undesirable penalties for the act only when the public emotional tide is moving in the right direction.

Social Emphasis in the Development of Attitudes

A T T I T U D E in relation to the individual has been thought of as a biological drive, a mental set, a state of readiness, a feeling, a verbal response, a muscular adjustment, or generalized conduct. Regardless of the interpretation, attitude elements are not found in isolation, but are interrelated in various ways and possess emotional qualities that are connected with an organic drive. These all serve to color opinion in the direction of the interests of the person concerned. In order to understand social behavior, we must consider the attitudes aroused in the group or crowd which conform to the characteristic behavior of the particular group. Preparations for specific responses are established in our nerve and muscular mechanisms. We are *set in attitude* to conform to the conduct expected of us by others. This readiness permits certain actions and inhibits others.

We have a prepared readiness to react to the mere presence of people, regardless of who they are. Certain set attitudes are presented in reference to many social situations, such as the problems of sex, courtesy of the road, respect for the rights of others, and other forms of social behavior. In fact, we have attitudes toward cooperation, courtesy, and dignity that determine the nature of our behavior.

Attitudes toward the behavior of others. How can those attitudes that best will serve individuals in society be developed? How can we insure the correct attitude toward parents, brothers, sisters, relatives, and friends? How can we be sure that attitudes will be used for our best interest? As we live and repeat experiences, as we give attention to suggestions from others, do we develop, definitely even though slowly, those emotional attitudes that help hold together the family, the work group, and society?

Attitudes are contagious; when they appear in the behavior of others it is likely that we will display the same attitude to some degree. Very often undesirable attitudes are caused by us as much as by the person whom we accuse of possessing them. If we are talking with a person who does not like another person whom we admire and he singles out some of that person's faults, it will be quite normal for us to experience some of his feelings toward the person whom we liked before this experience. At a later time, if we have a disagreement with the person with whom we were speaking, however, we begin to mistrust him.

The power of suggestion and the influence of an encouraging word can do much to stimulate attitudes that have desirable social values. The time to start the development of them is at birth. The patterns of social attitudes need to become as habituated as possible. To be trustful of people is an attitude that can be started in childhood. If a child discovers persons who are untrustworthy, he can become selective but he can continue to trust each member of his group until a person proves himself to be unworthy of that trust.

An attitude of honesty is a prized possession of anyone with whom it is associated. A person who is known for his integrity and his honesty, and whose word can be relied upon even in trying situations, exerts a positive influence upon any group, and helps to build desirable social attitudes. It is important that an individual so habituates the attitude of honesty that it becomes a part of him.

The growing person is entitled to seek and to discover the values of life. We enjoy a baseball game partly because our friends enjoy the game; we thrill at picnics largely because it is the thing to do; we enjoy a certain play because our friends say that they like it.

Servants in the home, parents, playmates, and teachers are to be included among the ever-present agencies that stimulate the formation of attitudes in the learning, developing individual who is the subject or the victim of the teaching. The child who matures among people who display desirable social attitudes enjoys possibilities for potential enrichment of life through numerous wholesome experiences.

Young people need the emotional experiences of the classroom, the praise of the teacher, the disapproval of a classmate, the reproof of a parent or teacher. They are entitled to experience the happiness that accompanies social success, or the hurt of disappointment. They need the social stimulation of meeting different groups. This can be made effective through planned social living, such as club work or organized interscholastic games.

School children learn to like a teacher partly because they have heard that he is *all right;* it must be kept in mind that the opinion of others merely makes it easier to develop an attitude of respect. To develop a real attitude of his own toward the teacher, a child becomes his pupil and is stirred by him. The child learns through personal experience that the teacher is fair and just; that he gives him a break if deserving; that he does not just hand out something for nothing, but that he rewards the child only when he has proven his worth.

Attitudes and discipline.   Attitude is the backbone of behavior that is characteristic of the well-disciplined child or group. Discipline relates to individual behavior in a social setting. The conception of discipline has changed in recent years. Today, it means to help develop in the child the capacity for self-discipline. We are interested not only in demanding outward conformity but also in helping the child to develop functional self-control. This means that we attempt to head off probable undesirable behavior by providing sufficient outlets for the child so that his energies are converted into desirable behavior channels.

We expect the adult to be able to direct his behavior in terms of inner controls. When he seems to lean on another, we think it strange. Yet we do not always give the child the training necessary to transfer his obedience to *external* authority to that of his own better judgment. Much of present misbehavior is caused by the fact that the child is challenging the authority that rests in the control of another—a parent, a teacher, or other social leader. If we could transfer the authority to the child at an early age and guide him in the wise use of it, he would develop self-control, and we would be saved much worry and effort. Give a person responsibility and help him to realize that he has the responsibility; then observe his development in power to use that freedom and responsibility.

An attitude toward others, an attitude toward self, and an underlying urge to do what is right are fundamental attributes of discipline. In connection with the mistakes made by modern parents in dealing with their children it may be noted that the former too often seem to believe that children are to yield without question to parental authority and dictation. Regardless of a child's own recognition of the relative injustice of a command, he is expected to respond to it with implicit obedience. It is better for all concerned to bring as much understanding into the situation as possible.

The following story illustrates the behavior of a boy who habitually acquiesced quietly to parental domination. When he began to assert himself, his mother, a dominant woman, and his teacher felt that he was questioning their authority and that his behavior was becoming anti-authority in general. He is a senior in a New York City high school, the oldest of three children, and a healthy boy. His teacher and his mother have reported better-than-average work until the past three months. During this time he secured a job as a soda dispenser, refusing to heed his parents' advice —"after all we have done for him." The mother places the blame on the husband, who depends upon his wife for all decisions. She complains that the boy spends all of his earnings on himself; he fails to give any money to her or to anyone else in the family. The boy expects to obtain a full-time job as soon as he finishes high school and be a "big shot." He says that college is all right, but not for him.

This is a case of an adolescent rebelling against parental or school authority as soon as he feels capable of earning his own livelihood. Had the mother not developed the sacrificial attitude toward him and had she helped him develop a fuller life during the formative years, he probably would have a better sense of values and would be more interested in continuing his education, thus preparing himself for the kind of vocational work of which he is capable.

Race attitudes. Most children imitate adult behavior and attitude without understanding the significance of the behavior expressions or attitudes that they are adopting as their own. The influence of social inheritance upon the development of attitudes toward other races is much greater than the observable reaction of the child. Such attitudes do not come to the child as a matter of course. His experience in the social environment of adults and of other children, of one race or of many races, stimulates attitudes within the child that he is certain to reflect in his behavior. When those attitudes are desirable, he is fortunate; when undesirable, he is their innocent victim. If, later, he displays attitudes of intolerance toward other races than his own he has his elders as well as himself to blame for his lack of intercultural understanding.

Effect of attitudes of others upon us. The presence of each person whom we know stimulates us toward a set of responses that operate especially in connection with that person. We not only appear to, but we actually do, give evidence of differences in attitude toward the respective people whom we meet and know. Likewise, the personality traits of the other person or persons serve as stimuli to evoke from us behavior that is unique and different from our responses to other individuals.

Through his behavior one person may earn our respect; another receives our contempt. A person who excels in a form of activity in which we are ambitious may be regarded by us as a rival. We learn to fear some people, and to scorn others. A person, through his charm or his helplessness, may encourage in us either love or pity. Our response to any one person is influenced by his observable behavior and its effect upon us. Our degree of readiness to respond to different persons differently is an outgrowth of habits of response developed through past experiences.

The behavior of people is greatly affected by what is expected of them by others. People attend church for social as well as for religious reasons. They participate in social service, partly to satisfy the wishes of their friends. They consciously attend to the interests and wishes of other people and modify their own behavior in terms of those stimuli.

If we achieve success in a project, we hope for recognition. If we fail, we try to evaluate the failure in terms of other people's reactions to it. If we fall short of another person's good opinion of us, we are likely to be ill at ease when we meet him. From the beginning of time man has been eager to achieve not only self-respect but also the good opinion of his associates.

As we develop the appreciation of certain traits and characteristics as desirable, we tend to want other people to recognize the fact that we possess these qualities. In order to achieve this aim, we attempt so to regulate and direct our conduct that the possession of the coveted traits is apparent. Behavior patterns thus developed in response to our desire for social approval gradually become a fixed and definite part of our personality.

The home, school, church, social clubs, radio, newspapers, books, television, and motion pictures are important social forces. They constantly influence the lives of growing children. These forces tend to direct young people's interests, motives, and attitudes toward respective life issues. Without these cultural forces an individual would rapidly revert to primitive life patterns.

An appreciation of values determines the quality of one's inner satisfactions. A set of values may function very effectively for an individual in one group; in another group, he may experience difficulty because of new or different values. Each social group has its own codes and scales of values for interpreting different behavior. Attitude development is conditioned by these influences.

▶ **Questions and Problems for Discussion**

1. Outline five practices that have affected the attitudes of students and discuss (a) the positive values which were derived, (b) the unwholesome effects. How could you change the influence in (b) for the better?

2. What is the relationship between attitude development and discipline?

3. What attitudes do you have that you count among your proud possessions? Name some that you would like to change. Trace the source and development of these undesirable attitudes.

4. Discuss ways of teacher-parent cooperation in inculcating desirable attitudes in a child.

5. Report differences that you have noticed in your own mental attitude toward the task you want to do; toward the task you do because you must do it; toward your employer when he grants your request; toward him when he denies your request; etc.

6. Describe reasons why some teachers or other persons seem not to be well liked by children.

7. What are among the important considerations in the development of self-control?

8. Differentiate between opinions and attitudes.

9. Discuss the relationship between ideals and attitudes.

10. Discuss the influence that you believe unconscious attitudes have upon human behavior.

11. What differences have you observed in the attitudes of people at different ages? Are these differences characteristic of the person, of his age, or of both?

12. Is your idea about your *self* the same as the ideas of others about you? Explain.

CHAPTER Seven

Significance of the Emotions

A N E M O T I O N is but one phase of a comprehensive internal adjustment that takes place in order to enable higher animals to react as coordinated entities and to be more completely the master of sudden changes in their environment. An emotion is dynamic; it stimulates behavior that makes the person less rational as the emotion takes possession of him. In general, an emotion is concerned with a mobilization of available energy reserves. By utilizing necessary movements and functions, and by inhibiting or accelerating them in terms of his needs, an emotion may affect an individual's entire being.

Arousal of Emotional Behavior

E M O T I O N S have both inherited and learned reaction patterns, involving visceral behavior and affective experiences that are generalized through the functioning of the autonomic activities, change in heart action, and release into the blood stream, by endocrine secretions, of energizing products. These inner experiences seem to have their focus in the internal organs of the body, from which they spread out and pervade the entire human being.

Stimulation of an emotional state. A specific stimulus is required to arouse inherited potentialities and to utilize the learned patterns in the fusion of the complex sensory experiences into what is called an emotional experience. An emotion is a stirred-up or diffused state of the organism that has been aroused by an appropriate stimulus. The same external stimulus may have differing effects upon different organisms or upon the same organism at different times.

An emotion appears only partly with the perception of the stimulus which caused it originally; it is fully experienced when the complete response is made to the stimulating force. An emotion signifies the state of feeling of the body after it reacts to stimuli through the functioning of the autonomic nervous system, together with the somatic responses. Every experience has an affective side. There are feeling tones that serve as functional mental qualities in the construction of emotional expression and in the building of the habit patterns which constitute the learned patterns of emotional behavior.

Importance of stimuli. A stimulus is required to arouse an emotion. It uses patterns that are inherited or acquired as its means of expression. Many psychologists, without becoming behaviorists, are accepting fear, tenderness, and rage as emotional tendencies whose patterns are fairly well established at birth. The stimulus that arouses any one of the emotional states is specific. The actual stimulus that may arouse fear seldom arouses tenderness or rage. However, under certain socializing influences, it may do so. For example, loud noises, when understood, will no longer stimulate a fear response but may arouse a tender emotion. Stroking and caressing may arouse affectionate responses; but if misunderstood, may excite fear or rage responses.

The duration of an emotional response is determined by the persistence of the stimuli. Evidence of good social adjustment is to be able to change the emotional experience rather rapidly if and when the stimuli that arouse these states are changed. It is possible for a person to be highly elated at one moment but, with the entrance upon the scene of a particular person, to experience quickly the emotion of hate, jealousy, fear, or envy. The normal human being, however, tends to be affected by many pleasant stimuli; the resulting emotional tension is quite satisfying to him.

The effectiveness of the stimulating force changes with situations. It is conditioned by an individual's desires at the moment, his state of health, and his understanding of all the attendant circumstances. The presence of a beautiful young woman may arouse emotions that are less potent in a man if he is happily married than if he is single. An undesirable social situation has little effect upon the emotional life of a person when he is not concerned with the problem. However, if he becomes actively interested in improving the situation, he is aroused by any slight comment about it that is presented. Likewise, a more powerful stimulus is required to arouse fear in a person when he is strong and healthy than when he is weak and ill.

Emotional states. The experience during an emotion is an individual one. It makes one intensely conscious of himself and tends to spread over the field of consciousness. We are "wild" with rage, "frozen stiff" with fear, "filled" with enthusiasm, "thrilled" with joy, "overwhelmed" by grief, "in the depth" of despair. Everything looks better to one who is in a cheerful mood than it does to one who has a case of the "blues." The experience that accompanies the release of energy during these bodily states can be described as representing the emotional state of the individual at any one time.

There is a continual flow of emotional experience that accompanies most of our behavior. These affective mental qualities arise from the facilitation, inhibition, and obstruction of the impulses resulting from external and internal stimuli. The resulting emotional states give richness to life and prevent monotony. Whether emotions are inherited or acquired, the long list of emotional states begins with the baser emotions, and extends through the socializing emotions to the more subtle emotions.

Emotions as Related to Adjustment

o f the numerous emotions we shall discuss the adjustment problems related to fear and anger. These emotional states appear so often during a person's waking hours that an understanding of their behavior and of methods of controlling them becomes essential to a better understanding of the theory and practice of adjusted living.

Fear. The characteristic response of fear is that of retreat. The growing child learns gradually how to make his fears less evident to his associates. By the time he reaches adolescence, he has evolved techniques of explaining many of them away. Nevertheless, young children have many fears. They are taught to be afraid of the dark, of some animals, of noises, or of any situation that can be used to direct their behavior through the use of this negative approach. It is much better to have the child engage in positive behavior for the values to be derived from that experience. It may seem easier to direct behavior through the use of fear controls, yet the child pays the price in nervousness.

People learn to fear and avoid situations that threaten their safety, that disturb their sense of security, or that alarm. A constant state of fear may be aroused by walking on a high precipice, looking down from a height, or skating on thin ice. Persons then try to avoid such experiences; they are not at ease watching others in such situations. Increased heart action may result from watching a tightrope walker, even though he is in little danger of falling.

Perhaps the fears that are most dynamic in their functioning are those that are aroused indirectly. The child is afraid to recite in public because his father has said over and over that he (the father) was always afraid to speak in public. The child learns to have fear of snakes, of lightning, or of certain diseases because he has heard of the dangers connected with them. When the general attitude in the home is one of fear of a specific activity, the child is almost certain to fear the activity before he experiences it. Fear of the dark or of being alone is an ill-at-ease feeling for the child and is relieved by the presence of the mother or other person. Illness or nervousness increases the child's timidity.

It is a normal reaction to avoid unpleasant sensations. The person who can let worms or caterpillars crawl up his arm is likely to be a hero to his peers. The harmless creatures are not to be feared, yet the very sight of bugs makes some people creep all over. The response is one of disgust. People avoid many things that they fear in part, such as insects, snakes, mice, or cold and clammy things. If fear is fed by an active imagination, disaster may result. A person may allow himself to anticipate robbers, contagion, ghosts, loss of investment, or anything that he would prefer not to have happen to him because it would interfere with his comfort or plans.

Teachers too often use the threat of failure as a device to awaken interest in schoolwork. However, instead of acting as a stimulant to the child to do his best, it may develop a fear of failure that will cause a detrimental emotional reaction. In order to promote emotional health in children, a competitive spirit is introduced so that it may function in the life of each child. Competing children, within the limits of general information and understanding for all competitive undertakings, ought to be equated in ability as closely as possible.

When fears become persistent and tend to control an individual's behavior to such an extent that he has difficulty in adjusting to social life, the term *phobias* is applied to them. Most persons who experience phobias are unable to explain the causes of them or to give a clear description of their own emotional experiences. Their life, nevertheless, is filled with anxiety. They are constantly worrying about the future and know that something terrible will happen.

These morbid or abnormal fears, called phobias, should not be confused with equally strong avoidances that are more like exaggerated disgusts, such as becoming sick or uneasy in the presence of certain sights or odors. Ordinary fears may result from unpleasant or harmful experiences that stimulate toward the avoidance or retreat from similar situations. Such fears are normal and may be experienced by all people. Phobias are more intense and persistent. They are *symbolic* of an intense fear which is connected with a feeling of guilt or of extreme anxiety. A person, alone in a small closed room, may have engaged in undesirable behavior and at the same time experienced extreme fear that his behavior might become known. Later, although the original incident has been forgotten, the fear of small rooms persists, and the individual is filled with an unreasonable dread of confinement in a small, closed room. He is reviving his former guilt or anxiety as symbolized by the present situation.

A person may suffer from a phobia, but may be normal in most situations that do not present stimuli which arouse his specific phobia. Phobias differ with people and conditions. A person may have a phobia of too close confinement in space, of open spaces, of darkness, or of disease. Phobias are built out of experience and are seldom found in children. An intense experience with prolonged fear is fertile ground for a phobia. During childhood and adolescence fear situations need to receive prompt treatment in order that a sense of guilt may not be attached to them and, at a later time, result in phobias.

Fear can serve as an effective control of behavior. It can keep a person from doing many things that, through curiosity, he otherwise might be impelled to do. Curiosity pulls one toward, fear away from, things. Yet in the development of his personality a person, through fear, may become timid or shy. He may exercise undue caution in every new situation, and make friends with difficulty. He may feel that others are taking advantage of him, and his feelings will be hurt easily. Very often in attempts at overcoming his lacks, caused by fear of the situation, he becomes overaggressive and develops an overbearing attitude.

Anger. This emotion is expressed through behavior that is determined by the training the person has received and his age at the time. In the child, the behavior may take the form of kicking, screaming, or sulking; in the adult, it may take the form of profanity, silence, or criticism. The habits which may govern the behavior are well established by the time adolescence is reached.

The persistence of the emotion of anger is found in the *temper tantrums* that are resorted to in order to gain one's desires. To be denied that which one wants immediately and to discover that, through persistence, the wish will be granted is an experience that may lead to the development of behavior patterns in the child, the adolescent, and the adult of forcing gratification of desire. If, by chance, the child obtains his desired end by a display of temper, he may learn to engage in temper tantrums early in his life. The child gets his way at first because the parents are not sure about his state of health, and they give him the benefit of the doubt. Consequently, the parents give in rather easily. Later, the child persists, since he has learned that if he continues in his behavior long enough, eventually he will win out. In too many cases he is successful because the parents are tired or are afraid that personal harm will result if they do not give in to him.

The temper tantrum is based upon an inadequacy of the individual. Once a child has learned that he can intimidate his parents by temper tantrums he makes good use of them at every opportunity. Temper tantrums are modified in form as the child grows through adolescence and adulthood, but they seldom are discarded completely. Some forms of the tantrum are so subtle that they are not easily detected; an observant person is alert to their onset and deals with them in a completely objective manner. Unfortunately, grandmothers and mothers-in-law may make effective use of tantrum behavior to the dismay of those who live with them.

If a child is to be helped to recondition his tantrum behavior, he needs the guidance of someone who will deny his demands with firmness but with justice. He needs to discover that his behavior is completely understood without the adult's saying it in so many words. His ego should be maintained and his pride spared, but his wishes should be denied when they are demanded in the form of a tantrum. The child knows his mother and what he may expect from her. It is well to be known as a parent who speaks when he wishes action and gets action before speaking again. This behavior will give the child valuable training and will spare the parents much trouble in the future.

If a child develops the tantrum technique, the problem can be met by all who come into contact with him: parents, teachers, or other group leaders. An effective way of dealing with the child while he is having his temper tantrum is to ignore him. If he discovers that his behavior is not gaining the attention of the proper persons, he will allow the tantrum to subside. He then can have explained to him that his wishes will be granted on the basis of their worth and not upon the basis of his demands expressed through persistent infantile behavior.

A second method of dealing with the child while he is having a temper tantrum is isolation. This method is used in social groups and in the school. During the tantrum, the child or older person is isolated from the group. If necessary, he is removed bodily with permission to return as soon as his behavior is in conformity with the rights and comforts of others; or the group may move from the room to let him have his tantrum alone.

The individual needs to learn through hard experience that he will fare better if he behaves in an acceptable fashion in the first place. No treatment is ever permanent, however. The individual's behavior is conditioned toward the specific situation and toward the person controlling the situation. For example, a child may never throw a tantrum in the presence of one parent, yet he may do so in the presence of the other; he may never have a tantrum in the presence of this teacher, but he does have a tantrum in the presence of that teacher.

Compulsions.   By compulsion is meant a drive to perform certain acts, or strong desires that are a part of the person when in the presence of certain stimuli. One person has a strong desire to place his toe on the crack of the sidewalk as he walks along; another draws squares during any thinking process; another winds a lock of hair around his finger; another puts his pipe into his mouth; another has a strong urge to look around since he has a fear that someone is behind him; another washes his hands an excessive number of times. Each person has his own personal compulsions.

Compulsions are behavior patterns that serve to reduce tension and relieve fear when it is present. There are definite reasons to be found in experience for the formulation of the compulsion even though these may seem to be baseless. These forms of behavior usually are not upsetting and, unless they are charged with excessive fears, are harmless.

Influence of the Emotions on Behavior

THE BRIGHT, the average, or the dull person may be maladjusted. The cause usually can be traced to an obstacle that has been faced and not resolved. Any interference of this kind should be removed, not ignored. To ignore the obstacle is to increase the difficulty that confronts the individual. It is better to face the actual conditions and to give the true cause for one's failure than to project the responsibility to a convenient person or cause. If we build up habits of running away from or of ignoring the issue, we merely permit the tension to increase until our defenses against nervous disorders are broken down.

Teachers and parents become aware of the habits and practices of children and develop an understanding of the causes of the undesirable behavior that is manifested by children. If a young person attempts to adjust through the use of bullying, stealing, sex offenses, or temper tantrums, it will not help much to administer punishment for the social behavior; adjustment is more effective if the cause of the undesirable act can be determined and controlled.

Influence of emotions in specific problems. Prolonged emotional stress, regardless of age, affects the efficiency, attitude, and physiological condition of the individual. These are the symptoms through which we become aware of the emotional strain.

(*a.*) *Retardation* is caused very often by emotional disturbances which, if they could be removed, would permit the child to pass his schoolwork. He may be emotionally upset about home conditions, be filled with intense hatred for his teacher, or possessed with deep fears which will not allow him to reach the degree of efficiency that he could if desirable emotional conditions prevailed in his life.

(*b.*) *Stammering* is another unfortunte effect of prolonged emotional strain. Since few children have anatomical defects that might result in the difficulty, it is considered to be caused by emotional stress. A careful observer can detect easily that the stammerer usually has trouble only in certain environmental situations. His difficulty is greatest when he is embarrassed or excited. His speech is quite normal when he is relaxed and at ease. The school situation offers many embarrassing situations; the social consciousness of the stammerer gives added strength to the state of excitement. The trouble is started by an emotion-arousing episode which contains many complex elements.

(*c.*) *Success.* A good emotional tonus is very helpful in putting to effective use the talents, energies, and abilities of a person in the solving of problems. The working man who is sufficiently stirred but not overexcited is in a better state to do the kind of thinking that will be required than is the worker who is not so stirred. The supervisor should not instill fear of failure, since this emotional drive may become the dominant one, and the worker may become so excited that he is not able to do his best work. He should be stimulated toward success so that he will have the desire to push ahead rather than have the feeling that he wants to run away from something.

Influence of the emotions on health. It is a well-known fact that the emotions exert a great influence upon digestion. A person's attitude at the time of eating and immediately thereafter has a decided effect upon the secretions of the digestive organs, including those of the salivary and gastric glands and the glands of the intestinal tract. Chronic fears and worries may cause subnormal secretion of the digestive system, and a consequent condition of constipation. If ill health results, a person begins treatment at the point of irritation instead of giving attention to whatever fundamental causes stimulated the arousal of the predisposing emotional state.

Physicians are becoming increasingly aware of the fact that stomach ulcers have for one of their chief causes that of emotional disturbance. Several years ago a young woman known to the writers was experiencing serious emotional disturbance. She was advised to eat proper food, secure sufficient rest, and avoid stimuli that might arouse undesirable emotions. Her intelligent adherence to this advice resulted in her complete recovery within a year. The removal of fear and worry is one of the most effective means of preserving or regaining health.

The success of the Christian Science movement results in part from the emphasis given by its advocates to the value of emotional control during illness. The attempts made by them to keep the body functioning normally at all times have significant and potent health values. The person as well as the disease must be treated.

Emotion as an asset. The tender emotions constitute the great driving force that stimulates the human to achieve that in which he is interested and which he is capable of doing. This emotion helps him to endure hardships, to take criticism, or to work at long intervals. Fear, on the other hand, serves as a check on behavior. It keeps man from becoming too reckless, thereby saving his reputation and, sometimes, even his life.

Human beings want to be near stimuli that arouse them. They want romantic love put into storybooks and fear put into the automobile. Emotions lend color to their existence and spur them on to do many daring deeds. The human craves emotional stimulation and desires emotional experiences. He tries to get them through books, movies, radio, television, and social gatherings. Nevertheless, he needs emotional balance in all of them. Overstimulation is unhealthful.

The poet, the musician, and the artist rely upon their emotions to serve as driving forces during their creative efforts. They are able to experience emotionally much more than many others and, consequently, have the ability to translate their emotional state into words, pictures, or music. Thus, through insight and integration of ideas do they produce the new, the beautiful, and the creative work of art. An emotional state in the right setting may give one an entirely new outlook on his own life.

Emotions as liabilities.   Excesses in the use and functioning of any of the emotions will produce a maladjusted person. Healthy emotional life is a decided asset; the emotions, when they are too powerful, can make life miserable for an individual and for those about him. Emotions become liabilities as soon as they interfere with a person's social success or work efficiency. It is because of these liabilities that education of the emotions is so necessary.

Emotional Conditioning

THE EXTENT to which the various patterns of effective behavior can be modified by conditioning is extremely important. The home and the school are faced with the problems of re-educating primitive patterns of behavior through which emotions express themselves, and of regulating and reconditioning the experiences of growing children in such manner that only socially desirable habits of emotional behavior will be fixed. The reconditioning of emotional behavior is complicated by conflicting interests and the affective elements in emotional experiences. Thus the problem of finding effective methods and procedures for inculcating wholesome emotional patterns is not a simple one of habit training.

Using attitudes for emotional direction.   Attitudes are useful because of the fact that they are most often related to self-interest. As the attitude patterns are formed, there is produced in an individual's mental processes a natural state of readiness that exerts directive and dynamic influences upon behavior. An individual's attitudinal habits or his attitude at the moment determines the extent to which certain environmental stimuli will arouse in him an emotional response such as jealousy, love, joy, resentment, fear, hate, or grief. The emotion-arousing stimulus is interpreted and responded to in terms of the individual's attitude. Loss of status, loss of security, or depth of grief can be described only in terms of the individual aspirations and interests by which the person is motivated at any one time.

Attitudes can be used to give positive direction to emotional development. An attitude toward success helps to bring success, just as an attitude toward failure helps to establish failure. The accompanying emotional experiences are powerful determiners of the degree of success or failure anticipated.

Using catharsis in emotional direction. It is important to find experiences that modify the emotions and at the same time make them more effective. Aristotle believed that music and drama could be used effectively to develop people artistically and, at the same time, to purge the emotions of their coarser elements.

It is sometimes asserted that strong emotional expression should not be restrained. If it is allowed to run its course, the individual will then be purged or freed from existing emotional tensions and be less likely to engage further in uncontrolled emotional behavior. As overindulgence in the eating of candy and its consequent results may free one from further abnormal longing for candy, so may excessive participation in uncontrolled emotional behavior exhaust the energy drives which motivated such conduct and allow one to develop into an emotionally well-controlled adult. Experiences of this kind are thought to give release to emotional energy connected with past experiences that have been emotionally charged.

Using sublimation for emotional direction. Through sublimation, opposing tendencies are coordinated for a common good. The conflicting influences of mental and emotional life are resolved into progressive development through the integrating processes. Attempts to direct primitive emotional reactions toward socially approved levels are efforts used to sublimate the emotions. Two emotions that are important factors in the determination of individual behavior and that constantly need to be sublimated are anger and fear.

(a.) Sublimation of anger. The emotion of anger has been associated with pugnacity. Pugnacity is a primary tendency that is likely to be aroused if a blocking occurs among any of the other

tendencies and their associated emotions. It is basic to the fighting attitude of man, serves him in defense, and operates as a self-protective reaction. Anger is aroused when any of the inherent emotions is thwarted. The emotion of anger kills happiness, for man cannot be truly happy when he is angry. Any interference with a person's pleasures is resented. Nevertheless, anger gives us courage, determination, and endurance. It aids in concentration of effort by clearing away detrimental inhibitions.

The pugnacity in human life is to be transformed rather than reduced. The fight attitude or the will to work is needed in the complete development of man. Attention can be directed toward giving it careful direction so that it may have effective expression. Critical disapproval can be administered in ways that are socially acceptable. Both society and individuals can be trained to use effective means of expressing disapproval without the use of violence.

Every person can be trained to exercise indignation, disapproval, or a critical attitude toward certain undesirable persons or conditions in his environment. These responsibilities cannot be evaded without violation of one's own self-respect. Moral character is built upon these evaluated qualities of life. The deserved disapproval of any faults of persons or institutions can be given effectively through controlled behavior, not dissipated through blustering or other overt pugnacious acts.

We ought to be certain that our critical, pugnacious, and antagonistic attitudes are expressed tactfully. Emotionally uncontrolled and unreasonable behavior rarely brings desired results. We first are convinced that we are logical, just, and reasonable in our critical evaluation of the situation and the persons concerned. We then attempt to present our point of view constructively by offering workable suggestions for the improvement of the situation and of individual behavior. If such suggestions are given sympathetically and objectively, most individuals can be led to accept the corrections offered, and are mentally and morally stimulated by their attempts to conform to more desirable standards of behavior.

Does avoiding a fight indicate lack of courage or is it an expression of good sense? Most boys have critical judgment that tells them not to fight. Nevertheless, it needs only a little prodding from several buddies to supersede that judgment and to start a fight. Too often, in an attempt to settle these issues, adults criticize the combatants rather than the instigators on the side lines. Disapproval should be directed against all who are guilty. This will help the person who is involved in the fist fight which he has entered with the mistaken idea that, in this way, he will be able to maintain his social dignity and standing in the group.

(*b*) *Sublimation of fear.* This emotion is usually associated with the tendency to flight. The relation of the fear response to the stimulus that causes it in sequence of time is a moot question. Whether one runs because he is frightened, or is possessed with fear because he runs is considered by some psychologists to be in favor of fear because of flight. Even though fear is consciously aroused in our mental processes after we flee from danger, the fear that we experience as we run contributes directly to our rate of running.

To fear is to have an attitude of avoiding, of retreating, of fleeing, or of concealing. Fear is the most persisting of the emotions and takes control of the person often to the extent of paralyzing his power of flight. Abnormal fear caused by a failure in adjustment is perhaps the most unhygienic emotional attitude.

Fear has been used as a control measure in political, religious, and other social groups. It also serves as a control of individual behavior. The inhibitions produced are often for an individual's social betterment. Fear acts as a check on development or advancement if it inhibits a person from doing the things that he should do for such advancement. He can benefit from ideas and ideals that keep him from doing personal harm to himself or to others, but it is better if his behavior is directed by forces other than those of fear.

The boy can be trained not to fear his teacher; he can be trained also to respect the rules of the school, the rights of others, and his own person. Self-control rather than fear can be developed to produce effective behavior in children. Nevertheless, fear can be used constructively. If it serves to caution the automobile driver, the pedestrian, or the bicyclist, many lives can be saved annually. Fear can be used as a protective tendency to preserve life, extend happiness, prevent pain, or alleviate suffering.

We have too many abnormal fears. It is unfortunate for a child to grow up in a home in which parents make a great fuss about the lightning that seldom strikes, the snake that never bites, the burglar that never comes, or the disease that seldom afflicts. The more valuable procedure is to teach intelligent understanding of the dangers and limitations of each of these so that proper precautions can be exercised at all times.

Suggestions to the College Student on Emotional Control

C R U Z E offers a few suggestions to college students on training for emotional control. He cautions that emotional control cannot be established in a few hours or days. Consistent effort over a long period of time is required. He suggests:

1. Learn as much as you can about emotions. Our public schools have been quick to include instruction in physical hygiene in their courses of study but rather reluctant to include anything in the field of mental hygiene. Certainly the high-school student is mature enough to master the fundamentals of emotional phenomena and it is absurd to believe that he will be better off if he remains ignorant in this area. No subject could be of more immediate practical value, for this information would assist high-school and college students with their everyday problems of adjustment. The individual who is well informed concerning the causes, reactions involved, and consequences of emotional activity will be in a better position to control his emotions than the person who knows little or nothing about these phenomena.

2. Avoid emergency situations. We have emphasized that emotions are emergency responses made when an individual does not have an appropriate response of a rational type ready to use to solve the problem he faces. The emotionally stable individual plans for the future. He acquires responses that he can use when he faces relatively unimportant situations. He does not allow these situations to develop into emergencies. Furthermore, he plans his activities carefully so that he will be able to avoid meeting people and situations which he knows will probably result in emotional tensions. Learning to avoid as many emergency situations as possible is an essential part of every program of training for emotional control.

3. Learn to control external expression of emotion. It is well to keep in mind that the external muscles involved in emotions are subject to voluntary control even though the visceral responses are not. The man or woman who has learned to keep a "poker face" during emotional tension has made decided progress in the battle for control of the emotions. Not only do these external responses tend to increase the intensity of the emotional experience, they also excite other people and encourage them to become emotional. If these people, in turn, allow themselves to show emotion, their emotional expressions will stimulate the first person to further emotional excitement. In this way a vicious circle of emotional reactions may be established.

4. Work is an excellent antidote for emotion. The person who is busily engaged in some interesting activity will not have the time or inclination to indulge in emotional sprees. If you feel depressed or apprehensive, or if you are filled with anger and resentment at some real or imaginary slight, the surest way of dispelling your depression, apprehension, or anger is to become busily engaged in some activity that will distract your attention from the emotion-provoking experience and, at the same time, use up some of the surplus energy that has been made available by the emotional reaction. Whistle when you are afraid and run around the block when you are angry. Devote your attention to these or other activities and relief from the tensions produced by the emotion will be forthcoming.

5. A sense of humor will save many difficult situations. The person who has a sense of humor will be able to avoid many emotional experiences. Try to develop a sense of humor by looking for the humorous or ridiculous elements in situations that are apparently going to be serious or trying.[1]

[1] W. W. Cruze, *General Psychology for College Students* (copyright, 1951, by Prentice-Hall, Inc., New York), pp. 475–476. Reprinted by permission of the publisher.

Emotional conditioning is complicated by inner conflicts and previous emotional experiences. The difficulty of the problem of developing emotional control is increased by an individual's inner drives and desires and by the respective affective qualities of his experience. Attitudes which are associated with self-interest are useful in giving positive direction to emotional behavior. As attitudes are established they produce a state of readiness that exerts dynamic influences upon the behavior of an individual. Hence an attitude toward success tends to establish success; an attitude of failure encourages failure.

Sometimes, through mental action, an individual is enabled to bring the past to the level of consciousness and, through this, secure a definite emotional discharge. This method (catharsis) is used as a means for the reduction of emotional tensions and for the avoidance of undesirable emotional reactions. Music and art sometimes are used to stimulate the emotions and at the same time to purge them of their coarser elements. Thus aesthetic expression becomes an emotion conditioner. Emotions under control add beauty to life. Hence the goal is to rule the emotions rather than to be ruled by them.

▶ Questions and Problems for Discussion

1. Illustrate the importance of the respective emotions mentioned in the chapter.

2. Differentiate between feelings and emotions.

3. Show how the approval of the teacher can become a motivating force in the life of a child.

4. What are desirable incentives that can be used to arouse children or adolescents to action?

5. What are some of the forces that interfere with the full development of an individual?

6. Explain the reason for emotions being contagious in crowds.

7. Name at least two useful purposes to which you have put anger; fear.

8. Discuss the relation of avocations to one's emotional life.

9. Report a case from your personal experience that shows the effect of the emotions on the health of a person.

10. What behavior shall a parent or a teacher display toward a child who is always talking about what he is going to be when he grows up?

11. List the unpleasant experiences you have had during the three age periods: before 5, between 6 and 12; between 12 and 16. How do they differ?

12. What stimuli easily aroused your emotions during childhood; during adolescence?

13. Discuss the relationship between emotional control and social adjustment.

14. Discuss the relationship between emotional life and industrial efficiency.

CHAPTER Eight

Frustration and Conflict

S INCE the mental and the emotional reactions of an individual are very closely related, it is difficult to discuss the one without implying a function of the other. A normal person possesses interests, desires, and drives that impel him to participate in many and varied activities. Moreover, he finds himself in a relatively complex environment to which he must adapt himself, both mentally and emotionally. As he lives and adjusts, he is constantly compelled to decide among situations, issues, and opposing forces of one kind or another.

Bases of Frustration

I T is difficult for any one of us to engage in activity without meeting an opposing force of one kind or another. The interests of other people, rules and regulations, social codes, unfulfilled desires, goals beyond achievement, and competitive situations are some of the social and individual factors that cause mental and emotional disturbance.

Meaning of frustration. Fundamentally, a baby's wants are centered in the achieving of physical needs. At one time he wants food; at another time he needs sleep. A healthy baby also wants to engage in kicking, cooing, and other forms of active behavior. At all times he wants to be comfortable—free from tight clothing and other restrictions. When or if any one of these wants, (which are recognized by the young child only in a relatively vague and diffused manner) is not satisfied, he engages in one or another form of disturbed behavior, such as crying, holding his breath, stiffening his little body or tossing it about. Even at this early age the child can be said to be *frustrated* in the achieving of his felt needs.

In general, a frustration can be defined as an unsatisfied need or desire. Throughout his life an individual encounters many frustrating situations. Some of the frustrations are relatively mild and can be overcome easily; others may be so serious, or seem so to the individual, that he comes to believe that there can be no satisfying way out of the difficulty.

Areas of frustration. As the child develops an increasing awareness of his relations with the objects and people that constitute his environment, his needs or wants also increase. Throughout life an individual continues to want and need physical satisfactions. The mode of achieving them becomes more and more complex as they are influenced by the developing tastes of the individual and the customs of his group.

Not only does the man or woman need to satisfy his physical needs, but he wants to satisfy them according to the accepted customs of his culture. Moreover, the fulfillment of desires and urges that grow out of his interpersonal relationships becomes increasingly more important to him. He wants attention; he craves the approval of his confreres; he needs to achieve success in one or more of his areas of activity; he feels the urge to gain security, both financially and socially.

To the extent that an individual becomes aware of the fact that he appears to be unable to satisfy a felt want he can be said to be frustrated. The causes of the failure may lie within himself; environmental conditions over which the individual has little or no control may interfere with the achievement of his need, urge, or ambition. In either case, conflict may arise within himself or between himself and the inhibiting forces outside himself. If his attempts to resolve the conflict are unsuccessful, his feelings of frustration are intensified and his conflict becomes more severe.

Frustration and the Individual

I F a strong emotional tension results from the blocking of an impulse it usually is considered to be a frustration. Experiences that seem to an onlooker to be no more than petty annoyances may be productive of many so-called frustrations. Emotional stresses may be induced by apparently trivial incidents: a shoestring tears apart when you are hurrying to catch a train; a newly painted window sticks when you attempt to open it; a short develops in your television set when you are watching a prize fight; an automobile passes by and dirty water is splashed on your clean clothes; you miss your train by thirty seconds and are forced to wait a half-hour for the next train, causing you to be late for work; your child disobeys your command or refuses to eat his cereal for breakfast; a member of your family offers to mail an important letter for you but forgets to do so; you are unable to convince another person of the worth of an idea; you have an unquenchable thirst on a hot summer day.

Situations similar to the ones listed are frequent occurrences in the daily life of most individuals; their frustrating effects usually are temporary, however. At the time of their occurrence they create definite stress and strain, and we become emotionally upset; later, after they have been met more or less satisfactorily, we can laugh at the strong emotional reactions aroused by them. Moreover, one such annoying incident seems to be followed by others of its kind. At times it seems as if everyone were conspiring to interfere with our planned activities.

Environmental sources of frustration. Unfortunately, not all thwartings and annoyances are overcome easily. Sometimes frustrations have their roots in environmental conditions that act as obstacles to the fulfillment of strong interests or desires. If the frustrating situations lie outside an individual's power to control, he may experience even greater emotional stresses and strains. To be caught in a sudden hurricane, to be affected by a contagious disease, to learn of the death of a close relative or friend, to have a chair pulled out from under you as you are about to sit, to be called to serve in the armed forces during a time of war—all represent environmentally stimulated frustration situations. The emotional reactions aroused by their occurrence varies with the degree of emo-

tional stability possessed by the respective persons directly affected
by them.

Other sources of frustration are associated with the cultural
and social aspects of experience. Laws and codes of behavior are
established for the general welfare; yet they interfere seriously
with an individual's desires or interests. For example, if we accept
the findings of the Kinsey report of sexual behavior, according to a
strict interpretation of existing laws, a large percentage of women
and men could be jailed for their sex acts. Some people have no
awareness of the fact that their accustomed sexual activities may
be contrary to law, however.

Many frustrating situations probably would appear if behavior-
restricting laws were known and followed. For example, every
driver of an automobile is expected to know and to obey traffic
regulations; in an emergency, a person believes that he has a good
reason for breaking one or more of them. Also, a businessman may
be tempted to disregard restrictions on unfair business practices if
these restrictions interfere too much with his ambition to achieve
financial gains.

The fact that groups vary in their social customs may become
a factor of frustration to a person who moves from one group to
another. Especially is it possible for a person to experience a strong
feeling of thwarting if he is eager to gain favor in a new group, but
discovers that his habitual behavior in social situations differs from
group custom. An ardent bridge player is expected to play canasta;
a vegetarian cannot find a vegetarian restaurant; a family that has
lived in a small neighborly town moves to an apartment house in a
large city and cannot become accustomed to the fact that no other
family in the house seems to know or care about next-door neighbors; a person who had lived in a city where he had been accustomed to a great deal of personal freedom in his choice of activities
is annoyed by the fact that in his new small-town home everything
that he does is known to his neighbors and openly approved or disapproved.

To the adaptable person the situations listed may seem to represent unimportant social differences to which one can learn to adjust easily. Yet some less emotionally controlled individuals may
consider them to be obstacles to the achieving of desired social
acceptance. In a graduate college class, for example, a discussion

concerning appropriate dress for high-school students and college undergraduates caused the display of emotional tension on the part of one of the younger members of the class.

This young man attempted to defend young people's "sloppiness" of dress; older members of the group disagreed with his expressed opinion, to the point of implying that he was exhibiting an immature attitude toward accepted social custom in matters concerning appearance and that, with increasing maturity, his opinions would change. His retort to the effect that, even though some of his classmates considered him to be a child, he would never become a social snob, led to a heated discussion concerning what constitutes social snobbery. It was asserted that sloppy dressers represent a group of social snobs to the same extent as do those who advocate greater conservatism in dress.

By the end of the session several members of the class gave evidence of strong feelings of frustration. Moreover, since all the members of the group are leaders of young people, many of them expressed their uncertainty as to what their attitude should be toward changing social custom.

Economic sources of frustration. There are few individuals who, at one time or another, do not experience strong desires to possess luxuries similar to those enjoyed by more affluent friends. Inability to satisfy this urge can become a strong frustration arouser. For example, a woman whose husband's salary is sufficient to supply necessities but few luxuries is motivated by a strong urge to compete with her neighbors. If one neighbor's house is painted, she wants her house painted; if another has a television set installed, she wants a television set; if an automatic washer is purchased, she wants the same kind of washing machine. Any luxury obtained by any neighbor impels this woman to prevail upon her husband to make a down payment on a similar article. This woman constantly indulges in self-pity because of her inability to compete in every way with her neighbors. Apparently, she cannot or will not recognize the fact that relatively few of her neighbors have all the things that she wants. They are selective in their interests, in terms of their financial ability to satisfy them.

In cultures where competition is between individuals of similar economic status rather than between members of differing financial levels the economic factor is less active as a frustration inducer. The frustration is experienced by the individual who attempts to rise from his economic group to one that is considered to represent a higher level of society. The democratic ideal, based upon the concept of equality of opportunity within individual limitations to attain desired goals, has tended to eliminate class distinctions in matters dealing with material possessions. For the able person, class leveling is an excellent stimulator of ambition to achieve a satisfying economic status. It is a frustration arouser for the individual who cannot meet competition.

Often an individual believes that if he were on a higher-income level than he now is he would not experience feelings of frustration associated with material possessions. He probably would discover, however, that his ambitions would induce him to strive toward still higher economic levels. Wants seem to increase with increased power to achieve them. The goal then becomes the achievement of superior business or social prestige. Anyone who becomes too involved in this kind of competition is likely to suffer feelings of frustration that are damaging to his total personality pattern.

Personal sources of frustration. The fundamental sources of frustration usually lie within the person himself. The level of his aspirations and the attitudes he develops in his daily living determine his degree of adjustment. Frustration arises if a person sets for himself the attaining of goals that cannot be achieved because of personal deficiencies.

The handicapped person becomes an easy victim of frustration. To the extent that his handicap denies him participation in activities common to those engaged in by the normal person he is likely to experience discontent, resentment, and frustration. He needs to possess sufficient emotional stability to combat the warping effects of these maladjustive factors.

As a result of his limitations, a mentally subnormal child or adult may not become frustrated unless he is brought into unfair competition with his mental superiors. A mentally normal but slow individual has enough intelligence to attempt to imitate the behavior of his more able associates. He fails in competition because he is unable to recognize and evaluate differences between himself and those who succeed. As a result, he may place the blame for his failure on factors outside himself. He becomes the victim of deep feelings of frustration. He does not have sufficient mental acuity to understand complex conditions and situations that are understood by his more able associate. This lack of understanding becomes for him the basis of emotional disturbance.

The intellectually superior young person or adult also may suffer feelings of frustration. His deeper insight and his exceptional powers of discrimination may lead to his evaluating conditions, situations, or other people more quickly and more accurately than can his less able associates. This is satisfying. If he attempts to explain his evaluation, however, he is likely to discover that his less able associates cannot understand his reasoning. This may be a frustrating situation. An intellectually gifted person often becomes impatient when his associates reject his conclusions as fantastic, and present what to him are specious arguments or evaluations.

The emotional development of the gifted does not always keep pace with their mental progress. Sometimes an extremely bright young person, whose thinking and reasoning ability already have reached adult level, cannot realize the fact that to the average adult the young person still is a child whose behavior and attitudes reflect lack of adult experience. The gifted child or adolescent attempts to perform duties beyond those expected of him by average adults. Consequently, if he is reprimanded by parents or teachers for assuming responsibility without adult invitation to do so, he is bewildered by and resentful of apparent discrimination against him. He may suffer intense feelings of frustration.

To suffer seemingly unjust reprisals for attempts to satisfy impulses and desires is frustrating; to develop an attitude of believing that one cannot attain a goal because of inherent personal lacks may be the cause of even deeper frustration. Feelings of personal inferiority can cause an individual to refrain from attempting to achieve in any area of activity, because he believes that he is doomed to failure. An attitude of superiority, unless it is an accompaniment of superior achievement, may lead to the display of aggressive behavior that eventually also may induce the experiencing of frustration situations. An attitude of inferiority is certain to intensify feelings of frustration.

Merely to have a feeling of inferiority does not necessarily arouse emotional disturbance. It may take only one failure experience to cause loss of self-respect and to arouse strong emotional reactions, however. The failure situation may have a lasting effect upon the individual, without his awareness of the fact that it is the cause of his lack of self-confidence. Nevertheless, he tends to avoid similar challenging situations in order not to become involved in another disagreeable experience. The unpleasant incident may be forgotten; yet the resulting feeling tones remain as a part of the individual's attitude pattern. Childhood experiences often are reflected in adult behavior. For example, a shy adult may be exhibiting attitudes that were developed during childhood. He fears failure in areas of activity in which his earlier experiences were unsuccessful. Hence he tends to avoid frustration-arousing situations.

Factors of frustration. Four important factors that influence an individual's response to frustration are (1) age, (2) health, (3) past experience, and (4) the nature of the motive that causes the frustration. Each factor exercises a specific effect upon the behavior reaction of the individual concerned.

The influence of the age factor can be illustrated by reference to reaction patterns at different age levels. The infant tends to display "angry" behavior when his desires are thwarted; he expresses his anger immediately; restraint of muscular activity induces tantrum behavior. Later, manifestations of emotional reaction become attached to many situations and considerations other than muscular restraint. The child struggles openly to remove any condition or object that to him represents an obstacle to the satisfaction of a desired activity or motive. The socially responsive adolescent or adult, however, has learned to control his inner annoyance and to direct his emotional responses in such a way that he may continue to receive the approval of his associates. The young person or adult learns that to avoid rejection by his peers, the anger factor serves him best when it is subdued or sublimated. People soon lose patience with an adolescent or adult who has a temper tantrum whenever his motives or wants are thwarted. The relatively mature individual is expected to inhibit overt symptoms of frustration when he cannot get his own way immediately.

A second important determiner of an individual's response to frustration is his physical health. Physical illness predisposes toward emotional disturbance; it sometimes becomes exceedingly difficult to control the emotions when one is ill. Although an individual exercises emotional control when he is well, a slight thwarting may provoke a temper tantrum if he is ill. A prolonged illness, an exces-

sive number of colds, and even a period of loss of sleep may constitute conditions that are favorable to the arousal of feelings of frustration.

The third important factor that influences an individual's responses to frustration situations is his past experience. To experience
the gratification of too many expressed desires predisposes toward
the use of tantrums when or if the fulfillment of a desire is denied.
The children of overindulgent parents become emotionally disorganized in frustrating situations. The helplessness of an infant or of
a crippled or frail child may stimulate parents and other adults who
are responsible for his welfare to adopt an oversolicitous attitude
toward him. Thereby he is denied the opportunity to develop gradually a reasonable control of his desires and an attitude of self-de-
pendence. If or when he reaches the stage of needing to assume personal responsibility for his welfare, he is likely to encounter many
frustration situations with which he will not be able to cope.

The nature of the motive itself is the fourth factor in determining an individual's response to a frustration. When a person's
wishes and desires are of minor or of transient importance, he may
adjust rather easily to their denial. If a strong desire so motivates
the individual that he is determined to find a way to gratify it, failure
to do so results in deep-rooted frustrations. His feeling of frustration intensifies his determination to satisfy his wishes: sometimes
through direct means; sometimes through substitute gratifications,
such as reading novels, attending motion pictures, joining clubs, or
indulging in excessive daydreaming. Or he may attempt to reduce
his state of frustration by seeking business, social-group, or community status. He runs for political office; he strives to become a high
executive in a club; he fights for power in business or industry.
Through intense concentration upon ego aggrandizement in one or
another such area of activity he hopes to reduce the emotional stress
and strain that have been evoked by his frustrating experience.

Individuals of any age differ temperamentally. A person who
has a generally cheerful outlook on life may not recognize a situation as a source of frustration. He takes the good with the bad. In
either situation he does the best that he can; he does not worry too
much if the results are not completely satisfactory.

The kind of individual a person is and the strength of the motive basic to the frustration influence the possible reactions that re-

sult. The way in which a person tends to meet thwarting or frustration represents what can be termed his *frustration tolerance*.

Frustration tolerance. The extent to which an individual is able to endure a frustration without becoming emotionally disorganized is considered to be his *frustration tolerance*. Frustration tolerance is individual. Individual differences in frustration tolerance are related to early experience. Some people seem to experience many disappointments, thwartings, and frustrations in their observable attitudes and behavior; other people appear to display freedom from involvement in frustration situations.

A certain situation may be a source of annoyance to each of two people; the reaction of either one in the situation is an indication of his degree of frustration tolerance. For example, two equally busy men are called for jury duty. The first reaction of one of the men is to attempt to be excused from his civic duty; his business would "go to pieces" if he were unable to give it daily direction. The second man recognizes his civic responsibility; he immediately starts plans for the maintenance of his business during his absence from it. This man gives evidence of high frustration tolerance; his responses are adequate and efficient in the presence of a frustration situation.

Most human beings experience frustration, and attempt to utilize one or more methods of escape. People differ, however, in the frequency and intensity of their utilization of any one method to resolve their difficulties. The kind and size of obstacles that are encountered and overcome give indication of an individual's degree of frustration tolerance. Individual degree of frustration tolerance can be illustrated through examples taken from any area of activity. Equally able high-school or college students are assigned the same problems to solve. The problems are difficult. Some of the students persevere until the assignment is completed, displaying a high frustration tolerance; others complete part of the assignment; still others look at the assignment, decide that it is too difficult, and give indication of their low frustration tolerance by their failure to attempt to solve any of the problems.

Similar examples could be cited from other areas of activity: business and industry, home responsibilities, social and community projects. There are many people who are sincere in their intention to do a good job and to be cooperative in their personal interrelationships. Whether these people carry out their good intentions depends upon the extent to which they are able to persist in an activity or remain in a situation when factors of annoyance, disappointment, thwarting, or frustration interfere with self-satisfaction.

Causes of Mental and Emotional Conflict

AN UNSATISFIED need or desire, or a frustration, may be the cause of mental or emotional conflict. The incompatibility of opposing desires sets up tension that often is increased by a repression of the unsatisfied drive, because of continued frustration. If these tensions are not properly resolved, many adjustment problems may arise in the mental and emotional life of the individual.

Meaning of conflict. Mental conflicts are related to the fact that the intellect of man is not a psychic unity. The human mind is developed through many thousands of more or less individualized experiences trying to find a place in the *psyche*. Mental conflict occurs when a person's ideas, feelings, and emotions, respectively, are pursuing their own outlets in the psychic life. This entails conflict. Adjustments are made to resolve the conflict. Some attempts at adjustment are helpful; some, called maladjustments, are harmful to the individual.

Most conflicts are undesirable because they are detrimental to the well-being of the person, dissipating his energy and creating emotional turmoil. They may be beneficial, however, if they serve to motivate behavior toward adjustment, provided that the emotional disturbance is not too severe.

Mental conflicts sometimes take the form of a combat with reality. When the demands of nature are too severe for the person, he begins to develop neurotic tendencies and tries to continue his life in a world of phantasy. It is easy for him to satisfy his desires in this dream world. Some persons find it difficult to subject themselves to the hardships encountered in routine activities, or they are unwilling to submit to any form of authority. Their emotions are highly sensitized; they dislike everything that interferes with their desire to assert their individuality or that increases the difficulty of dominating their associates or surroundings.

Areas of conflict. The child endows each new experience

with feeling and emotional values. Each day he utilizes behavior patterns that already are established; his daily experience is colored by the feeling tones of earlier experiences. The nature of these patterns determines the nature of the individual's ability to adjust to the many diverse conflicting forces and interests of his life.

Childish interests usually are fleeting. At one moment a child is deeply interested in his teacher; the next moment finds him interested in a classmate. Consequently, during these early years conflicts are of short duration and can be resolved easily by an effective change of stimuli. The wise mother does not talk about an injury done by another boy, but directs the child's attention to something else, thus reducing the emotional tension experienced by the child at this critical time. Later, she can help the child better to understand the problem in its proper setting. With the young person's increasing maturity, conflicts may become fewer in number but may tend to last longer. Older children learn to get along well together. Yet if they continually are thwarted they may develop a resentment of or a hatred of their young associates. These experiences then become the bases of subsequent conflicts. An increased appreciation of the respective rights and responsibilities of all individuals and groups that are concerned gradually will lessen the tension and modify demands.

Attitudes in relation to conflicts. An individual's attitudes usually reflect the traditions and customary thinking of his group. His attitudes, when he attempts to solve a personal problem, may become emotionally charged because of the conflict between his habitual attitudes and his momentary interest. A student, as a result of his training, may have developed an attitude of honesty, but if his graduation depends upon his passing a test for which he is not adequately prepared and if cheating is possible, he at once faces a conflict between his habitual ideals and his immediate need. To the extent that conflicts of this nature continue, emotional strain increases. If an individual always could be certain of what is socially right and socially wrong, positive attitudes could be developed and conflicts avoided.

Emotional disturbance of one kind or another is likely to be the cause of an undesirable attitude. The person who is emotionally stable and who is able to adjust to his daily activities with reasonable success is not likely to develop antagonistic attitudes toward those who may seem to achieve greater success or recognition than he does. The boy or the girl who enjoys security in his home is not tempted to run away or to engage in one or another form of delinquency. The antagonistic or unduly critical person engages in asocial behavior as a means of fighting his own feeling of inferiority or insecurity; he is attempting to impress others with his superiority.

If undesirable attitudes are to be improved, the emotional disturbances that cause them need to be resolved satisfactorily. Unless the individual can gain the security which he craves, any attempt to redirect his attitudes is likely to result in still greater conflict.

Behavior Patterns Resulting from Conflicts

AN INDIVIDUAL's past experiences and his attitudes toward them are mental and social factors that may cause feelings of insufficiency. In his daily experiences the child finds that he is scolded for his mistakes or ridiculed for his shortcomings more than he is praised for his accomplishments. If he is clumsy and needs assistance, he is likely to be scolded or snubbed, or his behavior criticized. He is constantly being denied the doing of the things he wants to do. Parents, teachers, playmates, and other persons inhibit him in one way or another. This kind of conditioning imposes handicaps that are difficult to overcome for the already inhibited and timid person. Later adjustment to social situations is difficult for the child who develops feelings of insecurity. If he learns during early years to meet, evaluate, and attempt to solve the simple problems that confront him, he is helped thereby to adjust to problems on the adult level.

Patterns of inferiority and insecurity. A feeling of insecurity is likely to be developed in children if they are permitted to attempt tasks beyond their age and ability. For a child to engage in schoolwork that is too difficult for his experience and ability level usually is disastrous. He seems to be destined to fail; he is likely to interpret the failure as something peculiar to himself. Consequently, he imagines that he is labeled by others as a failure; he develops strong feelings of inferiority.

Many persons feel that they have little chance to progress vocationally as a result of the fact that they entered industry without first having attended college. Even though they have engaged in self-education they still feel the lack of that academic label which the college degree can give them. A woman had completed only three years of college study before her marriage. On one occasion she was a member of a group of relatives and friends who were discussing the colleges from which each had been graduated. Embarrassed by the fact that she could not report the holding of a college degree, she withdrew from the group. She had reared two fine sons and had organized a successful nursery school, yet she experienced a feeling of inferiority in the presence of the degree-holding members of the group. Later she continued her studies. The eventual earning of a college degree was an ego-satisfying achievement that exercised a tremendous influence upon her attitude. She now feels secure among groups of college graduates.

Sometimes impatient parents and teachers discourage a child from completing a project in which he is much interested. Adults tend to be more concerned about the adequate completion of a project than they are in stimulating the individual growth of the child who is using his energies for self-improvement. A boy who forgot his lines in trying to recite a poem was reprimanded in the presence of his classmates by his teacher and informed that he would not be permitted to take part in a school program unless he could learn his lines. This public reproof so discouraged the boy that he was inhibited from making any more attempts to recite in public.

Conflict groupings. The serious effects upon an individual's chances of successful life adjustment of various conflict patterns are presented succinctly by Cameron:

> So prominent is the position occupied by conflict in modern theories of behavior pathology that the subject merits special consideration at this point. For adolescents and adults, in particular, conflict is usually harder to endure and harder to overcome or escape than either thwarting or delay alone. In ethical matters, for example, a conflict may go on and on indefinitely, debated by the unhappy person covertly or aloud, much as in the soliloquies that Shakespeare wrote for Hamlet. And sometimes the conflict and the debates end similarly, in suicide or

homicide. Just as thwarting usually precipitates delay, so conflict usually implies a delayed or thwarted person. If the individual in conflict carries through an act to apparent consummation in spite of it, he may eliminate delay and direct thwarting, but he does not as a rule succeed in reaching full satisfaction, and he is not likely to have an adequate after-reaction of gratification.

When we speak of *conflict*, we mean *the mutual interference of competing reactions which prevents the adequate development, continuation or consummation of ongoing motivated behavior*. The competing reactions may be conceived of (a) as overt or covert attitudes and responses, (b) as antagonistic patterns of change in muscle tension and relaxation, or (c) as mere shifts in action, potentials, demonstrated or inferred. For our purposes, conflicts can be conveniently grouped as *adient-avoidant*, *double-adient*, and *double-avoidant* reactions.

Adient-avoidant conflicts. The typical adient-avoidant conflict consists of two incompatible reactions, arising in the same act, one of them directed toward an object, activity, or goal (adient), and the other directed away from it (avoidant). Adient-avoidant conflicts appear early in childhood when punishment or restraint prevents the adequate development, continuation, or consummation of an act, but does not terminate it. If, for example, each time a child reaches toward some object, an adult slaps his hand, restrains him or scolds him, he may develop an avoidant reaction without, however, losing his original adient one. If reaching and withdrawing tendencies are approximately equal, the child's hand may remain suspended part way to the object or execute oscillatory movements toward and away from it, until fatigue, distraction, or a rage response tips the balance. The reverse situation develops when an adult coaxes or compels a child to face something toward which the child's original reaction, still present, is one of avoidance.

However, as every mother knows, even the certainty of punishment does not always prevent an adient reaction from going on to consummation, nor will the most attractive reward always overcome a child's avoidant reaction. Both children and adults do and refuse to do many things in spite of their accurately anticipating painful retaliation. One reason for this, of special importance in behavior pathology, is that the sustained tensions of conflict can become in themselves so intolerable that they make one reckless of consequences. The normal small child may terminate his conflict in an outburst of rage or aggression against an interference or an offending object. In young and old alike, an outburst has the immediate, though unplanned, effect of reducing the tensions of conflict. But as a child grows older, this technique becomes less and less successful in getting rid of conflict, because of society's rising scale of taboos against temper tantrums with increasing biosocial maturity.

Among children and adults, prolonged adient-avoidant conflicts are prime sources of anxiety, and anxiety is a prominent constituent of many behavior disorders. Thus, sustained conflict often leads directly into anxiety disorders, anxiety attacks, and panic reactions. The anxiety of adient-avoidant conflict may under some circumstances lead instead to phobic, compulsive, or hysterical reactions. These often protect the individual from direct anxiety at the high cost of chronic neurosis, but they do not actually resolve the conflict situations. What we call *guilt* is a special case of adient-avoidant conflict. The temptation to do something forbidden is the adient tendency while the partial inhibition of that forbidden adience, derived perhaps indirectly from previous punishment or threat, is the avoidant tendency which prevents or delays the adient consummation. The adient-avoidant conflict of guilt is clearly responsible for many delusional and hallucinatory developments, such as those we shall meet in paranoid disorders, in schizophrenia, and in mania, depressions, and delirium.

Double-adient conflicts. The typical double-adient conflict consists of two incompatible reactions arising in the same act, both of which are directed toward the same object, activity, or goal (*convergent adience*), or each of which is directed toward a different object, activity or goal (*divergent adience*). In *convergent adience* there is one object, activity or goal, but two competing, incompatible attitudes are aroused toward it. In *divergent adience* there are two objects, activities or goals, and one's adient attitude supports competing responses toward both at once.

Double-adient conflicts of both kinds develop in numerous common ambivalent situations. Convergent adience is seen, for example, in the simultaneous appearance of hostile aggressive attitudes and affectionate accepting attitudes toward one's parent, one's beloved, or one's child.[1] Divergent adience appears in situations that offer a person parental reward, filial, community, or celestial reward, in exchange for abandoning something else which he dearly wants. No matter which adient reaction he begins, he will find that he cannot escape the pull of the other adient-reaction tendency.

Double-avoidant conflicts. The typical double-avoidant conflict consists of two incompatible reactions, arising in the same act, each of which is directed away from an object, activity, or goal. The man in double-avoidant conflict is like a tennis ball in play; whichever way he travels he gets hurt. This is the dilemma of the child or adult who, for example, is threatened with pain, privation, or rejection if he does not go through with a disagreeable, humiliating, or frightening situation. It also was Hamlet's dilemma and the one confronting a great many suicides. Hysterical disabilities are not uncommonly the outcome of double-avoidant conflicts. Faced with the social demand that he perform some dangerous or distasteful duty, a person may be unable to escape it without incurring social retaliation and disgrace, unless there are extenuating circumstances. As we shall see, the momentary tremor, paresthesia, or paralysis that develops in the anxiety of such conflict may persist indefinitely there-

---

[1] *Adience* should not be confused with the so-called "pleasure principle." Adience refers to relative *direction*. A hostile aggression is adient in the same general sense that a loving approach is adient.

after, as an hysterical symptom, which provides an extenuating circumstance acceptable to the patient and his associates.[2]

Significant aspects of conflict. Conflict is an inevitable concomitant of human action and interaction. The intricate pattern of human nature and the complex character of human relationships preclude the possibility of anyone's achieving even for a short period during his lifetime a completely placid, non-thwarted state of self-satisfaction. A continuous vegetative existence or bovine calmness probably would become extremely boring to most, if not all, human beings.

During discussions concerning the emotions, the authors are accustomed to ask their students whether the latter would prefer to go about their affairs unhampered by emotional excitation. Student reaction always takes the form of a definitely negative response. They agree that their joys, sorrows, disappointments, frustrations, and conflicts give zest to life. The tragedies of childhood become the subject of adolescent amused retrospection. Upon the frustrations of adolescence are built adult emotional controls. Conflict situations during adulthood serve as proving grounds to develop strength of character.

Many of our unpleasant, thwarting, and frustrating experiences are relatively unimportant, temporary, and easily overcome. Hence they represent desirable elements of personality development and adjustment. Poor adjustment or maladjustment is a resultant of the inadequately resolved conflicts that tend to recur or of persistent conflicts that continue to defy attempts to resolve them.

The introduction of new interests, changing conditions, or participation in unaccustomed activities may weaken the force of a conflict situation. Although the conflict situation cannot be attacked directly and consequently resolved, its effect upon the individual wanes and the conflict situation eventually is forgotten. Later, however, a similar conflict situation may arise. The detrimental effects of the new conflict are intensified by the emotional residuum of the former experience.

For example, a college junior experienced a conflict between

[2] N. A. Cameron, *The Psychology of Behavior Disorders* (Boston: Houghton Mifflin Company, 1947), pp. 131-34.

his desire to continue his education and his equally strong interest in marrying. To marry meant to leave college for a job. Before he made a decision he was called to service in the Armed Forces. He had not resolved his original conflict but he gained satisfactory recognition of his military activities which prepared him for successful civilian employment. He married, enjoyed a happy home life, and continued to achieve successfully in his vocational work. Some years later he received an offer of a job that had challenging possibilities. Acceptance of the offer necessitated his spending several years in a foreign country but leaving his family at home. This was a conflict situation that brought to memory his conflicting interests as a college student. This time, however, no outside factor could remove the need for decision making. The new venture would give him added prestige and increased financial remuneration. His family left the decision to him. He thought through the situation, weighing its advantages and disadvantages; he could not sleep or eat; he suffered strong emotional stress; he wished that something might happen (as it had years earlier) to relieve him of the responsibility to resolve his conflict. So devastating were the effects upon him of his struggles that on the final day for his acceptance or rejection he suddenly became extremely ill. Attending physicians feared that his illness would be fatal. By the time he recovered from his illness the new job no longer was available. From a practical point of view, the man's illness had resolved his conflict. The emotional aftermath of the experience seriously affected his self-regarding attitudes, however. He continued alternately to reproach himself for his indecisiveness, to resent the job's not being held for him, and to accuse his family of failing to meet their responsibility in helping him resolve his conflict.

An unresolved conflict may persist in varying forms and differing situations. Unless the victim of the conflict finally can attack the conflict and achieve a reasonable resolution, he may be driven to escape from the situation by one of several avenues: withdrawal from group living by becoming a hermit; attempted suicide; aggressive criminal acts; retreat from reality into a world of self-preoccupation. Unresolved conflicts affect the victim's entire personality. To a more or less serious degree he suffers from personality or behavior disorders that appear to be unresolvable and that may predispose toward disintegration of personality.

The Resolution of Conflicts

T H E R E is no standard remedy that can be administered to a person who is suffering from a state of conflict. It is possible, however, for parents, educators, employers, and other community leaders to help young people develop attitudes and behavior patterns that will lead to the achievement of self-building experiences. In this way conflict arousing interpersonal relations can be prevented. Moreover, community leaders can do much to help the individual who already is experiencing a conflict situation.

School factors. Schoolmen who know the content of education better than they do the psychology of the educand often are heard to say that any one who uses *common sense* as a means of assisting high-school students in their adjustment problems is applying basic psychological principles. We do not object to this belief, but we know that some advisers are more successful than are others in helping high-school students. Can this greater success be explained only in terms of greater common sense? Is there any teacher who will admit that he does not make considerable use of common sense in his dealings with his learners? Common sense becomes a significant factor of counseling, if the term is interpreted to include a consideration of the problems of the student in light of his background, his interests, his limitations, and his attitudes. To help a confused adolescent resolve his conflicts, a counselor needs *uncommon sense* that is the resultant of intense training, broad experience, and adequate personal adjustment.

Social factors. On the social level the life-adjustment program has three objectives. First, the individual definitely needs to gain all those positive attitudes, ideals, practices, beliefs, and habits that are essential to his becoming an efficient member of the social groups of which he forms a part. Such qualities as cooperation, geniality, generosity, kindness, and courtesy are socially acceptable traits that, as they are born of experience, become effective agents in preventing and resolving mental and emotional conflicts. Second, it is important that care be exercised to eliminate or minimize all social influences that tend to produce major conflicts in the respective groups and institutions that form the framework of social experiences.

Finally, when maladjustments already have been acquired, attempts can be made to determine the social nature of the causative factors. Efforts then can be made to remove the social irritants and to change the social situation, or to correct the individual's attitude. The preventive program is confronted with innumerable problem possibilities on the social level. With an increase of interest among adults in the development of better adjusted children may come a more successful functioning of preventive measures.

Work factors. There probably is no more hygienic method of resolving conflicts than participation in interesting and challenging work. Every adolescent dreams of the time when he will be a successful economic factor of society. In fact, a college senior was heard to remark that every high-school graduate should have a year of work experience before continuing his education on the college level; thereby he can enrich his college life.

Too ambitious occupational aims, parental opposition to personal vocational interests, lack of opportunity to train adequately for a chosen vocation, or insufficient need of workers in a desired occupation for which ability and training are adequate are fundamental sources of youthful conflicts. Young persons who, for the reasons stated, see no hope of a satisfying occupational ambition may develop antisocial attitudes and actions. If young people recognize that they are being thwarted in their normal urge to be gainfully employed according to their interests, they tend to resolve their conflict by placing the responsibility of their failure upon the inadequacy of the society that they believe to be the cause of their unfortunate situation.

Recently some students of a trade school neglected their studies yet refused to withdraw from school, although they were over the compulsory school age. When they were asked their reasons for neither studying nor quitting, their answer was that there was no reason for them to learn a trade since they were just "sticking around" until they were eighteen, at which time they would let the government take care of them in the armed services. There is evidence here of an attempt to resolve conflict through *flight* from purposeful activity.

Several brilliant and well-educated young college tutors who were among a group of college teachers accused of un-American activities began their careers as enthusiastic and loyal Americans.

Because of their ability, they had been encouraged by their college advisers to prepare themselves for college teaching, and were given part-time jobs in teaching and assisting in the college. Confident of an eventual appointment, these men, at great sacrifice, continued their graduate studies and then married. Budgetary cuts interfered with their receiving permanent college appointments. They became embittered by what they considered false encouragement followed by unfair discrimination. Hence they were motivated to *fight* against the, to them, existing intolerable social order.

Quite different from these young people who resolved their vocational conflicts in an antisocial manner are those young adults who are strong enough emotionally to accept failure in the achievement of their desired vocational aims, and who are ready and able to engage in whatever work is available—doing an honest job, but alert to more desirable work possibilities. Many of these young people are so successful in their "forced" work that they not only develop an interest in it but also win promotion and economic security. Others are able, eventually, to achieve their original aims. Consequently, they believe that their temporary disappointment has made them more appreciative of their final success.

Numerous conflicts among workers are mitigated through the efforts of industry itself. Many firms are discovering that it is a good common-sense procedure to provide better working conditions, to permit rest periods, to arrange shorter hours, and to plan recreational programs for their workers. It took many years for the more foresighted companies, stimulated by the demands of organized labor groups, to demonstrate the benefits of these methods of satisfying workers.

The individual and his conflicts.   Society has a major responsibility for the prevention of and resolution of conflicts experienced by individuals or groups. In the final analysis, however, the individual who is experiencing a conflict is the one who must attempt to resolve that conflict.

To the extent that a younger or older person who finds himself in a frustrating or conflict-arousing situation possesses habitually stable emotional qualities, he usually can resolve the difficulty in a manner that will be satisfying to himself and acceptable to others. The emotionally insecure person is likely to attempt a resolution of an existing conflict in such a way that the situation becomes more serious. He may even come to lose whatever degree of stability he once possessed.

As we have said earlier, a conflict may be rooted in two or more warring urges or desires within the individual himself, or it may arise out of a frustrating situation which involves persons or conditions in his environment. Whatever the source of the conflict may be, the person who is experiencing it can approach the problem situation in one of three ways. (1) He decides that he no longer can endure the conflict, so he attacks it *directly*. He does something definite about it. (2) He recognizes the fact that the conflict situation does not permit an "all or nothing" approach. Compromise between the elements of the conflict situation appears to be the most effective means of resolving his emotional stresses and strains. (3) His conflict has become so severe that there appears to be no reasonable way of resolving it. He becomes the victim of the conflict situation and withdraws completely from realism; he becomes mentally ill.

We know that mild or more severe conflicts are common. A young man has an intense desire to be the proud possessor of a high-priced automobile; he also wishes to marry. His financial status does not allow him to do both. A young woman was teaching in the elementary school after the completion of a three-year teacher-training course. She had saved enough money to make a fourth year of study possible, but she was responsible for the support of a widowed mother. If neither became ill, her savings would take care of both of them while she was not earning any money. A man who was earning a relatively small salary fell in love with a girl whose parents were wealthy. The girl wanted the man to give up his job and work for her father. The girl's father was willing to give the young man a high salary, but the young man was not interested in the work and had no training background for it. Moreover, he enjoyed his present work. Hence he felt that accepting this man's proposition verged on the parasitical.

Many more instances of similar conflict situations could be cited. In any case, something needs to be done to preserve mental health. The person involved is the one to decide whether he should employ the direct approach or attempt to compromise. In the first case cited the man married, hoping that eventually he might be able to afford an expensive automobile. His hope was realized. The young teacher compromised. She continued to teach and earned her degree from a university at which she could complete her college work after regular school hours. The man gave up the girl, and remained in his chosen occupational field. He reached this decision, however, only after much conflict and some guidance. He still is not certain that he made a wise decision.

Relative value of direct action and compromise. Various factors need to be considered before a conflict situation is approached either by way of direct action or by compromise. Direct action may be impulsive, it may not take into consideration all of the factors that are basic to the conflict situation. An immediate solution to a problem is satisfying only if the person has an intelligent understanding of the whole situation and is certain that the action that is decided upon will resolve the conflict. For example, a woman teacher lives with her aged mother in an apartment house in a large city. Because of her mother's ill health the woman devotes all of her time to her schoolwork and to the care of her mother. She lacks opportunity to engage in relaxing social activities. Hence she is under continual pressure.

Although the woman can retire from teaching, she is very much interested in her schoolwork; but her mother resents her daughter's absence from the home during school hours and feels that she is being neglected. Here is a conflict situation that needs resolution through direct action. The daughter realizes that retirement means a reduction of income, but that careful planning will make it possible for the two of them to live comfortably on her pension. Hence she retires; she and her mother leave the city for a small town in a warm climate. The woman does not regret her decision. Her mother's health and attitude have improved and the daughter is enjoying the social relaxation which had been denied her for so many years. Moreover, since they are living in a college town, the teacher probably may do some part-time teaching for personal satisfaction.

Too often a person takes direct action to solve a conflict situation and later regrets his decision. A high-school girl was undecided about her plans for the future. She was a good student who would have gained much from a college education. She believed, however, that her family needed the money that she would earn if she went to work directly after graduation from high school. Consequently, in spite of the attempts to dissuade her by both the family and the school officials, she elected the commercial course. This action did not solve her conflict, however. By the time she was graduated, she knew that she wanted to go to college but did not meet college entrance requirements. At this point she compromised by working during the day and completing her college-entrance requirements in the evening division of the high school. This meant at least two years of evening study, but she persisted. She then entered college and worked during the late afternoons and evenings in order to support herself financially. Although this heavy program was difficult, she felt that she finally had resolved her conflict. She found further satisfaction from the fact that, upon graduation from college, she was able to enter a professional field in which she was successful.

Compromise usually is the first approach for a person who can meet his conflict situation with some intelligent understanding of its fundamental factors and who is willing to give a little rather than to demand the complete satisfaction of his own wants. At one time or another every person is faced with a situation in which there are present more or less serious elements of conflict. He does something to free himself from the problem situation. Any action that relieves tension is better than passive acceptance of emotion-disturbing conditions. If an individual is unable to resolve his conflict by means of satisfying direct action or intelligent compromise, he may attempt to settle the struggle for adjustment by adopting one or another unrealistic approach to his problem, or he may withdraw completely from the demands upon him of a realistic situation which he believes he cannot meet successfully.

A successful executive is invited to address a national gathering of important men in his field. Although he is an excellent organizer, he always has had an abnormal fear of public speaking. He believes that a refusal to speak before the group would be interpreted as an admission of weakness. He withdraws from the situation honorably (as he believes) by suddenly losing his voice. He is not shamming; he attempts to speak but no sounds emerge. Apparently his vocal cords have become paralyzed. It may take considerable therapeutic treatment to help him regain his power of speech, especially if normal speaking ability were to be associated with recurring invitations to address large audiences. Other conflicts that involve fear of engaging in a particular situation may cause a person to lose the power of locomotion or the ability to use one's hand for writing, for example.

Some of the more common devices referred to as unrealistic approaches are presented in the following chapter. The complete or almost complete repudiation of reality is discussed in the chapter that deals with mental illness.

▶ **Questions and Problems for Discussion**

1. Describe situations that make you unhappy. Are any basic needs interfered with?

2. What unresolved conflicts are you now experiencing? What can you do to resolve them?

3. What is the importance of decision making in the resolution of conflicts?

4. Describe your behavior when in conflict.

5. Have you resorted to the use of alcohol in times of frustration? What do you do when frustrated?

6. Differentiate your needs from your wants. Which are requisites for happiness?

7. Relate several social situations in which you found it difficult to know what to do. How did you meet these situations?

8. What do you do to adjust in situations in which you develop a feeling of inferiority or inadequacy?

9. As an adolescent, were you a member of a gang? If so, describe the role played by you. Also indicate the goals of the gang. Were these goals ever in conflict with your ideals? How?

10. At your present stage of development, what three things do you most wish for? If you were given three weeks to attain them, what would you seek?

11. What are two or more things that you are expected to do that you believe yourself incapable of doing?

12. If you were given $10,000 to spend for ten items during the next two weeks, what would you purchase?

13. Discuss the extent to which others agree with your life plans.

CHAPTER Nine

The Struggle for Adjustment

A s you know, human drives and urges are the bases of human ideals and actions. If an inner drive motivates an individual to engage in activities that are unsuccessful in their self-regarding effects, he is likely to seek a more satisfying form of behavior. This compensatory pattern of behavior may be defined as a learned set of reactions that tends to reduce the force of the stresses and strains that are caused by the non-fulfillment of an urge by way of customary modes of behavior.

Patterns of Adjustment

I T is almost repetitious to assert that all of man's behavior tends toward the attainment of a series of more or less socially accepted goals. The individual's concept of and evaluation of the goal itself may be incomplete or faulty; his appreciation of his ability to achieve that goal may be inadequate. If either of these two situations exists it is difficult for him to achieve personal satisfaction through participation in so-called normal or realistic experiences. Hence the individual attempts to adopt an adjustive form of behavior that satisfies his impulse to achieve. This substitute behavior continues until he no longer feels the need to achieve the desired goal, or until the actual achievement of the original goal can be realized.

We now shall describe briefly some generally recognized substitute forms of behavior, including their significance as adjustment-seeking techniques and their relationship to maladjustment.

Compensatory Behavior

THE TERM *compensation* is interpreted by some psychologists to be a general concept that includes many specific forms of adjustment to failure or inadequacy. For them, rationalization, criticism, sublimation, and other forms of substitute behavior are compensatory techniques. Other psychologists consider compensation to be a specific attempt to reduce tensions that result from a recognized defect. The individual emphasizes the functioning of another trait or characteristic which is likely to distract the attention of associates from the defect. The substitute or compensatory behavior may or may not receive approval.

Some common forms of compensatory behavior. Many examples could be cited of the utilization of compensatory behavior. A throat difficulty interferes with the continuance of a singer's musical career. To compensate for the disappointment, he either develops his histrionic talents or becomes a teacher of music. A boy who cannot excel in study may aim consciously to become a successful athlete.

Sometimes the adoption of this kind of behavior is unconscious. Small men often tend to become assertive or aggressive. They may develop superiority in a special skill whereby they gain social approval, in spite of their small stature. They may become meticulous in dress and grooming.

Some parents attempt to compensate for their own inadequacies through the achievement of their children. These parents want to make available for their child the opportunities that they themselves had desired but were denied. They insist upon selecting the child's career, his associates, and his mate, in terms of their own thwarted interests. The socially unpopular adolescent or adult may adopt a hobby, such as collecting stamps, signatures of well-known persons, rare coins, or other objects. The pride that he develops in his collection and the social recognition that he receives compensate for his social inadequacies. A childless woman may become concerned about the welfare of all young people and engage in some form of social work.

Ineffective compensatory behavior. A compensatory activity may be unrealistic, such as exaggerated manner, affected speech, or ultramodern dress. The individual may tend to compensate for a defect by overaggressiveness, bullying, false submissiveness, or overzealousness in denunciation of social or individual inadequacies. These compensatory habits are expressions of the individual's denial to himself of his own inadequacy. Ineffectiveness of compensation is illustrated by the behavior of M. Z. and J. L.

M. Z. is twenty-three years old. She is extremely conscious of the fact that she is only five feet tall; she complains that her friends seem to tower above her and call her a "shrimp." Her dress is very peculiar; her use of cosmetics seems to be directed toward compensating for her short stature. Her nails are very long and very red, her hats have tall crowns, and her heels are extremely high. When she was in her second year at high school she joined a liberal-youth group, as a revolt against general peer attitudes. Since then she has been intolerant of all people who do not share her views; she constantly asserts that she is proud of the fact that she is different from the "common crowd."

J. L., a college student, is shy and ill at ease with members of the opposite sex. As a result of this attitude she refuses to attend any mixed gatherings. She gives as her reason the fact that she is engaged to a young man in the army. Since he is gaining promotion rapidly, she must devote all of her time and energy to study so that he will not be ashamed of her. She is a brilliant student but is beginning to show the strain of overwork. Her classmates suspect that she is not truthful concerning her engagement. They are worried about her physical and mental health but are unable to help her make a better social adjustment.

There is danger in overcompensation. An individual may not be content to develop normal competence in the substitute activity but may strive for complete mastery. The energy expended in this way may be too great; the individual may break under the strain. Moreover, the substitute attitude or behavior pattern may be socially disapproved. Inner tensions are thereby increased rather than reduced.

Attention-Seeking Behavior

THE DESIRE for attention is a normal characteristic. Social approval or commendation usually is most satisfactory. To receive social disapproval, however, is more satisfying than it is to be ignored. If a person's adjustment is adequate, he earns desired attention. It is only when ordinary behavior fails to attract comment from others that he may feel the need of bringing attention to himself by means of spectacular or unconventional behavior. This urge is common among children but is characteristic also of adolescents and adults.

Attention-getting devices. Crying without physical cause, throwing things, strutting, imitating Mother's use of rouge and lipstick, among young children; boasting of personal or of family prowess, displaying bad manners of speech or writing, among adolescents; engaging in hobbies and collections and affecting peculiar dress or manner, among adults—these are only a few of many attention-getting techniques that are utilized when ordinary behavior does not gain for the individual the amount and kind of recognition he desires. Even though an individual is successful in his daily activities, his success may be taken for granted by his associates. Since this passive approval is not completely satisfactory he may strive to force a more active recognition of himself.

An amusing story is told of a six-year-old boy who started his school career in the same building in which his older brothers and sisters had received their early schooling. During his first few school days the family evinced flattering interest in his enthusiastic reports of his good work. Since his experiences were no different from those of the older children who also had shown superior ability in their schoolwork, displayed interest in his achieved "stars" and success stories gradually lessened. He announced to the family one day that his teacher had scolded him. This announcement was received without much comment, whereupon he reported that his teacher had not only scolded him but had hit him. He could give no reason for his teacher's behavior, but continued to bring home stories of undeserved punishment. Puzzled by the situation, an older sister, who knew his teacher well, visited the school to discover what this small child was doing. To her surprise, the teacher insisted that he was a model boy; he had not been punished; actually, he had received more commendation than had any other child in the class. Asked to explain his conduct, he burst out, "I tried to tell you all the nice things that I was getting but no one would listen to me. I said that my teacher was hitting me so that *you would pay attention to me.*"

A person may have won considerable public recognition because of unusual achievement in art, music, literature, or other activity. After his reputation has become established as that of an accepted artist, his performance no longer is regarded as sensational. He then may begin to display odd mannerisms, unusual style of dress, or other personal peculiarity. People notice these and often imitate them. His behavior becomes a "fad": he temporarily relives the thrills of his early triumphs.

An individual may use this form of adjustment in order to divert attention from one factor of his personality and focus it upon another. B. L. is an intelligent college graduate. As the result of an accident, one side of his face is badly scarred. Although he is conscious of this physical shortcoming and tends to be shy in social situations, he is an excellent salesman. He attributes his success to the fact that he always is ready with a laugh, a joke, or a quip. Since his humor is clever, the listener attends to what he says and is diverted from giving too much attention to his physical defect.

Many of these simple attempts at attention getting represent innocuous, possibly helpful adjustment techniques. For example, a boy is in a class with children mentally superior to himself. He is able to pass in his work, but is not good enough to win honors. Hence he tries to gain the attention of his classmates by collecting unusual specimens of whatever the current interest of the group may be: campaign buttons, shells, stones, marbles, or pictures. The approval that he receives acts as an impetus toward further achievement in this kind of activity. Although most children do some collecting, this specially motivated activation may be the start of a profitable adult career.

Overemphasis upon attention getting. The normal desire for attention may be so stimulated through the exercise of otherwise praiseworthy activities that maladjustment may result. For example, it is desirable to develop in young people a habit of thrift; the school bank is an excellent means to achieve this purpose. Yet if too much attention is given to the individual or to the group that deposits the most money in the bank there is danger that a child may become so interested in the size of his account that he develops miserliness, or is tempted to obtain the money for deposit in dishonest ways. Hence school leaders are careful not to emphasize class competition unduly.

The individual's desire for attention may be so strong that he is stimulated toward abnormal and socially undesirable means of satisfying his urge. There are many causes for the lies of children, among which are included that of attention getting. In order to gain prestige, the young person who believes that he is inferior to the other members of the group in commendable achievement regales his pals with tales about his great prowess or his unusual experiences. If the story is not convincing enough, he is forced to bring evidence of his "crime." Consequently, he is impelled to justify his boastings by participation in delinquent activities.

Other forms of attention-seeking behavior may be displayed. For several years the authors worked with a high-school girl who displayed symptoms of emotional disturbance. Her difficulty started with certain phobias that made her unwilling to come to school. As the result of the attention given her by her teachers, the girl's early fears were modified and she gradually made a good adjustment to her schoolwork. It was no longer necessary for her teachers to single her out for special attention. However, she still craved the attention from the authors that had been given consistently in the form of approval of her school success and of her improved cooperation at home. This general approval did not satisfy the girl. She needed special attention.

She told wild tales of her exploits with men. She claimed that she went daily to the furnished room of a man who was very much older than herself; she was treated to drinks and kissed by a married man whose wife employed her in a part-time job. Investigation revealed that these stories were false. Any expression of doubt concerning their authenticity, however, might have stimulated her to seek such experiences in order to bring back to her counselors proof of her delinquent behavior. Her rehabilitation then would bring her again into the focus of their attention. She was romantic, given to daydreams, extremely egocentric, and desirous of attention. Unfortunately, her behavior finally became so abnormal that she was committed to a hospital for the mentally ill.

Many youthful delinquencies can be traced to the urge for attention. Few persons are "born" criminals. The desire to excel, the unbearableness of being ignored, and the thrill of recognition are significant causes of juvenile delinquency.

Self-Bolstering through Criticism

CONSCIOUSNESS of inadequacy in one's ability to meet social demands often results in the development of an attitude of criticism toward other persons, especially if the latter appear to be well adjusted to situations in which the individual is experiencing failure. The discovery of weaknesses in the successful person mitigates the lack of self-esteem of the failing person. Gossip has its foundation in this attempt at adjustment. Although this attitude is found among normal persons, it may be a symptom of serious maladjustment.

Kinds of criticism. Tactful criticism *to* an individual of an observable fault usually is appreciated as a sign of friendly interest. Criticism *of* an individual to others generally is motivated by a feeling of inferiority to the person criticized. This feeling may be very slight; implied and expressed criticism in the form of gossip usually is not malicious. Since no one is perfect, it is taken for granted that the faults of an individual are proper material for common discussion. No matter how harmless the criticism is, however, any emphasis upon the weakness of another person arouses in the critic a comforting feeling of virtue.

A child often uses this method (which he has learned from listening to his parents discuss their friends) to counteract the effect of having other children held up to him as models to be imitated. He resents the fact that his parents appear to like another child better than they do him. Therefore, he looks for faults in the other child and consoles himself with the thought that he excels the other in the display of certain desirable qualities. He may strive toward personal improvement in these respects. The child is helped to overcome his original lack; his criticism of the model may have desirable rather than undesirable effects. He no longer resents the model child, but feels equal to him or even superior to him. Instances have been known in which the child or young person actually has tried to help his former object of criticism to overcome the faults that he has recognized in him.

Self-criticism, if based upon a normal desire to improve behavior, is desirable. However, self-criticism may be a form of adjustive behavior. The expected response of the listener to a person's belittling his own achievement is praise. If the listener seems to agree with the self-critic, the latter starts to justify his own degree of achievement in comparison with that of others. Unusual displays of modesty often follow this pattern. Persons who employ this technique are not sure of their status; they are attempting to bolster their ego.

Ineffective adjustment through criticism. Carried to an extreme, criticism may develop definite maladjustment. A father who was overzealous concerning his young daughter's deportment was accustomed to point out to her certain faults in the behavior of other girls. His purpose was to encourage her to refrain from behaving in a similar manner. The effect of this training was twofold. It helped her develop a keen power of observation, but it also cut her off from free associations with her peers. She constantly watched them for possible faults lest she imitate their behavior and receive reproof from her father for conduct unbecoming a lady. Her father's death during her adolescence stopped this training before she had developed a critical attitude that might have interfered seriously with her social adjustment.

Unless his energies are redirected into other channels, a person who develops the habit of gossiping as a self-bolstering device may become so intent upon picking up choice tidbits that he will lean more and more upon this method of self-realization. His chief desire is to be the first to thrill his associates with a new bit of scandal. His listeners' reaction to his tales is to him a most satisfying form of social approval. If actual facts are not available or not spectacular enough, he almost unconsciously embroiders the truth or resorts to the manufacture of stories based upon very slight threads of fact. These tales may be extremely damaging in their implications. The individual no longer is rational; he believes the stories that he has invented. The realization that his listeners come to discredit his gossip may have serious effects upon his mental health.

Sometimes the listener to criticism of another person encourages this criticism in order to convince himself that the speaker approves of him (the listener) or he would not take him into his confidence. A pathetic case of this kind is that of a mother whose love for her only child was extremely possessive. She resented any attention that the girl might give to friends, regardless of sex or age. If the girl praised anyone in her mother's presence the latter would use every means at her disposal to break up the friendship. The situation became so intolerable that the daughter found it necessary to meet her friends away from the home, or to satisfy her mother's ego by discovering real or imaginary faults in these young people. If she chose the latter course, her mother would become the stanch advocate of the criticized person and reprove her daughter for not recognizing the person's sterling qualities. The daughter could then agree that her mother's judgment was better than hers. The girl could not be too enthusiastic about the person or find virtues other than those that had been pointed out to her by her mother. In this way the mother satisfied her urge to maintain first place in her daughter's affection. As a matter of fact, however, the girl, as a result of her training and experience, was a much better judge of people than was her mother.

The Utilization of Identification

A SOCIAL group usually includes among its members one or more individuals who have demonstrated superior ability in a specific form of activity. It is normal for other members of the group to identify themselves with these superior persons and to experience personal satisfaction from the achievement of their successful associates. The rooter at a baseball game, for example, identifies himself with his favorite team; he regards the home runs made by his team as personal victories. This is a satisfaction that is achieved more easily than one that is earned through personal endeavor. Moreover, in case of failure on the part of one's chosen idol, it is relatively easy (though often temporarily disappointing) to satisfy one's desire to experience success by switching one's allegiance from the failing individual or group to another more successful one and by identifying himself with the latter.

Development of identification patterns. This is a common and relatively harmless form of adjustment. Most of us belong to a small group within a larger social group. It is usual for us to identify ourselves with or to experience pride in the achievement of noteworthy members of this select group. Such identification may interfere with an individual's active participation in group activity, however; it is easier to overcome a feeling of inferiority by basking in the reflected glory of the exploits of the other person than to gain recognition for personal achievement. Still, this diverted attention may prevent the arousal of emotional stress.

Identification as a means of compensation may begin very early in life. The small child identifies himself with his parents of whom he usually is proud. "My father can lick all your fathers put together"; "my mother is the prettiest woman in the world—my father says so"; "my father knows everything"—are remarks frequently made by children of well-adjusted parents. Because of this hero worship the child tends to imitate his parent's behavior so that someday he may be as fine as the adult is.

As children proceed through school and college they identify themselves with their various "adored" teachers or campus heroes. Witness the mannerisms of the little girl playing school and imitating her teacher. The child has so carefully observed gestures, intonations, and even vocabulary, that her teacher is given a chance—and sometimes not a flattering one—to see herself as others see her. The boy lives the life of his storybook or television hero—it may be an Indian chief or it may be Roy Rogers. The girl temporarily may be Red Riding Hood, Cinderella, or a glamorous motion-picture star.

A bright little girl, who was an ardent reader of well-chosen children's books, each evening became a different storybook character. This interest activated a game between herself and her father. When he arrived home from business she was accustomed to greet him with an imitation of the day's heroine. His part in the game was to address her by her heroine's name and to carry on with her an appropriate conversation. So good was her imitation, which at the time was not acting but living, that the practice thus acquired did much to help her later to become a famous character actress.

As the individual grows older he tends to identify himself with special groups: fraternities, select clubs, and civic and business organizations. He takes great pride in the good reputation of his organization. The more highly selected it is and the less outstanding his participation in the group activities, the greater is his tendency to boast of his group's achievements. Usually those persons who are responsible for maintaining the standards of the group are too busy to talk much about their achievements. Members of outstanding families, who themselves are relatively mediocre, have an inordinate pride in the family's history.

An individual's identification with a person who is worthy of imitation or with a group that has high ideals may develop a desire to become like these leaders. Gradually the individual, within his limitations, may imitate his heroes as the child imitates his parents. In this way he may acquire personality traits that cause him to be a model for others to imitate.

Effect of identification upon personality. Parents who have a feeling of personal failure sometimes identify themselves with the success of their children to an extent that exceeds justifiable parental pride. An individual may identify himself with his possessions to so great a degree that he boasts of his home, his automobile, his clothes, his jewelry, etc., as though his possessions were endowed with qualities of excellence that cannot be found elsewhere. Identifications of the types described are undesirable: first, because too much bragging becomes boring to listeners and so interferes with an individual's normal associations with his fellows; second, because the individual may waste his time in boasting rather than in doing. One criticism of American sport is that too many Americans are bleacher-seat athletes who exercise their lungs in yelling and their arms in waving hats rather than participate in healthful games. Another criticism of Americans is that they think more of what they have than what they are.

Identification is undesirable when the person so loses his individuality in that of his ideal that he is no longer conscious of himself as a person, but takes on in thought and in action the personality of his hero. Since his background and environment may be very different from that of the hero, the results may be disastrous.

If normal boys identify themselves with the heroes of undesirable motion pictures or thrilling badmen stories, their identification with the characters may go no further than the mental reliving of exciting exploits. No more serious effects may result than a waste of the time that should be given to study, or a reduction of power to meet routine duties. In its extreme form this identification may result in an attempt to emulate the behavior of the hero, with consequent danger to other persons or penalties to himself.

Among the mentally ill this form of compensation is quite common and may be one of the first observable symptoms of a mental disorder. The kindly, moral, and religious but ineffectual man suddenly becomes God; the brilliant, diligent student of history now is Napoleon; the derelict who is picked up on the park bench tells the policeman about the treasure which he has hidden safely at the bottom of the Pacific Ocean and which, as soon as he has finished his nap, he will have brought to the surface and distributed among his friends.

A young woman had been brought up very carefully by an uncle and an aunt. Because of their attitude against continued education for girls, she was not allowed to enter college or to study music. She resented her relatives and her enforced idleness. Finally, she left home and started on a trip to Europe. All her clothes and accessories were white. During the trip she informed fellow passengers that she was a princess who was returning to her native country to claim her fortune. She asserted vehemently that most of this fortune would be given to her uncle and aunt who had been good to her but whom she had treated badly.

Her behavior gave evidence of her identification with heroines of the historical novels and operas of which she had been exceedingly fond. She was returned to America and committed to a hospital for the mentally ill, where she is confined for life. She refuses to see any of her former associates; she devotes most of her time to reading and rereading historical romances. On occasions she is a brilliant conversationalist. She has lost her own identity in that of fictional heroines. She does not answer to her name.

Attitude Projection

MOST human beings dislike to admit their errors of judgment or their inability to perform successfully. It is much more satisfying to an individual to project the blame for his failure upon other persons or objects in the immediate environment. The teacher is to blame for the student's failure; the stone upon which the pedestrian stubbed his toe should not have been in the way. If this projection is understood by the person using it, the results are not serious and may even be a source of amusement to him and his associates. If, however, this behavior takes the form of irrational ideas of false persecution, it is a dangerous form of maladjustment.

Bases of projection. Examples of projection are common. The child fails in his test because the teacher gives the wrong questions or marks his paper unfairly. The cook's cake falls because someone shakes the stove by slamming the door. The adolescent girl is a wallflower because her mother makes her wear an unbecoming dress, or because boys have poor taste or want something for nothing. One's car hits the post because the road is not level.

Such projected reasons could be true, but in most instances the use of them is an excuse—a kind of grabbing in a specific situation at a straw of possibility that is not a probability. For most people the temporary conscience salver is accompanied by a suspicion that the fault lies in the individual himself. Usually, after an experience of projecting blame, a person will attempt to meet a similar situation with a form of behavior that will give more satisfying results. Yet the attitude of projection may be used for the justification of other personal mistakes. Used in this way, projection protects the individual from the feeling of futility that might result if he were affected too seriously by all of his minor behavior mistakes.

Effects of habitual projection. When projection becomes a habit, when all one's failures are blamed on others, when a deep-seated and unreasonable attitude of projection is developed toward a particular person or group, the resulting emotional state of bitterness may become a factor of mental disturbance. The habitual integration of projection results from conflicts that are induced by a recognition of personal failure, and attempts to explain failure in such a way that the personal fault will be minimized. An attitude of inferiority may dominate the experiences of an individual academically, economically, politically, and morally.

In connection with conflicts on the academic level we have referred to a student's tendency to blame his teacher for his failure.

More serious is the "self-made" man's denunciation of a college education, and his campaign against public support of parasites who have learned the easy way and who are being paid by public funds to continue ineffectual methods of superficial education. If a coveted position is won by a college graduate, the reason for the choice is not to be found in the superior ability and training of the person chosen but in the false standards of an effete civilization. The disappointed candidate may become so bitter that he withdraws from his group and goes to an unspoiled community where real merit is appreciated. He stays there until he loses out in competition. A series of such experiences, instead of convincing the man of his own need of self-improvement, may so exaggerate his feeling of thwarting that he develops a delusion of persecution.

An individual who is economically inferior to others may attempt to compensate for his ability to achieve desired financial or social status by engaging in the promulgation of radical ideas concerning political or social justice. For example, he believes that the cause of his obscurity or poverty lies not in his own lack of power to achieve but in the unfair competition to which he is subjected.

This man becomes the advocate of the thesis that all men are equal and should share equal rewards and recognition. He fails to appreciate differences in ability or willingness to achieve, or in the social value of the achievement. The radical thus projects the blame for his own incompetence upon an unfair and prejudiced social order of which he is an innocent victim. He often is unaware of his own power to achieve, and fails to recognize opportunities for success that may be offered to him. In fact, he may have become so imbued with attitudes of economic or social martyrdom that any attempt to change his status would be regarded as further evidence of political or social injustice. Moreover, it sometimes happens that in those cases where economically or socially underprivileged radicals have later become members of the group of "the overprivileged oppressors" they then have become bitter opponents of the "grabbing lower classes" who interfere with their progress, through unreasonable economic or social demands.

If an individual, because of lack of physical or emotional control or as a result of rigid childhood training, finds himself motivated to engage in behavior that he recognizes to be undesirable, he may develop the tendency to shift the responsibility from himself to environmental conditions. This attitude leads to a strong urge within him to reform the world. In this way his own sense of inferiority is lost in his appreciation of the sins of society or of the disastrous results to society of such evils. The converted sinner becomes the rabid reformer. Not all persons who advocate or attempt to bring about desirable social reforms should be included in this group, however. We are referring here to the neurotic, unreasonable, fanatic type of reformist.

Behavior Rationalization

RATIONALIZATION is an attempt to excuse behavior that is recognized by the person engaging in it to be undesirable or foolish but that produces certain emotional satisfactions. There is no valid reason for the self-satisfying behavior, so there must be manufactured an apparently sensible justification of it. For example, a woman sees a dress that she admires. It is expensive, she needs her money for other things, but she wants the dress and buys it. In order to justify her extravagance, she asserts that she and her husband are likely to receive an unexpected invitation to a social gathering of his business associates. Therefore, she must be prepared for such an occasion in order that she may not discredit her husband by her appearance.

Bases for the utilization of rationalization. It is difficult for an individual always to admit to himself the true reasons for his acts or the real motives behind his behavior. The higher his standards of conduct and the finer his ideals, the greater may be his attempted self-deception. It is almost unbearable to admit that one's behavior is actuated by unworthy motives. Hence, the average man is given to excusing his socially undesirable conduct by justifying it in terms of highly commendatory though false motives. Usually he is deceiving no one but himself. If he rationalizes his behavior too often, there is danger that he is not believed even when he gives an honest explanation of his behavior.

Anyone dealing with young people knows the difficulty encountered in obtaining from them straightforward accounts of the reasons for their misdeeds. One high-school dean has developed a relatively successful technique of dealing with this problem. She listens courteously to the student's explanation of non-conforming behavior. Then she remarks in a conversational tone, "Now let us get the real reason." Usually, after a few pointed questions by the dean, the student admits the real motive for the infraction. After a few such experiences a student meets a situation of this kind by saying, "I thought that I was doing it for this reason but I guess I had better find the real reason before you find it for me."

Many rationalizations have become almost social traditions and are used and accepted without much thought of their connotation. Some of these are: genius never could spell; great people write unintelligibly; the man who does things has no time to bother about superficial matters; attention to petty details is the sign of a small mind. The inference in each case is that if an individual has failed in one of these specific forms of desirable behavior, the failure itself is the sign of the possession of a more worthy quality. Many more such forms of self-justification are common. Our likes and dislikes; our fears; our tendencies to indolence, to selfishness, to jealousy, to spitefulness and envy, to extravagance or miserliness, to too great interest in or too little interest in appearance, to too much or to too little time spent in recreation or in work—all lend themselves to plausible and self-satisfying explanations.

Our consideration for the feelings or for the plans of other people, our sense of duty, our good manners, or our heavy responsibilities are favorite forms of excuse for failure to meet the ordinary daily demands of life. If with the rationalization goes the determination not to repeat the conduct that needs to be excused, the results are not serious.

Effects of rationalization.   An individual's associates accept his occasional utilization of rationalization, since they themselves sometimes may experience a similar self-bolstering need. If this device is utilized consistently as a means of self-justification, however, the group soon learns to resent its implication and the individual's social adjustment is hindered by the unfriendly attitudes of his associates.

The persistent use of rationalization may lead to the development of a false appreciation of one's own personality. For example, an elderly man was so absent-minded that he rarely did what was expected of him and almost never kept appointments. Consequently, he developed the habit of inventing startling and seemingly convincing alibis for his memory lapses. So fixed had become this habit that it was almost impossible for him to tell the truth. Occasionally he recognized his defect, and urged his listeners not to believe the story he had just told them; whereupon he would proceed to regale them with another tale no more truthful than the one he had branded as a falsehood.

As a result of extreme utilization of this device, reality becomes less and less a part of the mental content; delusions are imminent. A serious form of projection may accompany the rationalizing habit to the extent that the reasons for an individual's failures are completely divorced in his thinking from inability to achieve. He places the blame for his inadequate adjustments upon conditions outside himself, or upon other persons or groups. In extreme cases this shifting of responsibility for personal inadequacies develops into strong feelings of persecution.

Sublimation of Inner Drives

I N an earlier chapter sublimation was described as an effort to direct primitive emotional reactions toward socially approved levels. Psychologists do not agree completely in their interpretation of this form of adjustment. To some it is merely a form of conscious substitution of desirable behavior for that which may be impossible to achieve or which is socially undesirable. If an individual's fulfillment of a strong interest or a desired activity is thwarted, he is likely to display emotional stresses unless the interest or activity can be diverted or sublimated toward achievable ends. According to the Freudian·interpretation, the thwarting that needs to be sublimated is limited to the undesirable expression of the sex urge or the *libido*. For a person living in our present culture to avoid emotional stress, the primitive form of sex expression must be diverted toward higher, socially approved forms of behavior. The individual may be unconscious of the force of the original drive; he is unaware of the indirectness of his interest in the substitute activity. He honestly may believe that his "substitute" activity is motivated directly by highly social attitudes.

The functioning of sublimation. Sublimation has social significance. There is value in the sublimation of one's primitive urges or selfish desires toward behavior that will benefit other members of the group or of society at large. It is an excellent method of releasing human energy into channels of the kinds of activity that are satisfying both to the individual himself and to those who are affected by his behavior.

The substitution of behavior may be conscious, in that the individual, recognizing a certain ability in himself, definitely directs this talent toward humanitarian ends, e.g., a man who possesses persuasive powers of speech becomes the leader of propaganda for worthy social causes. Sublimation, in its strict interpretation, however, implies that the transference of interest or of activity is on the emotional rather than on the intellectual level.

Sublimation is used as a means of adjustment when, temporarily or permanently, a strong drive cannot be translated into drive-satisfying activity. Consequently, there may occur a gradual, unconscious change from interest in self-gratification toward concern with the welfare of others. If the enlarged activity is successful, feelings of thwarting or of personal tension are modified or eliminated, and the person becomes a well-adjusted member of society. A boy is larger and stronger than his schoolmates; instead of using his strength to plague his fellows, he may become the champion of smaller boys or of girls and fight their battles for them against other boys who have not sublimated their primitive fighting tendencies.

Much of literature, art, and music may be explained as the outpouring of emotional energy into creative compositions. The man or woman who, because of circumstances beyond his control, is denied the opportunity of having children of his own, may adopt all children and become active in fighting for their health and safety. The childless woman or the woman whose children have died or have grown up and moved away from her may direct her maternal urge into social-service work, teaching, or similar activities.

Value of sublimation. Many primitive inner urges or drives that motivate an individual to activity are concerned with the survival of the self. In so far as the realization of a drive is not antisocial, this is desirable. When society is harmed by an individual's satisfaction of such inner urges, however, functioning of sublimation becomes an excellent form of adjustment. Some writers claim that the progressive improvements in civilization constitute forms of sublimation. By nature, the individual is antisocial rather than social; all basic motives are directed toward selfish ends. Although one may not agree with this evaluation of human nature, to sublimate often has personal and social value.

Since sublimation is a tension-reducing form of behavior that gives opportunity for desirable or even highly commendable activity, it usually leads away from rather than toward inadequate adjustment. It is only when the sublimated behavior pattern becomes extreme that maladjustment is possible. The humanitarian may become a rabid emotional propagandist or a weak sentimentalist. The artist may try for the bizarre in his creation. The social "uplifter" may develop into an aggressive fanatic. In such cases the individual concerned probably is suffering extreme emotional imbalance that would make normal adjustment of any kind difficult if not impossible.

Daydreaming and Fantasy as Media of Adjustment

T O gain satisfaction from imaginary achievement of success and approval when these are not possible of actual attainment is a popular form of self-satisfying adjustment. There are very few persons who, at some time during their childhood, adolescence, or adulthood have not experienced the thrill of imaginary success achievement.

Purposes served by daydreams. Daydreaming represents a tendency to allow the imagination to play with ideas that are satisfying realizations of desired goals or purposes. If an individual recognizes the ephemeral character of his dreams or uses these dreams as preparation for actual accomplishment, this form of adjustment is helpful. It is only when the world of fantasy is divorced completely from reality that the utilization of this self-satisfying device leads to inadequate adjustment or maladjustment.

A great work of pictorial art, music, or literature is conceived and brought to the level of expression through the imaginative dreams and flights of fantasy of the creator. The author, the painter, the engineer, the architect, or the composer uses his daydreams as the means of building real and appreciated masterpieces. He is able to combine constructive imagination with practical realization.

The imaginative meanderings of his childhood and adolescent day-dreaming experiences constitute the background of his controlled utilization of revery as the basis of creative activity.

There is no definite line of demarcation between a child's dream world and his actual world. To him fairies, goblins, giants, brave princes, and beautiful princesses are as real as are his living associates. In his early life he may become too engrossed in fairy tales because he does not have sufficient opportunity to play with children of his own age. Consequently, these mythical figures are more real to him than are living people. Moreover, experience with his family and little friends may not always bring him desired satisfaction, but his book friends never fail him. Hence the young child may identify himself with a mythical hero or heroine; he creates highly satisfying stories of his own prowess and achievement.

During the child's school years, especially if he is brighter or slower than the average student in his class, actual classroom work may become boring to him; his early habits of telling himself stories may return in the form of daydreams. His apparent inattention to classroom routine may earn the disapproval of his teacher, in which case he may become more dissatisfied with the situation and, consequently, intensify his habit of daydreaming.

The healthy child is in no way harmed by his youthful dreams or fantasies, if he is given plenty of opportunity for successful achievement within his abilities. For example, the young child's supreme belief in Santa Claus as a giver of gifts to good children stimulates him to merit the approval of the donor. His discovery that his parents and friends are the givers of the gifts helps him to shift his loyalty from his childish ideal to his real associates.

During early adolescence dreams of adult accomplishment are common. The majority of young people are stimulated by stories of adult success long before they are old enough or sufficiently trained to experience similar successful achievement. A normal girl dreams about Prince Charming. A boy envisions himself as a noted physician, a stalwart policeman, or a successful businessman. Unless an adolescent's dreams of conquest are too unrealistic, they stimulate him toward the achievement of constructive goals. This is especially true if the dreams grow out of successful activities and are followed by continued success in the stimulating activity.

The more challenging an adult's program of activities is and the more opportunities it offers for further achievement, the more likelihood is there that each step in his career may be followed by dreams of further achievement. His dreams of future success act as an incentive for further activity and is, at the same time, an indication of lack of satisfaction with his present accomplishment. This is sometimes referred to as "noble discontent." The well-adjusted person knows when to transfer his dreaming into productive activity.

If the past experiences of an aging adult have been relatively satisfying, he tends to give much of his time and attention to retrospective dreaming of his past achievements. He again is telling himself stories; he is returning to the fairy-tale level of imagination, except that now his memories are embroidered in such a way as to make himself the hero of previously experienced feats of performance. In each reliving there is an increase in the glorification of the real experience as he had lived it earlier.

Besides these organized, continuous dreams or fantasies that have their foundations in an imagination permeated by romantic tales of achievement every individual indulges in idle dreaming of the kind that is common to the man who may be sitting in a comfortable armchair, facing a friendly fire and puffing at his favorite pipe. His thoughts wander idly from one half-formed dream to another; he is only mildly conscious of his surroundings. His dreams have little or no basis in reality; he is enjoying the satisfaction that comes temporarily from losing oneself in the world of make believe.

Ineffective utilization of daydreams and fantasy. Daydreaming or fantasy may be a symptom of inadequate adjustment or of serious mental illness. The individual who finds himself unable to make adequate adjustments to life situations gradually develops the habit of dream adjustment, almost to the point of losing complete contact with reality.

The child whose normal activities are unsatisfactory may become so engrossed with his dream world that failure to adjust in his actual experiences is no longer significant. He "sits through" his class periods, to the dismay of his teacher, who is unable to stimulate him to activity through any ordinary means of encouragement, scolding, or shaming. Disapproval from his parents for his lack of cooperation has no effect upon him; he is scarcely conscious of it.

Examples of this extreme form of fantasy are relatively uncommon, however.

Adolescents and young adults often use this type of escape technique as a compensation for unsatisfactory sex adjustment. Too strict parental control or awareness of personal unattractiveness may lead to the thwarting of normal sex impulses. Satisfaction is sought through erotic dreams. As these dreams become increasingly systematic, the likelihood of normal sex adjustment decreases. Similarly, failure or inadequate achievement in school or business may motivate an individual to seek self-realization in a dream life or world of fantasy. His power to improve his inadequate adjustment in realistic situations thereby is lessened or completely lost.

Repression as Conscious Forgetting

A N I N D I V I D U A L tends to avoid persons or places that are associated with previous unpleasant experiences. Similarly, a person may want to forget the details of a humiliating or embarrassing situation. This type of forgetting (repression) is different from failure to recall that is caused by lack of sufficient associations, or from temporary forgetfulness that results from the interference of distracting stimuli. Repression means that the individual *wants to forget*, although he may not be conscious of his desire to do so. This attitude tends to increase rather than decrease tensions. The memory of the unfortunate occurrence persists in its attempt to come to the foreground of attention; consciously or unconsciously, the individual wills it back to forgetfulness.

The bases of repression. Repression, the forgetting of the unpleasant, has been the subject of much controversy. The followers of Freud use the term to designate the relegation of an unpleasant memory into the "unconscious"; other psychologists who deny the existence of an unconscious mind attempt to explain repression as an element of attitudes. Regardless of the point of view of any particular school of psychology, reports of experiments dealing with the effects of pleasantness or unpleasantness upon retention seem to indicate that unpleasant experiences are forgotten more readily than are pleasant ones. Although there are individual differences among people in this respect, there is reason to believe that it is normal to forget or to try to forget an experience that arouses a feeling of shame, embarrassment, or extreme annoyance.

Individuals tend to relive mentally those personal experiences that are self-satisfying. This mental repetition of the experience fixes it in the memory. Ordinarily, a man or a woman dislikes to think or to talk about unpleasantness that is associated with personal inadequacy. He, therefore, does not fix any such experience in his thinking; he may forget it entirely. If he possesses a sufficient number of self-regarding memories to take the place of these "forgotten" ones, he is spared thereby the feeling of failure or of conflict that otherwise he might experience. For no apparent reason, however, a similarity between the repressed or forgotten experience and a non-conflict-arousing experience may cause him to forget the details of the second experience.

The emotional concomitants of repression. An individual may avoid or become emotionally excited in an apparently normal situation because of a suddenly aroused fear that seems to have no basis in fact. Although an earlier fear or embarrassment-producing experience is forgotten, its emotional coloring and attendant tension are still present. A tension of this kind is reduced through the continued placing of oneself in such situations with satisfying results and with an understanding of the basic cause of the fearful attitude.

For example, a young couple were strolling along a sandy beach under a boardwalk. The young people failed to notice that the rising tide apparently had cut off any means of exit from the beach. Not until they had crawled and dug their way through the sand were they able to get out from under the boardwalk. No physical damage was done and no reference was made by either one to the seriousness of their predicament, except a laughing remark concerning the narrowness of their escape. The memory of her undignified crawling and digging remained a source of embarrassment to the girl, however. Finally, the incident was forgotten, but for many years the girl could not tolerate to be in a crowd or in a small room. Intelligent efforts to discover the original cause of her phobia combined with pleasant experiences in former fear-producing situations has helped her overcome the stresses associated with her early fear-producing experience. She has continued to dislike low ceilings, however, but understands the reasons for her attitude.

Emotionally unstable persons often become the prey of intense and abnormal fears and phobias. These fears or phobias arise out of unpleasant or shameful experiences that are characteristic of this kind of personality. The result may be a form of maladjustment that is difficult to recondition. The tendency to repress the undesirable memory struggles with the recurrence of fear in any stimulating situation. The conscious recall to memory of the repressed material may bring about an adjustment. Contrariwise, such recall may intensify the fear of the actual situation. Moreover, a symbolic fear caused by the combination of a desirable and an undesirable experience may be so great that the fear response spreads to many stimuli.

Forms of Withdrawing Behavior

I N their social relationships some persons appear to be more outgoing in their attitudes than are others. Natural tendencies and environmental experiences cause individuals to differ from one another in their degree of ascendance or submissiveness in social situations. Withdrawing tendencies are rooted in temperament, personal interests, and ambitions and situations. An attitude of self-sufficiency may have little or no effect upon an individual's adequacy of adjustment. On the other hand, extreme withdrawal may be symptomatic of inadequate adjustment or severe emotional disorder. We shall consider briefly three forms of withdrawal: shyness and seclusiveness, negativism and refusal, and retrogression.

Shyness and seclusiveness. Because of overprotectiveness or too strict discipline on the part of parents, or because of a lonely childhood, a child may become very shy in the presence of strangers. He takes refuge in a passive attitude that deceives the unobservant adult into thinking that the child is well adjusted. The youngster is not naughty, nor does he indulge in temper tantrums. Yet beneath his quiet, unassuming exterior the child may be experiencing feelings of tension and frustration. The disturbed emotional state is the result of a conflict between his desire to participate in the activities of his peers and his fear that he may not be accepted by them. A continuance of the conflict state leads to still greater withdrawal.

The "good" child may become an inordinately shy, seclusive, and unhappy adult. Since most children are adaptable, however, they respond with relative ease to situations and relationships in which they can achieve some self-confidence, thereby overcoming their shyness.

Negativism and refusal. During some part of the early childhood years a child tends to respond negatively to requests or suggestions. He may comply with the request even while he is denying it. A child's refusal may be accompanied by active forms of resistance such as body stiffening or temper tantrums. The negativistic attitude usually disappears by the time a child is old enough to attend school.

Serious manifestations of negativism or refusal are manifested by the older child or the adult who has developed habits of contradictory attitudes, stubbornness, and rebellion against authority. Such behavior patterns often are the behavior resultants of physical or mental weakness that has made it impossible for an individual to perform successfully the tasks assigned him. Neither he nor other persons in the situation understand the cause of his difficulty; the victim's only adjustment seems to be that of refusal. If these conditions continue, the individual becomes suspicious of the intent of any requests or suggestions made to him by his associates. He is likely to develop habitual antagonistic attitudes.

An example of the functioning of negativism is the habitual attitude of a brilliant educational leader. She admits that, as a student, she worked hardest for those instructors whom she suspected of disliking her. Her purpose was to show them that they were wrong in their judgment of her. Her life has been one of challenge. If the members of her family wish her to agree with any of their plans or decisions, they suggest the opposite of their real interests. She is dogmatic, stubborn, and strong-willed. She does not recognize her own faults and is annoyed by the stupidity and lack of cooperation of her professional associates. She also is a lonely and unhappy woman. Her superior ability sets her apart from her peers. She has not learned to adjust to a society composed of her inferiors.

Retrogression. A child may be overprotected to the extent that he is not expected to make decisions for himself or to fight his own battles. He derives great satisfaction from this sheltered life. Later he may be unable to meet adequately the demands of a larger environment in which he is held responsible for the management of his own affairs. A feeling of failure and frustration results. Unconsciously he may revert to the stage of his life in which he experienced satisfying protection and concern for his welfare. Consequently, he may attempt to return to his earlier patterns of behavior and experience. He is displaying an attitude of retrogression.

This form of adjustment, that is more general in its application than is a specific behavior pattern, may show itself in the early years of an individual's life. A child of three or four may resent the diverting of parental attention from him to a new baby brother or sister. His resentment shows itself in his insistence upon being helped in activities that he can perform very well. He demands to be fed, to have help in putting on his shoes, or to be tucked into bed.

Adolescents who leave home for college or a job miss the family attention to which they are accustomed. A feeling of homesickness results. A young married woman is expected by her husband to be proficient in certain routine activities. He does not give her the praise that she feels is her due, or he is not properly sympathetic about burned fingers or a disagreeable tradesman. She reverts to an earlier stage of development. She either finds an excuse for returning to the shelter of her mother's protective care or she develops symptoms of illness that compel her husband to expect less from her or give her the attention that she craves.

These examples represent regressive attitudes that can be overcome through the experiencing of satisfying success in activities that are appropriate to the age and ability status of the individual. Retrogression may be a symptom of extreme withdrawal when or if an individual will not or cannot meet the demands of his life situations.

▶ **Questions and Problems for Discussion**

1. Describe a case in which a mental conflict has been the cause of a physical breakdown. A mental breakdown.
2. Recall one of your obsessions. Relate how it affected you, its cause, and how you resolved it.
3. An adolescent girl desires to wear a certain dress to a party and her mother forbids it. How can the girl solve her problem?

4. Report a personal experience in connection with joining new groups. What were some of the specific problems that you faced? How did you proceed to solve them? If you failed to solve them, what did you do?

5. List five experiences through which you have passed recently that threatened your self-respect. How did you meet these situations?

6. Observe a small child of your acquaintance and note as many expressions of attention getting as you can. Which of these are undesirable?

7. What rationalization do you practice?

8. Analyze the reasons given by some of your friends for their apparent failure. In how many cases do they engage in projective behavior?

9. Give as many examples as you can of daydreams that resulted in creative production.

10. What can be done for a person who exhibits a form of the withdrawing behavior?

11. Do you believe that children should read fairy stories? Should they be taught the Santa Claus myth? Justify your answer.

12. Try to recall the criticisms of others expressed by you during the past week. Analyze your motives for these criticisms.

13. Have you an abnormal fear? Can you trace its origin?

14. Describe a case in which the conflict was pronounced yet the individual was able to adjust to the trying conditions of the situation.

CHAPTER Ten

Mental and Emotional Disorders

IN the preceding chapter we described some of the devices that are utilized by frustrated or thwarted individuals in their struggle for adequate adjustment to conditions or people who constitute their daily environment. Inner controls may be lacking to overcome what appears to be an unsurmountable obstacle, however. The conflict may be so severe that its victim can find no way to resolve it in a socially satisfactory fashion. Consequently, his attitudes and behavior become increasingly unrealistic and unacceptable to his associates.

Basic Elements of Maladjustment

A SEVERE emotional strain may interfere with an individual's habitually well-adjusted reactions to function adequately. The death of a member of his family, a severe illness, a serious disappointment, or any other emotion-disturbing or frustrating situation may lead to poor adjustment. Extreme maladjustment usually is associated with generally inadequate emotional control. Yet the effect of a conflict situation upon a generally stable person may be so overwhelming that he suffers a temporary or more permanent mental or emotional disorder.

Behavior trends.   The first failure to make a satisfactory adjustment to an emotion-disturbing situation is likely to become the basis of continued failures and of decreasing power to withstand the unwholesome effects of maladjustment. Some children are born with potentialities that predispose toward mental and emotional imbalance. These inherent weaknesses become intensified through the effect upon them of the unfavorable environmental factors by which they are stimulated. The child of emotionally unstable parents not only may inherit possibilities of individual instability but during his early years and perhaps through much of his life is a victim of his parents' emotionally maladjusted behavior. Regardless of the stabilizing influences to which this young person may be exposed outside the home, the effect upon him of conflict in the home makes it difficult for him to free himself completely from experiencing overemotionalized attitudes and behavior.

Inability to master a disturbing situation may result either in flight from the annoying condition or in an unwarranted and abnormal attack upon the situation. An example from everyday life is that of a young woman who anticipates happiness in her married life. She believes that she is failing to achieve this desired goal. She may return to her sheltered girlhood home or she may launch a continued verbal attack upon her mate. Her attitude becomes so unbearable that her mate attempts to escape from the unpleasant situation through drink, extramarital relations, or complete repudiation of his home responsibilities.

Flight is characterized in varying degrees by retreat from the situation, self-dissatisfaction, abnormal envy, alcoholism, drug addiction, neurotic or psychotic state, or suicide. The *fight* response to failure may take the form of grouchiness, brutality, physical combat, juvenile delinquency or crime, or some other form of aggressive personality disorder.

In their milder forms, mental and emotional disorders usually are recognized by psychiatrists and many psychologists, but are little understood by the average person. The layman becomes aware of abnormal attitudes and behavior in another person only after these have reached a well-developed stage. Hence a person who is afflicted with a less easily recognized form of disturbance may remain in his home environment. Little or no attention is given to his abnormal state except that his family or friends consider him to be "queer." As a matter of fact he may suffer more than do those who display decidedly abnormal attitudes of fear or hostility in their behavior patterns, and are protected in hospitals for the mentally ill from emotion-arousing stimuli inherent in everyday living.

Fatigue, disappointment, or other emotional strains may lead to temporary mental disturbance. The majority of us, however, are able to attain and maintain a wholesome mental balance. It is the persistence of a disturbance that places the disorder in the field of the abnormal. This, in part, accounts for the difficulty that often is experienced in the legal interpretation of sanity. An individual may evince abnormality in a few situations but may be able to achieve rational adjustments in most phases of his personal and social life. Furthermore, with the removal of certain stresses and strains he may be able to regain desirable normal adjustment in all phases of his behavior patterns.

The advance of psychiatric knowledge has dispelled the concept that irrational or antisocial behavior is an indication of a pathological disorder. Abnormal behavior during an emotionally disturbed state may be the resultant of social and other life experiences, or of ineffectively functioning inherent traits and reaction tendencies. Many mental disorders originate in thought and feeling and need to be treated through constructive mental and emotional stimulation.

Causative factors of mental disorders.   A serious disorder may result from a failure to attain socially acceptable outlets for a primitive urge. An individual may suffer from sexual frustrations and inhibitions, or from an inability to satisfy a strong urge for superiority and power over animate and inanimate factors of his environment. His conflicts reach the surface of consciousness but the underlying causes may be unknown to him. He may not realize, for example, that fixed parental attitudes and prejudices or rigid disciplining experienced in his childhood may have caused the development of certain severe repressions, thereby weakening his mental and emotional immunity.

In general we may classify the causes of serious maladjustment as *predisposing* and *exciting*. Personal inability to adjust can be considered as a predisposing factor. Predisposing causes of disturbed states are built into the personality of an individual. They grow out of a conflict between his psychobiological drives and the restrictions of his environment. This conflict and its solution determine the course of his personality development. Social, occupational, and sexual readjustments are significant barriers that call for a detour into another path which often is the path of least resistance.

If his life is relatively free from unusual stresses or strains, even a relatively unstable person can achieve a satisfactory pattern of adjustment in his daily relationships with his associates. Conflict situations may arise in the person's life, however, that act as *exciting* causes of more or less serious mental and emotional disorders. Some exciting causes may result in no more than a temporary form of mental disturbance. Others, through their persistence, may lead to disturbed conditions that cannot be remedied or alleviated except by way of hospitalization and appropriate therapy.

Psychogenic disorders. Organic or mental disorders that are rooted in emotional disturbances, severe frustrations, or unresolvable mental and emotional conflicts can be referred to as *psychogenic* disorders. We already have listed some causative factors that underlie the onslaught of one or another form of illness. For discussion purposes we first are classifying roughly the various forms of disorder into two groups: (1) psychosomatic illness, (2) personality disorders. Since personality disorders differ in degree of seriousness, we can subdivide them into what are termed neurotic tendencies and psychotic states. We now shall consider briefly some of the causes and symptoms of psychosomatic illness, neurosis, and psychosis. Suggested therapies for the treatment of mentally and emotionally disturbed individuals are presented in Chapter 11.

Psychosomatic Illness

THE TERM *psychosomatic* implies an interrelationship of mind and body, with especial reference to disease. The diagnostic and remedial techniques employed by the Armed Forces in their care of servicemen who became "mental" patients were instrumental in bringing to public attention the close interrelationship that exists between emotional status and health condition.

Psychosomatic reactions. It is a recognized fact that a disturbed emotional state is accompanied by various physiological changes, e.g., increased heartbeat, gastronomical changes, and increased muscular strength during extreme anger or rage. Usually these bodily changes or emergency states return to their normal functioning with the reduction of emotional tension. The victim of a persistent fear or rage condition is unable to cope with the conflict situation, however. He may be more or less unaware of the strength of his emotional state; yet he continues to suffer physical discomfort or pain, which he interprets to be symptomatic of a diseased condition.

The mental and emotional conditions include fears, anxieties, compulsions, delusions, or hallucinations. The physical symptoms may be one or more of the following: aches and pains (especially visceral), sleeplessness, poor appetite, constipation, tics, labored breathing, and feelings of fatigue. Some physical disorders that formerly were considered to have an organic origin now are regarded as psychosomatic in that they involve emotional factors. Among the more common types of psychosomatic disorders or diseases are included ulcers, asthma, hay fever and other allergies, the common cold, colitis, eczema, arthritis, disorders of circulatory system, obesity, and sterility.

Beginnings of psychosomatic reactions. Organic changes that result from emotional stimulation of organic dysfunctioning differ between young children and older persons. The very young child who is exposed to a situation that gives evidence of emotional stress components may experience a generally reduced power to function physiologically. For example, an infant's separation from the mother or mother substitute denies him the loving care and the warm interpersonal relations that are experienced by the child whose mother is with him. The emotionally "neglected" baby may give evidence of the symptoms of marasmus: apathy, listlessness, a general physical "wasting away" that results in an early death. An increasing understanding of a young child's emotional as well as physical needs has resulted in a definite decrease of this form of psychosomatic disorder. Certain prenatal and postnatal factors may predispose toward psychosomatic reactions.

Prenatal factors. The first modification of an individual's overt behavior may result from disturbances during his prenatal life. It is an accepted fact that there are no communicating fibers between the nervous system of the mother and that of the fetus. The fetus is an intimate part of a "total" psychosomatic organism, however; therefore it is probably influenced by its emotional and metabolic processes.

Through the endocrine organs and cell metabolism emotions change the composition of the mother's blood, either momentarily or for longer periods. This proves irritating to the fetus as evidenced by increased bodily activity. It appears that the fetus is modified to the degree of the mother's somatized anxieties or fears.

This irritability may carry over to postnatal life along with hyperactivity, exaggerated bowel and gastrointestinal activity, and a higher fluctuation of heart rate. Physical symptoms of cardiospasm and rejection of food either by regurgitation or passing it as undigested curds may be of psychic origin.

Postnatal factors. When a child's growth in height, weight, intelligence, maturation of emotional processes, and sexual maturation does not develop evenly, certain psychosomatic reactions are likely to arise.

Retardation in sexual growth, as in the Froelich syndrome, is another example of the interrelationships between the psyche and soma. The patient becomes effeminate in appearance, obese, and generally infantile. Besides feelings of inadequacy and inferiority, such individuals develop deep-seated anxieties which in turn produce significant degrees of somatic dysfunctioning.

A severe illness or generally poor health can change the factors of the child's environment or the position of the child in it. It causes the withdrawal from normal social situations and from contacts and competition. If the child is acutely ill he becomes the center of attraction, is frequently spoon-fed by the mother or nurse, and is more or less pampered. The child gradually regresses or retreats to the infancy level. His modified patterns and the regression of his process of socialization are psychosomatic aspects of illness.

Since a balanced diet is necessary for mental growth and energy levels, poor eating habits tend to create anxiety in parents. The child, unaware of his needs and physical standards, sees pressure being put upon him to eat when he may be neither hungry nor like the food placed before him.

Some individuals have a constitutional ease of conformity while others seem to be entirely lacking in this quality; each child is endowed with certain constitutional characteristics and qualities which determine his potential resistive or reactive responses to environmental pressures. The strong, highly active, mentally alert child may respond to a restrictive parent with open rebellion, while his brother may make a passive adjustment, withdrawing from new or anxiety-producing situations.

In all cases this potential or energy is subject to modification through nutrition, disease, and the pressures of environment. This modification is not limited to childhood, but is extremely important during the early years. This is the period in which the individual is most rapidly expanding his social sphere. As he grows older, he comes in contact with an increasing number of people and an increasing number of expectations and demands. These pressures may be opportunities for rebellion both in overt behavior and in terms of somatic function.

Enuresis, encropresis, and vomiting are common means of expressing aggression or hostility, or of getting attention. The symptom does not necessarily mean organic defect or weakness. A child learns early that physical hurts or pains receive prompt and satisfying adult sympathy and attention.

In the home and the school many concessions are made for the sick child. He is excused from the fulfillment of home duties and preparation of homework. A child's emotional difficulties may be disregarded by adults, or may be interpreted as signs of stubbornness, lack of cooperation, laziness, or "naughty" behavior.

The tendency learned in childhood to emphasize the suffering of physical pain rather than to call attention to his experiencing of emotional stress can influence an adult's reactions in similar situations. Moreover, to complain of symptoms of physical illness is less embarrassing than it is to let it be known that one is suffering from mental or emotional disturbance.

Disorders of Personality

DISORDERS of personality represent maladaptive behavior and attitudes. The behavior disorders resulting from serious conflict situations are relatively set and require therapeutic treatment. The disorder may require temporary or prolonged treatment or hospitalization. Rehabilitation may be complete or partial. In the more serious cases, rehabilitation or cure may be doubtful, or the patient may never recover.

Classification of personality disorders. Various terms have been applied to serious personality disorders: *neurotic, neurasthenic, psychoneurotic, psychasthenic,* and *psychotic.* The term psychotic is applied to those persons whose behavior disorders are so serious that they are legally committable to a hospital for the mentally ill. Neurotics or psychoneurotics are permitted to be free, but receive expert care or treatment.

Difficulties arise when we attempt to distinguish between these general classifications from the point of view of symptomatic behavior. Neurotics, psychoneurotics, and psychotics are maladjusted persons. They attempt to solve their serious frustrations and conflicts through the display of unrealistic behavior. In extreme cases of the psychoses, the personal struggle for adjustment to accustomed life activities becomes a losing battle: the patient succumbs to his disordered state. Personality disorders require the services of trained therapists.

According to Freud, a neurosis is a physical process associated with sexual adjustment; a psychoneurosis represents mental disorientation. At present the terms *neurosis* and *psychoneurosis* are used interchangeably. Neurasthenia, described by Beard as weak nerves, and psychasthenia, associated by Jung with a weak psyche, are today considered to represent forms of psychoneurotic behavior.

The Psychoneuroses

A NEUROSIS or psychoneurosis is a mental disorder that generally is milder in form than a psychosis. A psychoneurotic disorder usually is caused by a conflict between an individual's strong desires or ambitions and the restrictive force of society's accustomed standards of conduct. The thwarted urges or wants may represent highly personal attitudes or faulty habits that were developed during childhood. These attitudes or habits serve as predisposing conditions of emotional disturbance. Definite symptoms of mental disorder are displayed when the individual meets a shock-inducing situation or no longer can repress successfully his conflict condition.

Psychoneurotic behavior may be characterized by the overt expression of differing symptoms. Although there is some difference of opinion concerning possible classification of psychoneurotic disorders, they can be considered to fall into four main groups, in terms of similarity of symptoms in each of the respective groupings. These groups are neurathenia, psychasthenia, anxiety states, and hysteria. Each of these types of psychoneurotic disorders is described briefly.

Neurasthenia.   The neurasthenic seems always to be suffering from feelings of physical and mental fatigue. He is self-preoccupied and depressed. He is also greatly concerned about the state of his health, although there may be no evidence of organic disorder. Certain areas of his body may be hypersensitive to pain; other areas may be insensitive. He tends to be irritable; his attention may be limited, and he may lack normal flow of ideas. He is likely to complain that he is suffering from one or another physical ailment: indigestion, constipation, heartache, eyestrain, spots before the eyes, shortness of breath, palpitation, hot or cold flashes, inability to swallow, or general aches and pains.

A neurasthenic recognizes the fact that he cannot cope with his problems. As an escape from meeting social or work demands he concentrates his attention upon his bodily processes. In rare cases this form of disorder is a result of overwork; it is more likely to be rooted in feelings of inadequacy. It may be possible that the inherited nervous system cannot meet successfully the demands upon it of complex modern life.

Psychasthenia.   Psychasthenia is characterized by symptoms of phobias, obsessions, or compulsions. The psychasthenic appears to be possessed by one or more of these inner states. In his daily activities he gives evidence of irrational subservience to his symptomatic condition. Basic to his disordered state are strong feelings of inadequacy and concern with his health status.

Phobias or abnormal fears were referred to in the discussion of emotions. Emotionally disturbed states aroused by possible phobia-inducing situations seem to originate in remembered childhood experiences that at the time of their occurrence produced strong fear reactions. A phobia is associated with various conditions or situations that are related to earlier unpleasant incidents, such as fear of high places (*acrophobia*), fear of closed places (*claustrophobia*), fear of open places (*agoraphobia*), fear of pain (*algophobia*), and fear of animals (*zoophobia*).

A person may not be able to free himself from an idea that he recognizes to be irrational. The idea or *obsession* usually is morbid. It persists against the individual's wishes. The obsession may lead to the development of compulsive behavior. A *compulsion* can be regarded as a tendency to perform meaningless motor acts that are recognized to be irrational. The engaging in compulsive behavior cannot be controlled, however. In order to avoid the recurrence of an obsession or to substitute for activity associated with it the individual may experience one or another compulsive tendency.

Obsessions may be mild, such as mental repetition of relatively innocuous ideas, or it may represent an irrational belief such as that the world is coming to an end before the year is over, that people who live in large cities are unfriendly, self-centered, or downright dishonest; that a particular political party or religious group is noneffective. Compulsive behavior may be no more serious than, for example, to throw a pinch of salt over one's shoulder if salt has been spilled, to attempt to divide the words of a sentence into groups of three words, or to compensate for an obsessive fear of failure by carrying a rabbit's foot in one's pocket and stroking it in a possible failure-producing situation. Some compulsions are extreme. The compulsive act may be personally or socially harmful, e.g., the impulse to steal (*kleptomania*), the compelling urge to drink hard liquor (*dipsomania*), or the impulse to set fires (*pyromania*).

Anxiety states.   Vague fears and feelings of apprehension are not uncommon experiences. One often hears a person say, "I know something terrible is going to happen." Usually the speaker is unable to tell what the "terrible" event will be. So great and so persistent may be the anxiety state, however, that the individual is unable to sleep or to breathe, or his pulse rate rises. During the anxious state he seems to be unable to concentrate, his mood alternates between depression and excitement, and he may be irritable or easily angered.

The victim of irrational anxieties usually possesses fear of inadequacy, especially in his strivings for security or self-assertion. For example, a man's business is prospering; vicariously gained knowledge of the effects of economic instability upon business conditions causes him to worry about possible disastrous conditions. He develops a persistent anxiety state that hinders his gaining any satisfaction from his present business success. A possessive mother exhibits irrational anxiety if her daughter does not return home from school or business at the usual time. By the time the daughter arrives, this mother is displaying symptoms of physical illness from which she recovers only after her daughter explains the reason for her delay, expresses regret, and applies remedial measures to relieve the mother's suffering.

Hysteria. In some ways hysteria is similar to psychosomatic illness. The patient reports that he is suffering from one or another form of physical difficulty and demands immediate treatment. Sometimes it is difficult for the diagnostician to discover whether the symptoms have an organic basis or are imagined. The hysterical patient often suffers severe disorder, although his symptoms tend to be variable and inconsistent.

The hysteria-induced symptoms may be associated with any area of physical and physiological functioning—sensory, mental, or motor. Apparently, hysteria is caused by unconscious attempts to escape an unresolvable conflict situation, to adjust to a partial repression of a real or fancied sexual shock or trauma (the current viewpoint of psychoanalysts), or to compensate for hereditary inability to develop a normal personality synthesis.

Whatever the cause of the hysterical condition may be, the patient complains of one or more of the following disorders: partial or complete inability to hear or to see; muscular habits such as tics or tremors or spasms; prolonged periods of forgetting (*amnesia*); ambulant behavior during sleep (*somnambulism*); clouded states of awareness of self and surroundings (*trances* or *fugues*), and apparent epileptic seizures (*idiopathic epilepsy*). Hysterical symptoms differ in form and intensity, but the development of a symptom represents a struggle to escape a conflict situation or a means to achieve the fulfillment of strong wishes or desires.

The Psychoses

A s we said earlier, the psychotic suffers from the most serious type of mental and emotional disorder. His behavior usually represents complete or almost complete withdrawal from reality. He appears to have given up the struggle for normal adjustment. The bases of some psychoses have been demonstrated to lie in bodily dysfunctioning (*organic psychosis*). For some psychoses there still is no known predisposing bodily cause. Hence these varieties of insanity or psychoses are regarded as functional disorders.

Causal factors. The basic causes of functional disorders constitute a complex hierarchy of factors that have their beginnings in native constitution and environmentally-stimulated experiences. Some causes can be regarded as predisposing; others are exciting in that a disturbing or conflict situation may give rise to relatively sudden disintegration and disorientation. In general, the cause of a psychosis or mental illness differs in strength and potential rather than in form from a condition or situation that arouses a relatively less serious personality disorder or psychoneurotic state. Common predisposing and exciting causes of temporary or persistent personality disorders are:

1. Shocks experienced during childhood, or habitual parental denials or prejudices.
2. Extreme worry, anxiety, fatigue, or boredom.
3. Exhaustion and toxemia produced indirectly by climatic conditions.
4. Lack of ability to satisfy a fundamental desire, such as the sex urge, according to social standards of conduct.
5. Stresses caused by unsettled social, economic, or political conditions.
6. Diseases (especially syphilis); trauma (especially spine or head injuries); toxic infections caused by narcotics, alcohol, or body poison usually forming in the gastrointestinal tract.
7. Periods of physiological change, such as puberty and the menopause.
8. Great emotional shock brought about by an extremely frightening experience, the sight of the wounded or dying (as in war or a serious accident), sudden death of a close relative or friend, and similar situations.

Common symptoms of mental illness. We know that any one of us probably gives evidence of behavior that is symptomatic of deviation from habitual good adjustment. The abnormal state has serious implications only to the extent that it persists and becomes relatively fixed. Hence the symptoms of serious emotional disturbance or mental illness differ in *degree* rather than in *kind* from those experienced occasionally by most of us. Furthermore, to determine whether apparently serious symptoms are real, imagined, or feigned requires trained insights, especially during the early stage of a psychotic condition.

Commonly experienced symptoms of mental disorder fall into four general categories: physical, mental, emotional, and behavioral. The various categories include the following:

1. *Physical symptoms:*
   a. Excessive or loss of appetite.
   b. Deviations in pulse rate, respiration, and body temperature.
   c. Abnormal weight changes.
   d. Headache, dizziness, nausea, vomiting.
   e. Abnormal pupillary activity, coughing, and real or imagined pain or fatigue.
2. *Mental symptoms:*
   a. Loss of memory (*amnesia*).
   b. Inability to perceive realistic relationships (*agnosia*).
   c. Failure to understand or produce language (*aphasia*).
   d. Delayed or retarded mental association, mental blocking, flight of ideas and distractibility.
   e. Phobias.
   f. Obsessions or fixed ideas that often take the form of unrealistic attitudes or beliefs (e.g., a close relative is planning the death of the patient; or the human race will be destroyed by insects).
   g. Strong compulsions to engage in antisocial behavior.
   h. Extremely unrealistic perceptual illusions resulting from an abnormal mind set toward sensory stimulation (e.g., a stranger is mistaken for a close relative who has been dead for many years; an inanimate object is recognized as an attacking enemy).
   i. Hallucinations or imaginary perceptions (e.g., the seeing of objects, hearing of sounds, tasting of food, etc., that are nonexistent except in the imagination of the individual).

    j. Delusions or false judgments—beliefs that have no factual basis, are unrelated to personal experience, and defy appeal to reason. They usually take the form of delusions of grandeur, delusions of persecution, and delusions of melancholia.

3. *Emotional symptoms:*
    a. Emotional apathy or indifference, expressed through crying, constant sighing and gloominess, brooding, and/or almost complete silence and refusal to eat.
    b. Emotional exhilaration and freedom from care or worry, expressed through excited talking, singing, dancing, and uncontrolled laughter.

4. *Behavior symptoms:*
    a. Excessive psychomotor activity that impels toward abnormal shouting or whispering, laughing or crying, and constant motion.
    b. Retarded psychomotor activity, inducing hesitation or indecision (*abulia*), halting speech or refusal to talk, body rigidity, and a general slowdown of motion.
    c. Abnormal impulsiveness or suggestibility (e.g., doing the reverse of what might be expected, persistently repeating the words or actions of another person).
    d. Continued, unreasonable repetition of the same movement or act (*stereotypy*).
    e. Nonhabitual behavior reactions (e.g., shuffling walk, facial grimaces, and other peculiar body mannerisms, unaccustomed use of profane or vulgar languages).

Not all of these symptoms are characteristic of every form of mental illness; neither can the symptoms be classified into definite patterns. They may show themselves in varying interrelated combinations. Some of the symptoms are not recognized unless or until they display themselves persistently in unrealistic behavior.

A delusion probably constitutes one of the most striking psychotic symptoms. Because of inadequate knowledge, a normal person may give expression to a false belief, but his error of judgment can be corrected through the acquisition of factual information. A completely unrealistic delusion suffered by the mentally disturbed tends to persist in spite of anything that may be done to change the patient's belief.

As a compensation for his basic, unsatisfactory adjustment, the tendency to daydream characteristic of normal individuals becomes an intense divorce from realism. The individual may come to imagine that he is superior to other humans, or is superhuman. His delusion of grandeur is a fixed belief that he possesses great authority or power and that others are or should be subservient to him. According to his earlier background of interests and experiences, he regards himself variously as a noted world figure, such as Napoleon, Hitler, Mussolini, Lincoln, Roosevelt, or even God. He demands that he receive the kind of treatment commensurate with his exalted state. At the same time he may display an extremely altruistic and beneficent attitude toward many or all his "inferiors."

The psychotic, unable to face the fact that he is responsible for his maladjusted state, may project the blame to others to so great degree that he develops a delusion of persecution. He is convinced that one, a few, or many of his associates, especially relatives and close friends (sometimes his physician or psychiatrist) are plotting against him because of their jealousy or envy, or their false belief that he has harmed them. Contrariwise, an appreciation of personal inadequacy may cause a disturbed individual to believe that he has committed an unpardonable sin, or that he has contracted an incurable illness because of his own shortcomings. A victim of the delusion of melancholia, suffering remorse for wrongs he has not committed, tries to compensate to others for hurts he believes he has inflicted, engages in acts of self-abasement and is convinced that there is no hope for him in this world or in any other.

Interpretation of Certain Forms of Mental Disorder

WHETHER the cause of a mental disorder is a single factor or a combination of factors, persistent abnormalities of behavior are organized by psychiatrists into twenty-four major classifications. In order to acquaint the reader with some of the more common forms of mental disorders a brief interpretation is given of each of five of the twenty-four classified types. The psychoses to be considered are:

Traumatic psychoses
Alcoholic psychoses
Manic-depressive psychoses
Senile psychoses
Dementia praecox (*schizophrenia*)

Traumatic psychoses. A brain or head injury may produce mental disorders that are accompanied by certain characteristic symptoms. Brain injuries vary in form and effect. There may be extensive destruction of tissue or a simple concussion that accompanies the physical shock, whether or not the skull is fractured. The immediate symptom may be delirium followed by hysteria, with a gradual development of memory defects and general mental deterioration. An injury of this type may lead to dementia praecox, paresis, and manic-depressive psychoses. Cerebral birth trauma may result in left-handedness, convulsions, stuttering, enuresis, or dull or subnormal intelligence.

Alcoholic psychoses. These psychoses develop as a result of excessive or continuous use of alcohol. There are different forms of alcohol-induced disorders that have their roots in the personality of the individual, his relative resistance to alcohol, and the extent of his indulgence. These forms are delirium tremens, Korsakow's psychosis, acute hallucinosis, and alchoholic deterioration. In delirium tremens, the patient may be restless and irritable, exhibiting varying hallucinations, as of snakes and worms. In acute hallucinosis, the hallucinations of hearing and the delusions of persecution are very acute, often driving the patient to suicide.

The symptoms of Korsakow's psychosis include paralysis of the extensor muscles, disorientation, lack of retention, suggestibility, mental fatigue, and sometimes hallucinations. Alcoholic deterioration caused by excessive and continued indulgence results in disturbances of motion, sensation, and intellect. If the patient cannot be cured of his indulgence in liquor he will show a history of progressive mental impairment.

The use of alcohol may be incidental to other psychoses. It may accompany general paralysis, manic-depressive psychosis, or epilepsy. If the patient has a psychopathic personality, however, and is not a chronic drinker, he may develop an alcoholic psychosis as a result of a few drinks during a relatively short spree.

Manic-depressive psychoses. Mental disorders traceable to emotional disturbances of a functional nature may be characterized by emotional oscillations and recurrences. A patient, however, may continue to display continued manic behavior, or give evidence of a consistently depressed state. The manic phase is characterized by overactivity and restlessness; slightly elevated temperature, and increased pulse rate; emotional elation; flight of ideas; violent or impulsive behavior. There may be little or no impairment of memory or clouding of consciousness, except in periods of great excitement during which time ideas seem to flow too rapidly for coherent expression. The patient is noisy, boisterous, and uncontrollable in his exuberance. He may quote poetry which he cannot recall during his normal periods, or repeat vulgar jokes or risqué stories which normally would be most distasteful to him.

During the depressed phase these symptoms are reversed. The pulse and temperature may be slightly subnormal, the skin feels cold and dull, and headaches may be common. The patient is emotionally depressed, and neither talks nor responds to questions, unless forced to do so. His answers to questions are given either by a movement of the head or in monosyllabic whispers. His mood is sad, hopeless, uneasy, or anxious; he seems to have a sense of physical and mental insufficiency and often exhibits suicidal tendencies. Extreme depression may be characterized by qualities of almost complete stupor similar in their appearance, although different in nature, to the catatonic type of dementia praecox. The patient usually suffers from ideas of death and self-destruction.

In the mixed phase, the respective symptoms of the other types are so mixed that the resulting state cannot be classified properly as belonging to any one of them. For instance, the patient may exhibit symptoms of depression with flight of ideas, agitated depression, or maniacal stupor. A patient may exhibit the symptoms of the manic at one time and those of the depressed at another, recurrently in circulatory fashion.

Senile psychoses. As the name suggests, senile dementia is a disease of old age in which there is brain atrophy, progressive mental deterioration with loss of memory, and physical deterioration. The patient loses his accustomed acuity of sensation and keenness of perception, and may become disoriented. His memory is defective for the immediate past but may be unusually clear concerning details of his earlier experiences. Attention wanders and ideas become limited and fixed; illusions, hallucinations, and delusions are common; irritability, suspicion, quarrelsomeness, abusiveness, and resistance may be marked.

Dementia praecox (schizophrenia).   Included in this classification are mental disorders that usually occur during adolescence or early adulthood and that are characterized by a number of symptoms. The exact causes of this disorder have not been determined. However, the disease usually finds its basis in unstable personality development that may result from any of many factors—physical weakness, inherited tendencies, unhealthful responses to inherent urges and desires, and consistent failure to adjust successfully to changing demands of childhood and adolescence.

Dementia praecox usually is classified according to four categories: simple, hebephrenic, catatonic, and paranoid. These types cannot always be definitely distinguished, however. The simple form is characterized by carelessness of personal appearance and personal hygiene, idleness, secretiveness, lack of interest in others, and daydreaming. The hebephrenic type can be recognized by behavior that is silly, laughter without reason, grimaces and peculiar mannerisms of speech and action, and hallucinations of sight and hearing. Delusions may be of a neurotic or a religious nature. The patient may be depressed and tend toward threats of self-destruction. His listlessness and lack of interest in the world about him gradually may develop into a retreat from the world of reality into a world of dreams or fantasy.

In the catatonic type there are found many negativistic reactions, stupor and rigidity of body muscles, and occasional impulsive excitement that is queer and absurd. The paranoid form is characterized by numerous delusions, ideas of persecution, and dreams of grandeur that are connected with hallucinations which the patient may exhibit in many fields of activity.

Seriousness of the Problem

I T has been estimated by leading psychiatrists that at least one out of every ten persons of our present population will suffer at one time or another from some form of mental disorder, and that for one out of every twenty the disturbance will be serious enough to require hospitalization. This is a situation that calls for intelligent consideration on the part of the entire citizenry. Moreover, improvement of existing conditions becomes the responsibility of medical, civic, and educational leaders.

Extent of the problem. The incidence of mental illness is recognized by most of us as a to-be-expected accompaniment of our present disturbed national and world conditions. Actual figures are almost staggering. There are at least 9,000,000 persons (representing more than 6 per cent of the total population of the United States) who are suffering from one or another form of severe emotional disturbance. Mental patients occupy more than one half of available hospital beds. We need at least 14,000 psychiatrists, instead of the nearly 5,000 that we now have.

Looking to the future. That our national leaders are aware of the needs in this area is evidenced by the fact that Congress passed the National Mental Health Act (1946), aimed at the improvement of the mental health of the American people. To the extent that funds are appropriated for the carrying out of the provisions of this Act, not only are more adequate services being provided for the treatment of the mentally ill, but there is being organized a broad program for the prevention of mental and emotional instability.

Adequate provision for the prevention and cure of mental disorders necessitates the setting up of research facilities for the discovery of causes; the expansion of agencies that are devoted to the giving of services aimed at prevention and treatment; the development of systematized education for all persons so that they become acquainted with ways in which they can help themselves to preserve mental health; and the removal of the stigma that at present is associated with the experiencing of mental illness.

Everyone—the parent, the teacher, the employer, and the individual himself—needs to be vitally concerned with the prevention of emotional disturbances and conflicts that interfere with healthful living. Adults need to be alert to the appearance in a young person of subtle behavior symptoms that may be indicative of the beginning stages of a mental disorder. Not only can such symptoms be recognized but therapeutic help may be sought, even though the individual is a member of one's own family. Mental illness can be regarded as objectively as is physical illness, and treated accordingly. No more social stigma need be attached to the fact that a person has suffered from a mental illness than is associated with the experiencing of a stomach or heart disorder.

The possession by every member of the adult citizenry of sound mental health is a personal as well as a social responsibility. Publicly supported and privately endowed agencies can be financed adequately through the media of taxation and voluntary contributions, so that there is no lack of equipment and of trained personnel for the meeting of the problem.

▶ Questions and Problems for Discussion

1. Why is it better to use the expression "mental illness" rather than "insanity"?

2. Discuss the multiplicity of causes and factors that enter into the development of mental disorders.

3. What information do you have that helps you believe that mental illness is not a disgrace?

4. Plan a trip to a hospital for the mentally ill at a time a psychiatrist is presenting individual case histories. Report what you learn from his analysis and discussion.

5. Explain what is meant by hallucinations, delusions, and compulsions.

6. Describe the behavior of anyone known to you who gives evidence of the following symptoms: negativism, blocking, stupor, delirium, or depression.

7. Discuss the implications of the National Mental Health Act of 1946.

8. Describe a program of education that would be aimed at the prevention of mental disorder.

9. Indicate by specific examples the ways in which parents, teachers, and employers can meet their responsibility for the mental health of young people.

10. What is being done in your community to prevent mental disorders?

CHAPTER Eleven

Therapeutic Treatment of Mental and Emotional Disorders

*F*ᴏʀ the well-trained physician the diagnosis and treatment of physical disorders are relatively simple in comparison with the diagnosis and treatment of mental and emotional disorders. The inner reactions that comprise human personality and the subtle interactions that constitute human interrelationships make it difficult for therapists to diagnose behavior disorders correctly and to apply appropriate therapeutic measures successfully.

The degree of successful rehabilitation that can be expected from the utilization of remedial or therapeutic techniques depends in large measure upon fundamental personal factors. Progress toward ultimate recovery is possible for the disturbed person whose difficulty is recognized early and appropriate treatment administered. The development of the mental-hygiene point of view and growth in scientific understanding of mental illness are reflected in improved methods of treatment. Some of the more commonly utilized modern therapeutic techniques for the treatment of mental and emotional disorders include psychosomatic medicine, psycho-

therapy, psychiatry and psychoanalysis, group therapy, and occupational and recreational therapy.

Psychosomatic Medicine

THE COMBINING of scientifically acquired knowledge
concerning psychiatric and clinical treatment with an improved
understanding of the significance of psychogenic illness has resulted
in an increased appreciation of the importance of psychosomatic
medicine. In this area of therapeutic treatment emphasis is placed
upon the relationships that exist between emotional reactions and
the onset and course of a physical disease.

According to estimates, from one third to one half of all persons who believe they need medical care exhibit symptoms of physical disorder that are rooted in emotional disturbances. These patients are not hypochondriacs to the extent of imagining symptoms
of illness. They may suffer as much pain as does the victim of a
purely organic disorder. The physician or psychiatrist recognizes
the fact that psychosomatic illness requires treatment of the organism as a whole. It is impossible to separate the *psyche* from the
soma. The classification of ailments as either functional or organic
is outmoded. Diseases and disorders involve the whole personality
and, consequently, the whole personality needs to be treated.

It is difficult to explain to an individual that his illness may
have an emotional origin. At the same time, he can be helped to
understand (1) that emotional maladjustments and illnesses are
not evidences of weakness, (2) that much of behavior, even the
functioning of body organs, is motivated by strong forces of unconscious origin, and (3) that these forces often are beyond the
influence of consciousness. The individual then can be assured that
he has a strong and normal mind, but that he needs help so far as
his emotions are concerned. The person who helps him readjust his
emotional life needs to possess a reassuring personality.

Importance of the physician's personality. The physician
who deals with a psychosomatic patient not only has an understanding of disease but also displays a sympathetic attitude toward
the behavior of sick people. He is concerned with the emotional
reactions of the patient as well as challenged by the patient's physi-

cal disorder. To a certain extent he identifies himself with the emotional pain which his patient suffers. He understands psychopathology as well as tissue pathology. Most important of all, he realizes that his patient is an emotionally disturbed person who is expressing emotional pain in physical form.

Physicians and nurses recognize the effect of the emotions upon a patient who is suffering from a physical ailment. A patient's chances of recovery are associated closely with his attitude toward his illness, his degree of cooperation with the physician and nurse, and the kind and amount of worry caused by the temporary interruption of accustomed activities. The onslaught of a serious disease may cause an emotionally unstable person to become so depressed that he is unable or unwilling to cooperate with the physician toward an amelioration of the disease condition or to help in the fight for recovery. According to Vaughan:

> The value of the psychosomatic approach is in its emphasis upon the treatment of the *whole* person, involving a study of his *physical* condition *and* an exploration of his *mental* outlook. The traditional medical concentration upon the organic will be corrected by the psychosomaticists who call attention to the importance of including the psychological angle too. The doctor who is wise will consider the personality of the sick person in addition to taking his temperature, thus obeying the famous dictum of Sir William Osler: "It is more important to know what kind of patient has a disease than to know what kind of disease a patient has." [1]

Psychotherapeutic Techniques

THE UTILIZATION of psychotherapeutic techniques is expanding rapidly. Yet there is still a gap between the needs of human beings for aid in re-establishing adequate individual and social patterns of behavior and the application of scientifically evolved therapeutic techniques.

[1] W. F. Vaughan, *Personal and Social Adjustment* (New York: The Odyssey Press, 1952), p. 210.

Psychotherapy and psychiatric treatment. It is important to distinguish between psychotherapy and psychiatric treatment. Too often their meanings are confused, or the terms are used synonymously. Essentially, the confusion stems from the fact that the difference in emphasis between the two is not generally understood. Therapeutic or mental-hygiene approaches are utilized in situations that represent a wide range of individual and social maladaptations which are not forms of serious mental illness. Moreover, it often is difficult to achieve a clear-cut differential diagnosis of the disturbed condition, and to select an appropriate form of therapy. For cases of relatively mild disorder, rehabilitation probably can be brought about through the utilization of one or more of the following types of community-service agencies: medical, psychological, social, educational, religious, and recreational. All of these community agencies utilize the resources of one another as ancillary services when the nature of the individual's adjustment problem seems to require such cooperation. Many of these community services utilize psychotherapeutic techniques to aid an individual resolve his conflicts. If a person is the victim of a severe mental disorder, however, he needs the services of a psychiatrist. Psychiatric treatment involves the utilization of various types of intensive therapy, including the administration of appropriate drugs.

Psychotherapy can be defined as any "non-physical" technique that is aimed at the improvement of the client's attitudes, emotional reactions, and overt behavior. The utilization of this technique implies the treatment of mental and emotional disturbances through suggestion and re-education. The sufferer may not be so ill that he needs to be treated by a psychiatrist; he can be helped by a physician or another trained service worker in whom he has confidence. Similarly, a mentally ill patient's confidence in his psychiatrist often is as effective, if not more so, than is prescribed medication.

Suggestion and reassurance can relieve tensions. Whenever it is possible, the psychotherapist appeals to the intelligent understanding of the patient by explaining the relationship that exists between physical illness and emotional disturbance. If a patient, for example, believes that he has a cancer, the use of X ray, in addition to reassurance, helps the individual understand that he is physically sound. The therapeutic treatment may take the form of repeated encouragement that reassures the patient who seeks help because he believes he is suffering from one or another ailment.

Most physicians, psychologists, and social workers apply therapeutic techniques in several ways. According to Maslow:

> . . . psychotherapy takes place in six main ways: (1) by expression (act completion, release, catharsis) as exemplified in Levy's release therapy; (2) by basic need gratification (giving support, reassurance, protection, love, respect); (3) by removing threat (protection, good social, political, and economic conditions); (4) by improved insight, knowledge, and understanding; (5) by suggestion or authority, and (6) by positive self-actualization, individuation, or growth. It is probable that all systems of psychotherapy use all these basic medicines in varying proportions." [2]

It may be difficult for an emotionally disturbed person to gain an adequate appreciation of the origin of his existing conflict situation. He needs to evaluate, in light of his total experience pattern, his fears, anxieties, feelings of insecurity, and general lack of adjustment. Some insight can be achieved through his informal, permissive talks with the psychiatrist. Some psychologists, physicians, and psychiatrists believe that self-understanding is achieved best through psychoanalysis, a technique that has been used extensively by Sigmund Freud and his followers.

Psychoanalysis

PSYCHOANALYSIS is the process of eliciting from a patient a body of significant information concerning his past emotional and mental life. The client discloses past incidents in his life that may have continued to exert a potent influence upon his emotional reactions. The psychoanalyst hopes to discover through psychoanalytic techniques the ways in which a pathological state has been produced. He then attempts to offer suggestions concerning definite methods of treatment.

[2] A. H. Maslow, *Motivation and Personality* (New York: Harper and Brothers, 1945), p. 306.

A fundamental distinction between psychoanalysis and other procedures, somatic or psychic, is that it attacks the underlying emotional conflict rather than symptomatic behavior. In psychoanalysis, little attention is given to the symptoms as such. It may be comparatively easy to remove a particular symptom by suggestion; but if nothing is done about the underlying causative conflict the patient soon displays a new symptom. An example of this is the "eternal patient" who, as soon as he apparently is cured of one symptom, is back with another.

Freud was convinced that the symptoms of neurotic patients were in reality the expressions of mental conflicts. Emotional impulses were transformed into abnormal physiological functions through a process which was called conversion. Consequently, a hysterical paralysis was called a conversion symptom, since it represented an unconscious resolution of mental conflict of which the patient was completely unaware. The emotional catharsis, under hypnosis, of the original traumatic memories and their attendant emotions brought relief only temporarily since it was not fused with the consciousness of the patient when he was brought out of the hypnotic state.

Consequently, Freud cast about for another method of securing the recall of repressed memories in the waking or conscious state. He essayed a direct attack upon this problem by utilizing direct suggestion. He assured the patient that he could recall the past if he tried. Freud soon discovered that this frontal attack was futile. He then developed a new technique called *free association* which remains the cornerstone of the psychoanalytic procedure.

Freud reasoned that ideas were associated in the mind in two ways: (1) by logical relationships and (2) by emotional relationships. It was the latter type of association in which Freud was particularly interested. By having the patient recline on a couch with back to the physician, it was possible for the patient to relax and to speak his mind freely, i.e., to say whatever came to him. It did not matter whether it made sense or not, whether it was conventional or objectionable. The important principle was to report anything and everything that came to mind.

Freud evolved the theory, which has been confirmed by countless analyses, that the patient is relieved of the necessity for logical thinking; he reacts to the pressure of feelings and emotions rising to express themselves. Hence he reveals, through a free association of ideas and feelings, those clues which provide the analyst with the content of the deeper layers of the motivating factors. Through this method the patient gradually brings into consciousness the repressed memories and emotions which had been prevented from being recalled into consciousness because of resistances. This finally was the technique utilized by Freud to unlock the unconscious mind while the patient was conscious. The major problem, however, was how to overcome habitual resistances so that repressed memories could flow into consciousness.

In this connection Freud made an important discovery, which he called the *transference neurosis*. This was the essential dynamic mechanism for the resolution of resistances. Transference is a powerful instrument in accomplishing this end, since the patient inevitably transfers to the analyst his neurotic behavior patterns. Essentially, the patient relives his neurotic past in his present relationship. It is a type of *facsimile* of the patient's real-life neurosis of which the patient is cured step by step, as he is led through it with insight from one growth-stimulating experience to another. This aspect of the analysis came to be called *emotional re-education*, since it was a procedure arrived at for establishing permanent changes in the personality.

In this process of uncovering repressed material Freud found that his patients frequently reported dreams. The utilization of free association was an excellent technique for making an intensive study of these dreams as they related to the mental and emotional life of the patient. Repeatedly he discovered that a dream essentially was a "wish fulfillment." Like neurotic symptoms, it had definite meaning; it was a conscious expression of unconscious wishes or fantasies. By the skillful application of free association to the *manifest content* of the dream (which almost invariably was a disguise for the *latent content* or meaning), he was able to elicit the actual meanings which the censorship of the unconscious prevented from coming into waking life, except as they were disguised or masked in symbolic form.

Psychoanalysis, both as a depth psychology of personality and a therapeutic method, has had a pervading influence upon the development of psychotherapy and upon the course of psychological theory in general. Its most fundamental contributions have been the introduction of a dynamic approach to the study of personality, and the elaboration of a systematic theory of personality and behavior which encompasses the human personality in all its aspects, and throughout its life span. Moreover, Freud's theories were singularly fruitful in that they led coworkers and students to further discoveries and to the elaboration of additional psychotherapeutic methods and psychiatric techniques.

Group Therapy

THERE is an increasing need for help in resolving problems of adjustment. Moreover, there exists a serious dearth of psychotherapists for individual treatment. Hence professional workers have been experimenting with other ways of dealing with maladjustments. A practical answer to the quest for rehabilitating techniques to be applied to mentally disturbed men during World War II was found in *group psychotherapy*. The first conscious and deliberate utilization of group psychotherapy, however, was not included in the treatment of neurotic or psychotic patients. It was used with tubercular patients by Dr. Pratt, in Boston, about 1905. He called it class treatment, but it was the first attempt to apply group influences aimed at specific therapeutic goals.

Psychodrama. The application of group psychotherapy in the field of mental disorders began in 1911. Dr. Moreno encouraged children to participate in what he has called psychodrama, in which they were encouraged to act out their fantasies in groups. Since then several "spontaneity" theaters have been constructed for psychodramatic use. It is Moreno's view that all the important elements of psychotherapy are available through psychodrama, with the additional advantage of reaching the larger group of the audience as well as the cast. For both cast and audience there is cathartic aid in different degrees. Both in an analysis of acted-out events as well as in subsequent discussion there is re-education value.

The most important dynamic concept involved in psychodrama is that of the auxiliary ego. A child is dependent upon his mother who, as an auxiliary ego, assumes full responsibility for him until he begins to share with her this responsibility for his behavior. Finally, he matures and contributes to the welfare of others.

The psychotic and the neurotic cannot meet their life problems on a mature adult level. Hence the attempt is made to wean them from dependency by gradual steps, and to bring them to maturity in easy stages, through the efforts of trained personnel as auxiliary egos. The procedure includes the interviewing of all patients who will participate; an analysis of data about each one (in order to plan the action), and a classification of each patient according to his dominant psychopathological pattern. This type of therapy, Moreno indicates, is of greatest value in cases of neurosis, incipient neurosis, and simple interpersonal conflicts.

Lay group psychotherapy. In recent years there has developed a movement among organized lay groups which can be considered as participation in effective group therapy. The well-known Alcoholics Anonymous is a remarkable organization of this type. Its inception occurred in 1935, through the efforts of an Ohio physician and a New York broker who found, through their mutual friendship and support, a solution to their problem of alcoholism. They then began to treat others. The movement grew to such proportions that now there are centers in most major cities in the United States. It is a completely voluntary form of therapy and does not function like a typical organization; there are no dues or other organizational requirements. It is a self-perpetuating group, since one of the important aspects of an alcoholic's rehabilitation is that he devote his energies to helping other alcoholics.

Psychologically, the essential therapeutic effects are gained through the patient's sincere desire to cure himself, a close identification with his sponsor who has been cured, and a spiritual rebirth experience which results in a complete personality transformation. The entire process may be completed in a few months. Relapse is avoided by constructive aid to others, regular weekly meetings, and the development of hobbies, avocations, and social experiences with other ex-alcoholics.

Other applications of group therapy. Group therapy has been successful in the treatment of veterans. It affords the psychiatrist an opportunity to see many patients at one time, thereby having great economic value. It provides emotional support to patients through participation in group relationships; it encourages the release of pent-up aggression and anxiety-ridden conflicts. Another aim is to foster some insight into one's difficulties. In many cases the group represents family life and dependable social realities to the individuals. For many groups of servicemen this method has special value, since the problems experienced by them have common psychological and social factors.

Occupational and Recreational Therapy

THE PURPOSE is to re-educate the patient mentally, physically, and socially. Occupational therapy diverts the patient's attention from himself and gives him an opportunity for self-expression. One of its most important features is that it helps prevent invalid habits. Physically, it helps mobilize disabled joints, or keeps healthy ones in good condition. It also is a great aid in developing mental and physical coordination. Another therapeutic value is derived from participation with other patients in normal activities. It thus becomes a morale builder. In this type of therapy the work can be adapted to the individual's ability and interest. The product is not important; the work itself is. The choice of occupational activity can be adjusted to the personal interests, cultural background, intelligence, aptitudes, and psychiatric clinical status of each patient.

The significance of psychotherapy in occupational therapy is indicated by Fidler and Fidler in the following:

Psychotherapy and the understanding of psychodynamics depend upon understanding and manipulating the relationships between individuals. For that reason, when occupational therapy is used as a psychotherapeutic procedure, it must necessarily follow that the product being made and the work expended in making it are considerations which must be secondary to judgments about how that product and this process of making it affect his relations with others. The occupation then becomes the tool of manipulating his relationships to other people and not the primary end in itself.

The determination of the treatment program for any specific patient must consider the planning for both the material activity of the patient and the social activity of the patient in one's presence. All of the numerous factors which must be considered have already been enumerated.

Here is where one must anticipate response and plan what situation the patient will be made to face, whether that situation be a material one of occupation or a personal one.[3]

The therapeutic effects of work and play as adjustment techniques for use with the normal individual are no less significant in the treatment of persons who are suffering from mental and emotional disturbance. The majority of hospitals that care for such patients are equipped with facilities for patient participation in various types of occupations suited to their needs and stage of improvement. Such forms of activity include raveling, sorting, sewing, crocheting, basket weaving, simple woodwork, painting, typewriting, printing, clay and soap modeling, photography, flower gardening, and road repairing.

One of the most important therapeutic requirements for these patients is the diversion of their attention from the fears, worries, and other emotional disturbances which may be the bases of their present disorder. It is essential, therefore, that new interests be developed. This can be done through occupational activities, through physical recreation, and through participation in programs that include music, vaudeville, motion pictures, books, magazines, radio, television, and picnics. Great care is to be taken in the selection of the therapeutic activity, in terms of the psychosis or the attitude of the patient. For example, the singing of "Auld Lang Syne" may calm one patient and stimulate another to violence.

Physiotherapy

THE TREATMENT of mental and emotional disorders through physiotherapy includes electrotherapy, heliotherapy, hydrotherapy, and massage. These forms of treatment usually have a psychic or calming effect which often is as important as, if not more so, than their physical value. The use of the bath has shown itself to be very successful. A prolonged warm bath reduces nerve tension, produces relaxation, and induces sleep. Patients who are wake-

[3] G. S. Fidler and J. W. Fidler, *Introduction to Psychiatric Occupational Therapy* (New York: The Macmillan Company, 1954), p. 27. Used with the permission of The Macmillan Company.

ful, anxious, elated, or excited often respond extremely well to the application of a cold pack.

► Questions and Problems for Discussion

1. Explain what is meant by psychosomatic medicine.
2. Discuss the effect of the personality of the psychiatrist upon his patient.
3. Give examples of adjustment through psychotherapy.
4. Illustrate the use of group therapy.
5. Discuss the value of psychoanalysis in the resolution of conflicts.
6. Illustrate what is meant by the use of *free association.*
7. Utilize the class situation to demonstrate the technique of psychodrama. What complications did you find?
8. Give examples of adjustment through psychotherapy.
9. Present the aims of psychotherapy.
10. What do you consider to be your greatest adjustment problem? Describe what you have done or are doing to improve.
11. What psychotherapeutic help is available in your community to those who may have need of it?
12. To what extent are community facilities for personal difficulties being utilized?
13. Look up and report on the educational qualifications of a neurologist, a psychiatrist, a psychoanalyst, a psychologist.
14. If possible, visit a hospital for the mentally ill and observe therapies applied for patient improvement.

CHAPTER Twelve

Adjustment Problems Associated with Sex

T H E S E X drive is one of the strongest of the human urges. Sexual behavior not only is an individual matter, but becomes the concern of other people, since at least one other individual usually is involved. Hence the problems of sexual behavior as they affect the individual or the members of a group are extremely complex. At numerous points throughout the book consideration has been given to many aspects of human relationships that are associated with sexual behavior and sex adjustment. This discussion deals with the more technical and personal phases of sex life.

Sexual Behavior in Human Beings

I T is believed that sexual behavior involves all parts of the body rather than the functioning merely of the sex organs. Nevertheless, the sex organs are of primary concern in the study of sexual behavior and adjustment. Although the sex organs of the male and of the female differ structurally, many of the physiological func-

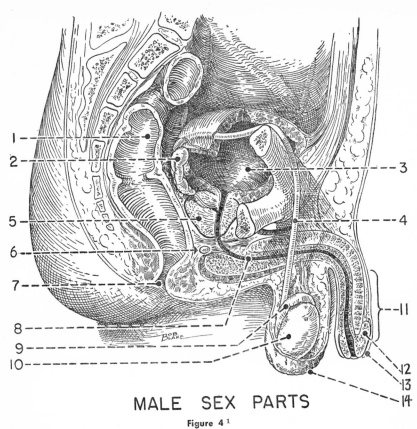

MALE SEX PARTS

Figure 4 [1]

The sex parts are: (2) seminal vesicles, (4) vas deferens, (5) prostate gland, (6) Cowper's gland, (8) urethra, (9) epididymis, (10) testicle, (11) penis, (12) glans penis, (13) foreskin, (14) scrotum. Each numbered nonsex part is: (1) colon, (3) bladder, (7) anus.

tions of the sex organs are similar. Structural differences are shown in Figure 4 and Figure 5.

Basically, reproduction is dependent upon the functioning of the primary sex glands or *gonads*. In the female, the primary sex glands are the ovaries, which produce *ova*, or eggs; in the male, the gonads, or *testes*, produce spermatozoa or sperm cells. The gonads not only function in reproduction but also secrete certain chemical substances (*hormones*) that affect the development of the repro-

[1] From G. McHugh, *Sex Knowledge Inventory*, Form Y (Durham, N.C.: Family Life Publications, 1950), p. 2.

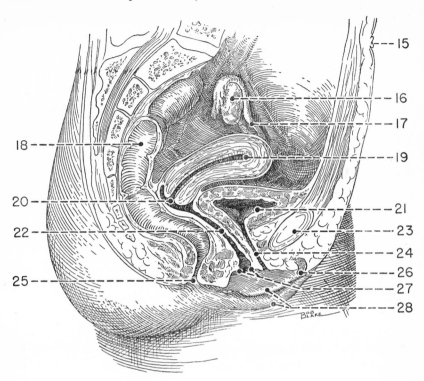

FEMALE SEX PARTS

Figure 5 [2]

The name for each sex part is: (16) ovary, (17) Fallopian tube, (19) uterus or womb, (20) cervix, (22) vagina, (24) urethra, (26) clitoris, (27) hymen, (28) labia. Each numbered nonsex part is: (15) navel, (18) colon, (21) bladder, (23) symphysis, (25) anus.

ductive tract and of the skeletal form. During the pubertal period the sex hormones are responsible for the development of secondary sex characteristics. In the female, these include growth of pubic hair, broadening of hips, increase of subcutaneous fat, and enlargement of the breasts; in the male, the recognizable signs of sexual maturing are greater voice depth, growth of body hair (especially the beard and pubic hair), and increased breadth of shoulders, depth of chest, and muscular strength.

The genital organs, or *genitalia*, usually are referred to as the

[2] Ibid., p. 2.

primary characters of sex. The external genital organs of the male are the penis (*phallus*) and the testes which, in the scrotum (a *small sac*), secrete the sperm cells; in the female, the external genitals consist of the major lips (*labia majora*) by which the internal genitalia are protected. The internal sex structures of the female include the ovaries, the uterus or womb, the Fallopian tube (*uterine tube*), and the vagina.

Fertilization of the ovum requires the deposit by the male into the vagina of the female of the semen which contain spermatozoa or sperm cells, during coitus or sexual intercourse. Under their own power the spermatozoa then make their way into the uterus and sometimes into the Fallopian tube until an ovum is fertilized. The ovum passes through the Fallopian tube to the uterus where the fertilized egg cell is nourished and protected during the period of prenatal development.

The proper functioning of the sexual organs as outlined is essential for reproductive purposes. Malfunctioning or non-functioning of certain primary sex characteristics seriously interferes with the performance of coitus or with the fertilization of the ovum. The removal of the testes (castration) in males produces eunuchs. Removal of a woman's ovaries is known as ovariectomy. Castration or ovariectomy results in sterility, but does not necessarily interfere with participation in sexual activity.

In normal coitus, the deposit of the semen is accomplished through the male orgasm, a rhythmic contraction of the urethra which ejects the semen through the phallus. Normally, the female orgasm is a rhythmic contraction of the musular coats of the vagina, sometimes accompanied by a rhythmetic contraction of the uterus. This facilitates the entrance of the semen into the uterus. The female orgasm, however, is not essential to conception. The intensity of the orgasm in women ranges from a complete orgasm in which vagina and uterus both participate, through the type in which only the vagina responds, to the non-experiencing of any orgasm or so-called *frigidity*.

Turgescence (tumescence) is a swelling of the tissues in the sex organ; normally it occurs in both sexes. Turgescence in the male is essential for coitus. A man's inability to achieve turgescence is referred to as *impotence*. Except in cases of actual frigidity, women experience some degree of turgescence; the tissue swelling may precede coitus or follow the penetration of the penis into the vagina.

The orgasm represents the climax or height of both venereal and emotional excitement in coitus. After the climax of the sexual act, the man usually is relaxed; he may fall asleep. After a brief period of rest, however, he again may experience turgescence and desire coitus. For a woman, reactions following coitus vary. Immediate and restful sleep usually follows a complete orgasm. If there has been a less complete orgasm or no orgasm she may remain in an excited condition and require repeated coitus to relax her. Continued inability to reach a climax may result in a condition of frigidity or neurotic behavior.

Although the orgasm is a muscular response, the processes that precede it are partly vascular. Stimulation of the sensitive areas of the genital organs produces excitation of the circulatory and nervous system. Sensory stimulation of the woman's clitoris or vagina and of the man's penis usually is necessary to produce an orgasm, although erotic thoughts can arouse orgiastic activity without sensory stimulation. Either sex may experience an orgasm during sleep, although the actual cause of it is still a matter of dispute. More research is needed to obtain a definite explanation of the so-called "wet dream." What appears to happen, however, is that a sexually stimulated dream starts turgescence which results in the experiencing of an orgasm.

As was suggested earlier in the chapter males and females exhibit some general similarity in their sexual behavior. Certain specific aspects of the sexual processes reflect physical and anatomical differences between the sexes. Kinsey summarizes some of the comparisons between the male and the female as follows:

> Because of differences in anatomy, the processes in the two sexes may differ in details. Tumescence, for instance, is most noticeable in the male in the erection of his penis, and most noticeable in the female in the erection of the nipples of her breasts and of the clitoris and labia minora; but the physiologic bases of these several events are essentially identical. The female and male are quite alike, as far as the data yet show, in regard to the changes in pulse rate, the changes in blood pressure, the peripheral

circulation of blood, the tumescence, the increase in respiration, the possible development of an anoxia, the loss of sensory perception, and the development of rhythmic muscular movements, even including rhythmic pelvic thrusts.[3]

Erotic Aspects of Sexual Behavior

T H E synonyms *erotic* and *amatory* are generally used to describe love feelings toward and sexual desire for a person of the opposite sex. In psychoanalysis, *erotism* is a term applied to sexual life in all its phases of physical and mental development and behavior manifestations. The term *sexual life*, as used in this connection, refers to all the conditions and processes that are in any way associated with interest in or desire for a person of the opposite sex who stirs one emotionally.

Erotic feelings toward a member of the opposite sex may manifest themselves solely in attempts to be with and enjoy the company of the object of the erotic attraction. Usually, however, the emotional state is accompanied by a strong desire for physical contact with the other person, and/or coitus, if the conditions are favorable for sexual intercourse. It can be noted that sexual activity, in a more narrow interpretation of the term, is not necessarily a manifestation of erotic feelings. For example, an individual may engage in coitus as a means of reducing physical tensions, regardless of the presence of erotic or amatory feelings for the other person with whom sexual intercourse is being experienced.

Stimulation of erogenous areas. Erotic desires, feelings, or thoughts are aroused by appropriate sensory stimuli: tactile, visual, auditory, or olfactory. Bodily areas that are especially sensitive to touch and pressure stimulation are called erogenous areas. The penis of the male and the clitoris and vagina of the female are considered to be the primary areas of stimulation. Secondary areas that are common to both sexes, in varying degrees, include the nipples, the lips, the ears and the skin back of the ears, and the flat area on the small of the back. These areas can be stimulated by pressure and touch, especially tickling. An erotic response may be aroused

[3] A. C. Kinsey, et al., *Sexual Behavior in the Human Female* (Philadelphia: W. B. Saunders Company, 1953), p. 640.

under some conditions, but not under others; certain skin areas are erogenic only for some persons.

The sight of a loved one or the sound of her voice may cause a man to experience erotic thoughts or feelings. The olfactory is an erotic or erogenic stimulation for many men. There seems to be a functional connection between the erectile tissue in the nasal passages and the erectile tissue in the genital organs. In a state of erotic excitement nasal turgescence may be so great that breathing becomes difficult. Characteristic female odors are erogenic for some men and may produce genital processes; for other men, these odors produce no erotic stimulation.

Stimulation of erotic areas may produce erotic desire, erotic feeling, or erotic thought without producing any general effects. Further, a response to a sensory stimulus is not erotic unless it produces erotic processes of some conscious sort, even though the genital processes are not involved. Sometimes stimulation of the genitalia may produce disgust instead of erotic feeling. It cannot then be called erogenic.

Erotic perversions.   A perverted desire or urge is abnormal in that it is directed away from what can be considered to be its normal object or objects. A perverted urge that becomes habitual is known as a *perversion*. Perversions may not always be harmful, yet they may be the cause of worry and maladjustment. Autoerotism and homosexuality (homoerotism) are two erotic perversions that give rise to considerable concern in some cultures. Their impact upon the individual who practices them and upon others who are affected by his behavior is discussed briefly.

Autoerotism.   The production of erotic responses by oneself without stimulation by another person is known as *autoerotism*. Autoerotic activities include any type of self-induced sex pleasure in which the genital organs or other parts of the body are stimulated until an orgasm is produced. Autoerotism is more commonly known as *masturbation*. It means sexual stimulation through the use of the hand.

Autoerotism is a common practice during the period of pubescence; it may be continued through adulthood. Among the men and women interviewed by Kinsey and his staff it was found that most of the men and more than half of the women had used self-stimulation at some time in their life.

Masturbation that has its beginning during early childhood, whether discovered by the child himself or taught to him by others, is likely to become an obsessive habit. Usually, however, masturbation in the male begins shortly before puberty, when erotic responses are developing rapidly and when the orgasm becomes possible.

Symptoms of autoerotic behavior are sometimes observable by parents, but the symptoms are not completely reliable. The boy may tend to withdraw from social contacts with other children, or display psychological changes that are subtle and difficult to detect or describe. He may become moody and irritable. The frequency of the masturbation may decrease in a few years but in some cases it may continue into adult life. The effects of the perversion depend upon the age of the individual, the frequency of masturbation, and the length of time the habit persists.

Homosexuality.   Homosexuality refers to the production of erotic responses through the cooperation of a person of the same sex. It sometimes is referred to as *homoerotism.* Homosexual experiences are more common than many people realize. Kinsey found that homosexuality was practiced to a greater extent by men than by women. His research revealed that, although more than half of the women studied had engaged in self-stimulation, only about one fifth of them had had sexual contact with other females. Among the men interviewed he found that at least 37 per cent had had homosexual experiences to the point of orgasm. His findings are contrary to the widespread belief that homosexual responses and completed contacts occur more frequently among females than among males.

Some persons who are homosexuals are inverts. The inversion may be physiological or it may be psychological. Some pairs of homosexuals stimulate one another with no differentiation of roles; usually, however, one of the male pair plays the role of a female and is referred to as "passive." He experiences inversion. In the case of women, the "active" person is considered to be inverted. These roles may be temporary; the inverted roles may change from time to time. Also inverts are likely to adopt the dress and mannerisms of the adopted sex.

Although secondary sex characteristics are modified in the direction of the invert they are not reliable signs of erotic perversion. Homosexuality has a debilitating effect upon those who become addicted to it. It is disastrous to those who acquire the perversion in youth before a normal heterosexual life has been established. Homosexual practices among women seem to be responsible for certain cases of frigidity. Likewise most male homosexuals who marry are usually frigid with their wives. A woman usually fails to stimulate erotic desire in a man who has for a long period obtained erotic and genital stimulation from another male. Some men homosexuals marry and force themselves to have intercourse with their wives. If the individual is a strong invert, sexual incompatibility results and divorce is the usual outcome. However, a male homosexual may marry to avert a scandal that already has reached the whisper stage.

Homosexuals are considered to be deviates in society; if they are apprehended, they become socially unacceptable. Thus homosexuals tend to be drawn closer together. If a high-school boy's initial homosexual experience is discovered, for example, he is likely to want to leave school and perhaps the community in which he is known. He finds it increasingly difficult to make heterosexual contacts and seeks the company of other homosexual individuals; eventually he develops a definite homosexual pattern. In many cases the first homosexual experience has been thrust upon the individual. It is important, therefore, that a boy be removed from a situation of this kind, lest social disapproval of this one act forces him into the company of homosexuals.

Homosexuality is a social problem to the extent that the relationships with others is involved. The concern of society with the problem is clearly stated by Dr. K. M. Bowman and Bernice Engle in the following statement:

> Society is interested mainly in the overt homosexual who leads a fairly active homosexual life and who may be responsible for initiating others into homosexual activities. The latent homosexual is ordinarily no legal or sociological problem, although his latent homosexuality may result in all sorts of neurotic behavior which makes him a problem to the psychiatrist.[4]

---

[4] K. M. Bowman and B. Engle, "The Problem of Homosexuality." Reprinted with the permission of the American Social Hygiene Association, 1790 Broadway, New York 19, N.Y., from the *Journal of Social Hygiene*, Vol. 39, No. 1, p. 3, copyright, 1953, by the American Social Hygiene Association.

Concerning the value of psychiatric treatment, Bowman and Engle suggest that:

> Reports on individual and group psychotherapy of homosexuals in cases followed for considerable periods are discouraging. Many psychiatrists state that treatment does not influence the homosexuality but may help in the patient's better adjustment. This opinion was expressed by the founder of psychoanalysis in his letter to an American mother. Freud declared that homosexuality is "nothing to be ashamed of, no vice, no degradation," and it is a "great injustice to persecute (it) as a crime and cruelty too."
>
> Although cure is no longer possible, analytic treatment may perhaps bring harmony, peace of mind and full efficiency to the unhappy neurotic patient . . . and sometimes it succeeds in "developing the blighted germs of heterosexual tendencies" present in every homosexual.[5]

Social Aspects of Sexual Behavior

HETEROSEXUAL activity, of course, is fundamental to the continuance of the human species. Hence at every stage of civilization and in every culture every societal group is interested in and concerned about the social significance of the sexual behavior of its members.

Cultural advancement and sexual behavior. In theory, if not in practice, an existing society wants to produce physically and mentally healthy children. By this means it is hoped that the next generation may be able to continue and to improve its cultural contributions. Consequently, matters dealing with sex receive considerable attention from the men and women who constitute the leaders of the society.

Societies differ in their traditional customs and social and religious acceptances and taboos as these affect sex relationships. Historical and comparative studies concerning attitudes toward sex among the various cultures give evidence of differing practices. These differences range from rigid control of sex activity to extreme permissiveness. In some primitive societies strict taboos are

⁵ K. M. Bowman and B. Engle, "The Problem of Homosexuality," p. 11.

found. At the same time, greater freedom in sexual activities is allowed, especially to the male, than is supposedly characteristic of modern Western societies.

To the present most cultures have appeared to permit considerable freedom to the male but have emphasized the need of chastity on the part of the female. As a result of changes in social conditions and attitudes that grew out of an extended war period and a confused world state, women have gained greater independence of action in the conduct of their lives than previously had been socially acceptable. The growing independence of women combined to some extent with a weakening of religious controls has led to demands by some women of sexual freedom comparable to that permitted men.

Difficulties in the study of sexual behavior.   In the past it was generally believed that the sex urge was stronger in the male than in the female; in the sex act, the man was the active aggressor and the woman the passive recipient, in spite of certain historical evidence to the contrary.

The changed sexual relationships that have resulted from women's increasing independence of action have given rise to various attempts to conduct comparative studies of the sex lives of men and women. Since an individual's sexual urges and activities are highly personalized experiences, however, it is difficult to obtain completely accurate data from which adequate generalizations can be established. For the most part, the investigator must rely upon the report of individuals whom he interviews. Of necessity, such interviews involve the voluntary participation of the person interviewed. Certain traditionally rooted prejudices against talking frankly about one's sexual behavior either may cause a person to refuse to be interviewed or may inhibit him from reporting accurately concerning his sex activities. Further, self-satisfying or attention-getting motives rather than scientific interest may stimulate some persons to become eager reporters of actual or imagined sexual experiences.

Various investigators have attempted to make such studies. The subtle psychological elements that enter into a project of this kind and their sociological implications are important factors that exercise a potent influence upon the extent to which the general public is willing to accept the findings of the investigators.

The most comprehensive study of the sexual behavior of human males and females has been conducted by Dr. Alfred C. Kinsey and his associates. Their conclusions are based upon data obtained from the voluntary reports of 5,300 males and 5,940 females interviewed. The study represents an age and a geographic cross section of American males and females. Dr. Kinsey emphasizes the fact that the relatively small samplings make it impossible to arrive at a scientifically sound generalization concerning the sexual behavior of all human males and females in the United States. Moreover, the validity of the conclusions based upon the samplings is dependent upon the correctness of the voluntary reports. The ideas presented here are based on the findings of Kinsey and his associates.[6]

The public has been greatly aroused by the Kinsey findings. Some of the unfortunate social outcomes of the publication of the Kinsey reports are the results of unintelligent misunderstanding of the number limitation of the studies and an unscientific proneness to draw sweeping conclusions from particular data. Regardless of the reactions of public opinion concerning the work of Dr. Kinsey and his associates, their investigation presents evidence of certain significant characteristics of male and female sexual behavior and trends in modern sex life that pose serious problems of sexual adjustment. Some of the characteristic likenesses and differences in the sex life of males and females, as reported by Kinsey, already have been referred to; certain other developmental tendencies and practices are presented here. The facts and percentages given are based upon *a limited sample that may or may not be representative of the population as a whole.*

Significant aspects in sexual behavior. The Kinsey reports reveal significant data relative to sexual practices of males and females at different stages of their development and during single and married life. Kinsey emphasized the fact that all individuals differ in their sex responses and practices; no one person fits into an assumed normal or average pattern. There appears to be a considerable change in the sex habits of women since World War I; heavy petting and premarital sexual intercourse are engaged in by a larger number of girls and women; since 1900 frigidity has declined among women by about one third.

[6] A. C. Kinsey, W. B. Pomeroy, and C. E. Martin, *Sexual Behavior in the Human Male.* Philadelphia: W. B. Saunders Co., 1948; and *Sexual Behavior in the Human Female.* Philadelphia: W. B. Saunders Co., 1953.

The peak of sexual strength is reached by men before the age of twenty; for most women the age is twenty-seven or twenty-eight. Once women reach their peak of sexual activity they usually maintain a steady level until their fifties, sometimes into their sixties. The male peak is far higher than that of women; male sexual activity remains higher for a long period of time. In spite of this fact, most men are growing old in sexual capacity when their wives are becoming more interested in and often less inhibited in sex, especially if a wife is younger than her husband. The fact that women do not show aging effects may create problems of compatibility between the married partners.

Venereal Diseases as Social Problems

VENEREAL disease is a general term that is applied to a group of extremely contagious and serious diseases that usually are introduced into the body through the genital organs by means of sexual contact. Since they are likely to be contracted as a result of sexual intercourse with an infected person, they often are referred to as the social diseases.

Syphilis and gonorrhea—cause and effect.   Syphilis is induced by the introduction into the body of the spirochete pallida, a corkscrew-shaped microorganism. After infection, these germs multiply rapidly as they make their way into the blood stream and are distributed throughout the body. The infected individual may notice a pimple at the point of infection. Since the pimple may disappear within a short time, he may not realize that the germs are active within his body. The devastating effects of the disease are experienced later in the form of severe impairment of many vital organs. The final stage is paresis—a destruction of the brain cells, resulting in mental enfeeblement. The disease is highly contagious during the first and second stages.

Gonorrhea, a disease that is more prevalent than syphilis, is caused by a paired germ called gonococcus. Gonorrhea is a localized disease, in that it attacks the mucous membranes of the genital organs and does not spread to other parts of the body. The affliction may cause severe damage to the reproductive system, however. Although its total effects upon the inflicted individual may not be severe, it may cause sterility. The child of an infected mother may be blind at birth. The germ can be killed, however, if the newborn baby's eyes are washed with nitrate of silver. In some states this treatment is requirement for all newborn children, as a precautionary measure.

Occasionally syphilis is contracted by the germ entering the body through a lesion in the skin or mucous membrane elsewhere than in the genital region. Fortunately, these germs cannot live long outside the body. Hence there is little likelihood that a person will acquire the disease from ordinary contacts. In order to achieve recovery from either syphilis or gonorrhea it is essential that the symptoms of infection be recognized early and treatment applied immediately. The germs usually can be killed easily if they are attacked before they have had a chance to multiply. It is important, therefore, that a person who suspects that he has been exposed to possible infection lose no time in consulting a physician for diagnosis and treatment.

Changing attitudes toward venereal disease. Historically, the incidence of venereal disease has been high. Popular attitudes toward venereal infection have varied among differing cultures and developing stages of civilization. Venereal infection has been regarded by some cultural groups as a more or less natural concomitant of sexual intercourse. In other societies, an infected individual became a social outcast, unworthy of medical care.

A relatively recent recognition of the serious personal and social implications of these dread diseases has stimulated considerable concern over the effect of their spread upon human resources and adjustment. Vigorous campaigns are being waged to prevent their spread. Medical science is conducting extensive research that is aimed at arresting the progress of the disease or curing the afflicted person. One of the primary objectives of the American Social Hygiene Association is to fight the spread of the social diseases. The aftermath of World War I in this respect alerted military personnel to the dangers of contagion during a war period. Consequently, through the efforts of the medical profession, the ASHA and military staff officers, much was done for the members of the Armed Forces of World War II. The spread of the diseases was checked somewhat as a result of periodic physical examination for all service men and women, lecturers concerning the physical and mental effects of the diseases, and other precautionary measures. Community leaders are attempting to awaken the general public to an appreciation of the VD menace to physical and mental health.

Mate Selection and Marriage

THE SELECTION of a marriage partner has had an interesting history. Respective cultures have imposed specific regulations concerning who shall marry. Political, religious, economic, and family restrictions of one kind or another have controlled and still control mate selection among differing societal groups.

Marriage concepts. Polyandry (one woman with several husbands) and polygamy (one husband having several wives) still are conventional forms of marriage among some of the more primitive peoples. The so-called civilized world, however, is committed to the concept of monogomy, or one mate for each person. Moreover, in those cultures in which only the monogamous form of marriage has legal status most marriage rituals imply, through the words "till death do us part," that the one marriage shall be a permanent relationship until the death of one of the mates.

Traditionally, the female mate was expected to be chaste before her marriage. The discovery by her husband, during the couple's first sexual intercourse, that his wife's hymen had been broken was legal cause for an annulment of the marriage. Real or imagined evidence of a wife's infidelity to her husband also constituted grounds for the husband's dissolving the marital relationship.

With a few exceptions societal groups always have and still continue to display a generally accepting attitude toward male sexual activities. This attitude probably is rooted in a traditional belief that for the male sexual intercourse is a necessary activity for the maintenance of good health, strength, and virility. The female, as we noted earlier, was expected to be the passive recipient of the male's sexual aggression; she subjected herself to, rather than desired, the sex act. We now know, of course, that the sex desire is as strong in the female as in the male.

There still are parents who attempt to guard jealously the chastity of their unmarried daughters, but they prefer sons-in-law who have had considerable experience in sexual activity or "have sowed their wild oats." The implication of this expressed parental attitude was the fact that an "experienced" man probably would be less likely to engage in extramarital sex relations. The possibility of the man's having contracted a venereal disease before his marriage was not considered a significant factor of suitability for marriage. Many states, however, have enacted legislation requiring that both the man and the woman submit to a premarriage physical examination to detect symptoms of venereal disease.

Traditional bases for mate selection. In many of the older cultures marriages were arranged by parents on the bases of parent-determined suitability of the match. Socioeconomic status and degree of prestige of the families concerned often were considered to be the determining factors of suitability; the girl's parents supplied the dowry, the man's contribution was his superior social status. In many instances the man had the privilege of selecting a girl to whom, at the time, he was sexually attracted or who would be likely to bear him children and establish a comfortable home environment. Whether the girl was emotionally stirred by her suitor was not important. It was taken for granted that the marriage relationship would stimulate in the woman the development of wifely attitudes of loyalty to and respect and liking for her husband.

In spite of traditionally established controls over mate selection, many young people managed to marry persons of their own selection. History has given us stories of great lovers, either married or unmarried. Romantic love, as a generally accepted basis of mate selection, however, is a relatively recent concept. At present a mate may be selected for reasons other than strong emotional attachment; yet it is customary for friends and relatives of the couple to express the conviction, at least superficially, that the contemplated marriage be based on "true love." Many problems of marital adjustment stem from this sentimental attitude toward the marriage relationship in conjunction with the social acceptance of freedom in mate selection as a democratic ideal.

Modern bases of mate selection. Each state enacts legislation concerning the age at which a young person may marry without parental consent. When a young man or woman has reached the legal status of an adult, as prescribed in his or her state, the person is at liberty to marry and to be unrestricted in the choice of mate. In fact, except in cases of extreme sex perversion or of venereal-disease infection, much latitude is permitted an individual in connection with his sexual activities and relationships.

Thoughtless mate selection and "quick" marriages are the resultants of various sex-stimulated phases and conditions of modern life. Some of the inducers of mate selection that are likely to give rise to marital problems of adjustment can be summarized briefly as:

1. Increased freedom of opportunity for the two sexes to participate in social activities of their own choosing without older adult chaperonage.

2. Increased participation by adolescents and young adults in cocktail parties and similar social activities.

3. Twosome night automobile drives and stops on deserted roads.

4. The tacitly accepted, though openly disapproved, participation by "respectable" girls in premarital experimental heterosexual activities.

5. The knowledge that the broken hymen does not necessarily represent loss of virginity.

6. The impact upon sexually developing young people of glamorous and detailed newspaper, radio, and television reports of the love life of national celebrities, of unrealistic love stories in some of the popular magazines, of highly sexual novels and motion pictures, of sexually arousing music, representative art, and dancing, and similar exciting media of entertainment.

7. The decrease of religious influence in some homes.

8. The apparently easy procural of a divorce and the high divorce rate.

9. The knowledge about and availability of contraceptives.

10. The seeming ease of setting up a home by means of instalment-plan buying.

11. The exposure to examples of lack of sexual control among older adults, married or unmarried.

12. The confused state of world conditions and the possible outbreak of war, especially the fact that young men who have no family responsibility are required to do their stint in military service.

Not all young people are motivated by these influences toward hasty, non-considered mate selection and marriage. Other stabilizing factors can offset the effects of unwholesome or abnormal sex-stimulating situations, conditions, or experiences. It cannot be denied, however, that changes are taking place in man-woman relationships, bases of mate selection, premarital attitudes, and marriage status.

The equalization between the sexes of educational, occupational, and political opportunities and freedom of behavior has led to the development in members of each sex of a better understanding of and respect for members of the opposite sex. The "veil of mystery" in which one sex was enshrouded for the other has given way to the possibilities of objective evaluation of one another. During the early days of the feminist movement some older, conventionally minded men and women expressed the fear that equalization of the rights of men and women would cause women to lose their femininity and men to become less masculine. Inherent physical and temperamental differences between the sexes are such, however, that, with few exceptions, each sex apparently is continuing to maintain his or her particular sex role.

Problems of mate selection. From the societal and religious point of view the fundamental purpose of marriage is to establish a home and raise a family. In earlier times the selection of a mate and consequent marriage followed this pattern. An important factor of the woman's choice of mate was the man's ability to provide a good living for his family; the man sought a woman who would bear him many children, and be an efficient wife and mother. When the home constituted the center for the provision of life necessities, a large family was an asset. Especially was this the case on a farm. Religious teachings encouraged this attitude toward the function of marriage; among some societal groups a large family was also regarded to be parental insurance against a destitute old age.

During the past half century or more the marriage function changed. Life necessities were made available through mass production outside the home; as a result of their increased educational and career opportunities, women no longer accept marriage as their only ultimate destiny. They have come to exercise greater freedom of choice concerning mate selection and marriage. Successful career achievement and economic independence, especially among more able women, have altered the bases of mate selection, marriage relations, and size of family. For the economically secure woman, the choice of a mate who will be a good provider is not imperative. Moreover, a woman who can or wishes to continue to be gainfully employed after marriage usually is interested in having a small and planned family. This attitude is strengthened by the fact that many couples believe that they owe their children whatever luxuries and success-achieving educational and vocational opportunities are available. Hence, in urban areas especially, there are many childless couples or families that consist of two gainfully employed parents and one or two children.

In rural areas the establishment of a home that contains a large family, financially provided for by the father and cared for by the mother, continues to be a purpose of mate selection and marriage; at present there is also an observable trend in this direction among city dwellers. Various personal desires, interests, or conditions determine an individual's decision to marry and the choice of mate.

Among the factors that are basic to mate selection in our modern American culture can be included one or more of the following: sexual attraction, romantic love, companionship, emotional security, desire for home and a family, escape from an unsatisfactory home situation, parental influence, loneliness, adventure, social position and prestige, financial security, gratitude, urge to reform (especially among women), notoriety, example set by members of one's intimate social group, premarital pregnancy, self-assertion in face of parental opposition, military or occupational pressure, and a felt need to regain self-esteem that may have been lost or severely damaged by being "jilted" by the first selected mate.

Unless the mate has been selected in terms of mutual attraction and respect, and similarity of interests and ideals, the chances are slim for the achievement of marital adjustment. If other factors are favorable, it is generally believed that a marriage is likely to succeed if the woman is younger than the man (optimal age for the woman is between 20 and 25 years, actual median age is 21.6 years at marriage); for the man it is between 22 and 27 years (actual median age is 24.3); if both have the same religious affiliation; if they have equal intelligence and educational status, or if the man's is slightly higher than the woman's; if the couple became acquainted in educational or occupational surroundings rather than in a social situation only; if the marriage represents freedom in mate selection; if the parents of either mate accept the other mate, and if the socioeconomic level of both mates is similar.

Important as these factors may seem, many marriages have been successful regardless of the lack of one or more of the favorable factors listed. The possible marital problems that might arise from differences in age, socioeconomic or educational status, religious affiliation, parental attitudes, or any other differences can be recognized before marriage by both the man and the woman, discussed frankly by them, and agreement reached concerning their solution. Marriage counselors have discovered that the primary cause of marital discord and mate incompatibility appears to be rooted in the personal inadequacies of either or both mates.

The emotionally uncontrolled, self-centered, and self-indulging child and adolescent becomes the uncooperative, adversely critical husband or wife who displays an inconsiderate and rejecting attitude toward the mate. As we have said earlier, sexual incompatibility or an abnormal attitude toward marital sex relations is conducive to sexual unfaithfulness to the spouse. Too great difference in ideals, interests, or behavior habits may give rise to feelings of boredom, lack of respect, or disgust. It is during the period of courtship that the couple can evaluate each other's personal characteristics and decide whether they can be tolerated. If not, a broken engagement is better than an unhappy marriage or a marriage that ends in separation or divorce.

Problems of courtship. The nature and intensity of the adjustment problems that may arise during the period of courtship are closely related to personality characteristics of each of the two persons concerned and the bases upon which mate selection is founded. The term *courting* can be interpreted to include an older adolescent's or an adult's relationships with members of the opposite sex which may eventuate in mate selection and marriage. In a narrow connotation of the term, courtship refers to behavior during the period of time between final mate selection and marriage, commonly referred to as *the engagement period.*

In either case, the length of time that elapses between first acquaintance with the future mate and marriage and the extent of knowledge about each other that is achieved during that period of time are important factors of marital adjustment. Some research studies in this area of human relationship yield results that would seem to indicate that the optimum period is at least one year in length. According to statistical data, a whirlwind courtship followed by marriage after a brief period of acquaintance is provocative of marital incompatibility. Regardless of the cause, an engagement period that is prolonged beyond the point of emotional involvement also constitutes inadequate preparation for successful marriage relationships. These conclusions apply generally; yet, in some instances, too short or too long a courtship period in no way interfered with the success of the marriage.

Intensity of sexual attraction is closely related to the effectiveness of courtship as preparation for marriage. Petting is coming to be considered a normal accompaniment of courtship. Holding hands, embracing, and occasional kissing are accepted activities of young people who think that they are "in love." Such physical contacts can arouse strong sexual urges unless both individuals possess considerable self-control. To control further erotically stimulated physical activities short of the point of coitus is a tension-arousing and frustrating experience. The exercise of sexual control is particularly difficult for the engaged couple.

The engaged man and woman desire physical contact with each other. They become emotionally and physically stirred through their petting activities. Then arises the question concerning the possible harm of coitus, especially if the marriage date has been set for the immediate future. There is difference of opinion concerning premarital sexual intercourse. Its advocates assert that the young couple thereby can discover the extent to which they are sexually compatible. On the debit side, however, must be taken into account the possible results of coitus: arousal of guilt feelings, fear of pregnancy, repulsion, or lack of interest in the experience on the part of one of them. Strong feelings of frustration may result if the situational factors make coitus impossible or unsatisfying; the frustrated partner may decide that he or she is sexually impotent or unfitted for marital sexual relations.

There are other problems that are associated with engagement: what one should tell the other concerning his past; whether an engaged person should limit his or her social activities to those which can be shared with the other; the extent to which the engaged couple should plan ahead concerning income and budgeting, the continuation after marriage of the present occupational activity of the woman, the bearing and rearing of children, the kind of home which they shall establish, and the elaborateness of their wed-

ding. The final decisions vary with conditions and individual interests of the couple. To attempt a satisfactory settlement of these
issues becomes a test of the ability of each to cooperate and to compromise. It provides each with an opportunity to evaluate the other's degree of emotional control and intelligent approach to problem solving, and alerts each to what may be the marital attitude and
behavior of the other.

The exercise of personal restraint in all phases of premarital
adjustment is important. In no area is it more important, however,
than it is in sex-stimulated behavior during courtship and marriage. Hence we shall conclude this discussion of adjustment problems associated with sex by suggesting that sexual restraint is
not suppression, inhibition, or denial of one of the strongest human
urges. In every culture and during every period of history, can be
found a few men and women who have completely sublimated their
sex desires and behavior. For many others youthful control of these
desires have earned for them later satisfying outlets through marriage and the raising of a family.

► **Questions and Problems for Discussion**

1. Name important conflicts that arise in problems associated
with sex.
2. To what extent, if any, should the sexes be separated for education?
3. What are the values to be derived from coeducation in the elementary school? In the high school? In college?
4. What objectives should sex education aim to achieve?
5. To what extent should sex education be given in the school?
6. How do the sex roles as defined by our culture affect sexual
conduct?
7. How do the dating problems of our teen-agers differ from
those of our grandparents?
8. Discuss the impact of the freedom permitted between the sexes
upon their social life.
9. Enumerate reasons for adolescents' being in doubt relative to
present-day behavior codes.
10. What values, if any, can come from the Kinsey findings?

11. What are the major problems associated with mate selection?

12. Whose responsibility is it to maintain proper behavior on a date?

13. In what way will knowledge about sex anatomy and hygiene be of value to young people?

14. Why is it so difficult to cope with the problem of prostitution?

15. Discuss the problem of venereal disease and sex adjustment.

16. To what extent may the emotional stresses during courtship become harmful?

17. How may childhood emotional attachment to family members affect the achievement of successful marital adjustment?

CHAPTER Thirteen

Living with the Family

*M*ᴀɴ's relationship to his home and his emotional reactions to all that it signifies to him are traditional themes of prose, poetry, and song. The importance to humans of their home associations is reflected in such well-known expressions as "home, sweet home," "home is where the heart is," "homesickness," "home cooking," and "I want to go home." No matter what the actual living conditions in the home may have been, memory tends to keep green only those incidents of past home life that cause desire for the reliving of the remembered happenings. The possession of a home with all its opportunities for self-expression and development appears to be a general human urge.

The Individual, His Home, and His Family

ꜰᴀᴍɪʟʏ life embodies human craving for security, understanding, sympathy, privacy, and intimate relationships. The home environment is a molder of human habits, ideals, and attitudes. It is supreme in its opportunities for self-development, self-realization, and social interaction. In the home, the individual first learns to appreciate himself as a member of a group bound by ties of kinship and by similarity of interests and abilities. Here, too, he meets his first conflicts between rights and responsibilities. In his home an individual may experience his greatest thrills of successful achievement or his most serious thwartings. The individual is fundamentally a reflection of his home environment.

Concept of home and family. Although it is possible for an individual to regard as *home* that place in which he lives alone, the word *home* usually implies the presence of other persons who generally are referred to as the *family*. All members of a family, however, need not at any one time live in the same home. The term family sometimes is limited to those immediate relatives who share with an individual his place of residence and general plan of life, but it also is used to include all persons who are related to the individual by birth or marriage.

The average family reflects in its accustomed behavior and interactions the standards and ideals of the social group or community of which the family is an integral part. On the other hand, in the family itself as a primary social unit are developed those attitudes, ideals, and practices that the members of the family carry into their associations with other members of the social group. These later become the bases of the general cultural ideals and standards of that group. In this way a family's attitudes and ideals tend to mold not only the customs and traditions of the community in which it functions but also predetermine to a great extent the traditional and cultural patterns that govern the behavior and ideals of succeeding generations. No family or community can be evaluated apart from its debt to the past or to its effect upon the future. Anyone interested in the problem of adjustment cannot treat lightly the influence of the home and of the family in the development of well-adjusted or inadequate behavior patterns.

Individual rights and privileges in the family. One of the basic causes of family adjustment or maladjustment is found in the type of relationship which exists among the various members of any specific family. Inherent in every normal individual are two fundamental urges—one for power and the other for personal freedom of thought and of action. If the members of a family are to live together amicably there must be a complete understanding concerning the extent to which each member of the group assumes specific responsibility for the well-being of himself and of his kin, and the amount of and direction of his own freedom of behavior in relation to the rights and responsibilities of the other members. The history of family development gives indication of the fact that there have been varying emphases upon the authority and freedom within the family group. The modern family exemplifies remnants of traditional attitudes combined with struggles for emancipation from one or another earlier custom. The family of today as compared with the family of the past is independent, loosely integrated, and democratic rather than dependent and closely knit; it is small rather than large, and democratic rather than autocratically controlled. Demonstrated affection is more common than was the case in earlier family relationships. Also with the decrease in the authority of the father has come an increase in family freedom.

There are apparent in modern family relationships, however, sufficient remnants of older traditions and mores to cause dissatisfaction with the newer family concept. Conflicts arise between struggles for authority and demands for further freedom from actual or imagined family controls. It is in these conflicts and struggles that the seeds of family maladjustment lie. In differences of individual interests are found the psychological bases for these conflicts. Hence we need to determine as scientifically as is possible the relative value of the old versus the new in the meeting of fundamental human needs. This could lead to the development of a program of education in family life that (1) can function as a basis for family adjustment; (2) can be psychologically and socially sound; (3) in its successful application can encourage a healthy and happy family life upon which can be built a well-adjusted and harmonious society.

Functions of the Family

A s the family is, so will be society; contrariwise, what society is, so will be the family. Since the family is a primary social unit, attitudes and behavior patterns that are characteristic of family interrelationships will be carried over into larger group relationships. At the same time family members are responding constantly to the societal influences by which they are surrounded. A child's first educational experiences are centered in the home; his teachers are the older members of the family; their ideals, attitudes, and general pattern of behavior are the resultants of their own childhood rearing and the effect upon them of the social, religious, economic, and educational influences of their out-of-home experiences.

Patterns of family life.   Primarily, the family is a social institution that is concerned with the care of the young. The extended period of human growth and development is basic to the significant position of the family as a social unit. The concept of home and family relationships has varied with different cultures and stages of civilization, however.

Although the pattern of marriage and home relationships differed among various primitive peoples, family life was characterized by strict patriarchal or matriarchal authority, rigorous systems of taboos, and pride in clan or entire family accomplishments and relationships. The modern American home reflects the influence upon family members of successive stages of societal development: Greek, Roman, and Hebrew stress upon patriarchal rule; monogamy and exogamy; Christian emphasis upon an individual's responsibility for his acts; the production of life necessities, as an outgrowth of the Industrial Revolution, and the ideal of democratic rights and responsibilities upon which our form of government was founded.

Factors of the home in society.   The complexities of modern civilization have given rise to a kind of social climate that, according to some writers, is unfavorable to the development of wholesome home life and good personal and social adjustment of the individual members of the group. It cannot be denied that the characteristics of modern society include some undesirable aspects. Practically every day one can read newspaper reports of antisocial behavior that is rooted in extreme self-interest, jealousy, impetuosity, intolerance, fearfulness, or unintelligent loyalties. Unfortunately, emotionally controlled, adequately adjusted behavior and constructive attitudes do not produce exciting newspaper headlines. It probably is not being too optimistic to believe that most American homes represent wholesome family and social adjustment, in spite of an increasing concern about the possible disintegration of the home.

In his home a young person can learn early to respect the rights of others, to develop an understanding and accepting attitude, to gain satisfaction from participation in the cooperative efforts of his family toward a common good, to tackle difficult problems unemotionally and purposefully, and to weigh decisions before he acts. A child who achieves emotional security in his family relationships probably will be enabled thereby to make satisfactory adjustments in his larger group experiences. In their discussion of the close relationships of the home, Patty and Johnson have this to say:

> With this preparation as a basis, the family is the primary atmosphere for practice in the social skills. When these foundations are laid with the family's encouragement, the social horizons can be extended for practice in dealing with diverse types of individuals. The family attitude should be a welcoming one to friends of all its members. Interest in extra-family contacts will aid in broadening the basis of social life. Participation in family recreation groups is important, as is joining hands in community enterprises. The opportunities for in-service training in human relationships are endless. All age combinations gain from this laboratory for experimenting with the social skills.[1]

Whether or not the family of the present produces individuals who will be healthy, intelligent, and emotionally controlled citizens of the future depends upon society's present standards for the family. It is necessary to find answers to questions such as these: Who shall marry and bear children? What responsibility do parents have for the rearing of their children? What are the economic and social needs of a family? What are the rights of the individual members of a family? What especially can organized society do to encourage and assure socially desirable child inception and life?

Marital function. The sex urge and the desire for the companionship of the opposite sex are inherent human drives. History has shown that experiments in segregated living have been unsuccessful except for a very few individuals. The two sexes so complement each other that an individual of either sex finds his complete self-realization only in harmonious association with and stimulation by a member of the opposite sex.

Extramarital sexual experiences in the satisfaction of the sex

---

[1] By permission from *Personality and Adjustment*, by W. L. Patty and L. S. Johnson. Copyright, 1953. McGraw-Hill Book Company, Inc., p. 283.

urge not only is undesirable for the general social welfare, but also is unsatisfying to the individual who practices it. The marriage relationship gives a couple an opportunity for stability in the satisfaction of this normal drive. Although the gratification of the sex urge is not generally accepted as the sole basis of the marital relation, the marital state affords a relaxation of sex tension and a socially approved avenue for the satisfaction of a normal need.

Intellectual parity, similarity of interests, dispositional likeness, and sufficiency of activity provide for husband and wife the fundamentals of cooperative living and companionship in the atmosphere of which there can be experienced desirable individual growth accompanied by healthful relaxation and freedom from strain. The mutual interest in and care of children fit into this pattern of marital life, enriching it and giving to it a purpose beyond that of individual development and self-satisfaction. Although the complete family unit presupposes the presence of children, the marital function of the family can be achieved by the childless couple if they project their abilities and their energies into activities outside their own personal interests, and work together toward the realization of a wider social good.

Factors Influencing Family Life

P E R H A P S the most outstanding characteristic of modern family life is its variation. In America today there is probably no "typical" family. The family may be large or small; it may include in its immediate circle only the members of the immediate family, or it may have added to it, in the same home environment, other relatives. The family may be rural or urban; it may represent a high degree of education and wide culture, or its members may be relatively uneducated and crude; its members may be engaged in highly trained professions or may earn their livelihood in unskilled occupations. The family members may be closely knit by similarity of interests and well adjusted to one another, or the members of the group may be indifferent to or antagonistic to the interests and activities of other members. In short, the complexity of modern civilization is reflected in many different kinds of modern American homes.

Factors of acculturation. It is a proven fact that peoples who come to America from other countries and who have been reared in cultures different from our own seem to be able easily and often quickly to assimilate American ideals and customs. However, certain Old World attitudes that are hard to change, tend to persist in family relationships. Traditionally, parental authority is greater than now is customary in the American home. The young person's choice of a mate or of a vocation, leisure-time activities, religious affiliations, friends, foods, and speech are influenced by the wishes and the habits of his foreign-born parents. Since the older members of the family tend to associate with persons of their own kind or nationality, they cannot understand or tolerate the desire of the younger members of the family to drift away from family friends and customs.

This situation gives rise to family conflicts which may disrupt the family, cause suffering to all its members, and result in socially undesirable behavior. Each successive generation feels less of the compulsion of the foreign tradition. If other factors are favorable, the assimilation of the traditions and ideals of the adopted country leads to their becoming the dominating influence not only upon the individual's relations with persons outside his home but also upon his family attitudes.

Influence of economic status. Economic status exercises a potent influence upon family adjustment. The members of a financially affluent family may not experience any need to participate in constructive, socially beneficial activities; habitual self-indulging attitudes and behavior can result eventually in boredom, restlessness, feelings of frustration, or emotional disorders. Even more serious are the maladjusting effects of the limitations of activity imposed upon the members of an economically underprivileged family. There probably is a medial economic status that can insure for all the members of a family the self-satisfying comforts and luxuries that have personal and social value.

For the underprivileged, the struggle for mere existence may be so difficult and the financial returns so meager that all members of the family except the very young need to expend most of their energy in uninteresting work. There is little time left for participation in relaxing social activities. Discontent, irritation, feelings of insecurity and of resentment may cause family dissension and unhappiness. Fortunately, public interest and legislation are bringing about some amelioration of the maladjustive conditions caused by extreme poverty.

Maladjusting factors can be found in some homes of the economically privileged or overprivileged. The responsibility for supplying an abundant family income may be the lot of one member of the family, usually the husband and father. The other members may indicate through their attitudes and behavior that it is their right to spend money lavishly for the satisfaction of self-centered interests. In a family situation of this kind the father may break under the strain of attempting to meet the extravagant demands of his wife and children; they may succumb to the effects of boredom caused by their aimless activities, or may continue feverishly to seek new and thrilling experiences. No close family unity is developed; family friction, discontent, and conflict are likely to characterize home relationships.

Best adjustments in family life seem to be established (1) if one or more members of the family are supplying adequately the fundamental needs of the group; (2) if all members understand and appreciate the occupational activities of those who are gainfully employed; (3) if there is time, opportunity, and money enough for the family to take part in socially desirable activities, sometimes together and sometimes apart; and (4) if each member of the group feels a personal responsibility for the family money, either through successful earning or by intelligent spending.

The kind of home in which a family lives, the neighborhood of this home, the satisfactoriness of clothes and of food, and the type of cultural and recreational activities in which the members participate depend to a great extent upon the economic status of the family. Ordinarily, we are not much concerned with the activities of persons far removed from us in geographic distance or social status. We very definitely are interested in the activities and possessions of our immediate associates. Family accord or discord may be based upon no more important factor than the extent to which the members of the family are economically able to afford those privileges which are enjoyed by their neighbors.

Occupational influence. Apart from the financial success of occupational activity, the form of occupation itself has an effect upon the lives of all the members of the family. It influences the family's interest in and the attitude expressed by the family toward social, political, and economic conditions of the country. If the father is an employer, the family attitude toward labor and labor legislation and toward class distinctions is different from the attitude of the family of an employee. The social level of the occupations in which members of the family are employed affects the social status of the entire family, and, consequently, the attitude of its members toward persons in their own social class and in other classes. The length of the work day and of the work week affect not only the leisure-time activities of the worker himself but also those of the other members of the family.

If the mother is gainfully employed outside of the home, the organization of home activities and responsibilities must be adjusted to meet her work program. Often the circle of friends and acquaintances reflects the occupational interests of the family. Parents' choice of a vocation for their children and the children's own vocational choices may be influenced by the family attitude toward the occupations of the various members of the family. A parent who is dissatisfied with his own vocational life may be willing to make many sacrifices in order that his children can be prepared to enter vocations that seem to be more desirable than his own. A parent who enjoys his work may try to force his children to enter the same field, even though their interests and abilities lie in other directions. The children themselves may be influenced toward or away from the occupational work of their father, as a result of the attitudes which they have developed toward it.

The status of the home as the center for the provision of food necessities is found at present only among families who still live on the farm. The increasing trend toward specialized farming, however, makes it not unusual for the farm wife and mother to buy her vegetables, milk, and other food products in town or from various other farmer specialists. Hence even the modern farm child fails to experience those forms of cooperative family life that were common in the past.

In general, city children are denied the experience of working with other members of the family in the care of the home. Even in humble homes, the laundry is sent out; canned and preserved foods are used; mechanical devices minimize the time and energy required to keep the home clean, and, in many cases, the meals are eaten away from the home. Girls, as well as boys, are accustomed to earn the money required to provide for the needs of the family by working away from the home rather than to provide these necessities directly in the home. In this way, instead of the members of the family being drawn together by cooperative activities, they are forced apart by their separate vocational interests and activities.

Educational influence. The child's first training is received in the home, and his early and permanent habits are established through this training. The educational level of the members of the family who are responsible for this early education is reflected in the habits and attitudes of the children. The family's attitude toward the value of systematic education affects the attitude of the children toward their educational ambitions. Important factors are the parents' interest in the school progress of their child, their cooperation with school authorities, their efforts to provide time and a suitable place for the child's home study, their understanding and willingness to accept their child's mental limitations, and their efforts to provide sufficient and suitable education for their child. The extent to which these factors become functional indicates not only parents' attitude toward the value of formal education but also their interest in providing a home environment that will insure good educational opportunities for their child.

Some American families still exhibit a traditional attitude of differentiation of educational opportunities for boys and girls. Parents may be willing to make tremendous sacrifices for the education of their sons. At the same time, they not only may deny similar privileges to their daughters, but expect and demand that the girls of the family leave school as early as the law will permit and go to work. The girls then can assist their brothers to acquire an expensive college education. This attitude may prevail in spite of the fact that the girls have demonstrated their ability to profit from further educational opportunities to a much greater extent than can their brothers. A situation of this kind has its roots in the belief that the girl should and will marry early and that she needs only the minimum of formal education in order to be a successful wife and mother.

Cultural influences. The cultural atmosphere of the home has a potent effect upon the developing personality of a child. The child reared in an apartment house in the center of a crowded city has an outlook upon the relative values of life different from that of the child who spends his early life in a detached suburban home, or the child who has learned early about the beauty of nature in his home on the farm.

The kinds of books read by the family; the conversation of elders; the religious affiliations and practices of the family; their tastes in music, art, clothes, and furniture affect the child's interests. The family choice of leisure-time activities influences the recreational habits of the child. His behavior both in and out of the home will reflect the social standards that govern the conduct of the family. Wealth or poverty alone cannot be accepted as a criterion of the cultural influences to which the young members of the family may be exposed.

A well-known business school, in which are trained many of the secretaries employed by the important business houses of the city in which it is located, selects its students very carefully. Before a young woman is accepted by the school, a visit is made to the home of the applicant. The purpose of this visit is to ascertain her cultural background. The school is not interested in the economic status of its students, but it does insist that the girls come from homes that give evidence of those cultural ideals which will make it possible for its trainees to fit into positions demanding an appreciation of acceptable social values. The school administrators admit that, unless such appreciation has been developed in the home life of the individual, they cannot, through their training, supply the deficiency.

Influence of intra-family relations. The children of a family usually reflect in their behavior and attitudes the attitudes of husband and wife toward each other, the attitudes of both toward their children, the relationships that exist among the children themselves, and the attitudes of grandparents, aunts and uncles, and cousins. We find in any family a subtle interplay of varying mental appreciations, of emotional drives, and of habitual modes of response that may effect desirable adjustment, or may cause unhappiness and failure in family relationships.

The displayed attitude of the husband and wife toward each other probably exercises a most potent influence upon general family behavior. The wholesomeness of their influence depends in great measure upon the extent to which they respect and admire each other, the satisfaction which they derive from their physical life together, their similarity of educational background and of interests, their accord in matters dealing with the rearing of their children, their willingness to defer to each other's wishes, their relations with their own and their mate's family, their religious accord, and their relative degree of independence of and dependence upon the other.

If children are aware of a close, intelligent, and emotionally stable relationship between their parents, they cannot avoid being influenced by it in their own relationships with their parents, with their brothers and sisters, and with their other relatives. Good social adjustment usually is achieved by young people, if these ideals are characteristic of family life: parents evidence a tolerance and an understanding of the rights of others; they accept their family responsibilities and expect others to assume theirs; the children are held to the high standards of conduct which the parents themselves practice; other family relatives are treated with consideration and respect but are expected to know and to observe their rightful place in the family; affection and care are given by the father and mother, and encouraged but not demanded from the other members of the family. It is equally true that the members of a family in which such attitudes prevail carry over to their other social associations the same understanding appreciation of their place in the larger group as they exhibit in their more intimate family relations.

Maladjustments in the Family

MALADJUSTMENTS in home and family relationships may result from the predominance of any one of many personal factors that may be present, regardless of the economic, occupational, educational, or cultural status of the home. Many of the maladjustments could be avoided if the members of a family were led to recognize the serious consequences of undesirable attitudes and behavior, and were helped to prevent the development of them. Domestic relations courts are filled with persons who, if they had used foresight instead of hindsight, might have avoided the humiliation of bringing their troubles to public notice. A complete survey of the many petty and relatively unimportant causes of family discord is impossible, but a few of the major maladjustive factors in family life are described here briefly.

Emotional immaturity. Too often young people enter into marriage with little or no appreciation of the responsibilities inherent in their new life together. Marriage, especially for a young woman, may seem to be an easy way out of an intolerable or unsatisfactory home, school, or occupational situation. The writers recall a high-school girl who was not succeeding in her studies, who was very much dissatisfied with her mother's overreligious strictness, and who saw no prospect of obtaining a desirable job. She informed the writers that she just did not want to be bothered by any attempts to adjust her school program, insisting that she expected to leave school on her seventeenth birthday and marry. She admitted that she had no particular boy in mind, but that the finding of a husband would be easy and that then she would be able to enjoy life. Since she would be careful to pick a man who had a good job, she would have no further worries. The attitude of this girl gave evidence of unrealistic romanticism born of too great concern with motion pictures, light fiction, and daydreaming.

This concept of marriage as a way out of existing difficulties is not confined to the young and immature. Adults often display the same lack of understanding of the meaning of marriage. They enter into the relationship without planning beyond the honeymoon. When they awaken to the realities of adjusting to the idiosyncrasies of their mate, and recognize the need of establishing an orderly and well-regulated life with the person who was a comparative stranger before marriage, they cannot accept the prosaic aspects of married life. They fall back upon their former discontent with life. They may neglect their responsibilities, hurl recriminations upon their mate, or withdraw completely from the marriage relation through a tacit agreement to live apart or by a legal separation or divorce.

Inadequate sex adjustment. Since the early Christian era there has existed among religiously minded persons a constant struggle between their natural urges and their religious teachings. Although the sex act is admitted to be necessary for the continuance of the human race, it seems difficult for society to agree upon the kind of training to be given to young people in preparation for marriage. As a result, much of the information which individuals have received concerning their sex life has come to them indirectly or in undesirable ways.

Parents are embarrassed by questions about sexual matters. This conspiracy of silence has affected girls even more than boys. Combined with the double standard of morality, it has been one of the most serious causes of marital incompatibility. Very often the husband and the wife exhibit very different attitudes toward sex relations. The husband does not always understand his wife's attitude, and mistakes her fear and ignorance for frigidity. The husband does not know the art of love-making or the preparation for the sexual act. Hence he either adds to the fear of the wife or arouses her disgust. The modern tendency toward smaller and planned families has further increased this tension between husband and wife. Psychologists, psychiatrists, and mental hygienists are attempting to develop a more rational attitude toward sexual relations. They are hampered in their efforts by a certain amount of social disapproval, and by their recognition of the possible difficulties inherent in the development of an adequate program of sex education.

Unless parents have achieved a normal and satisfying attitude toward their own sex relations, their children recognize the sex tension between their parents and are affected by it. Not only does the home life of the family suffer, but the children carry into their own adult sex lives an inadequate sex adjustment which may cause serious conflicts in their own marital and family relations.

Parental rejection of children. Children are aware of parental attitudes toward them and, in their behavior, respond to this awareness. It is normal for an individual to crave approval from the members of his group; it is imperative that a child recognize that he is "wanted" by his family, and that he is accepted as a desired and respected member of this close social unit. If he fails to gain this assurance, the effects upon his developing personality are serious.

Rejected children tend to exhibit behavior characterized by indifference, lack of emotional control, social antagonisms, and undue motor activity. Such behavior requires wise treatment. These children may seek, outside the home, the attention and love which they fail to obtain from their parents. Usually, however, they are unfriendly, and may be rebellious, confused, discontented, and discouraged. Parental attitude is responsible for these maladjustments and it is only through a correction of the parents' attitude that these undesirable traits in children can be overcome.

A child may be unwanted for one of several reasons. The coming of the child may interfere with other parental plans, or the family already may be larger than the parents desire or feel that they can care for adequately. Child rejection by one or both of the parents may be caused by lack of harmony between the parents themselves, resulting from inadequate sex adjustment or from undesirable family background of one or both of the parents. Whatever the cause of the rejection, the results are dangerous enough to engage the attention of all persons concerned with the wholesome development of our citizens. Prospective parents need to understand what the outcomes of their parental attitude may be.

Parental overprotection of children. Almost as serious as rejection is the situation which results from parental overprotection of their children. A child born after many years of married life without children may be so overwhelmed by the solicitous care of his parents that normal tendencies toward personal independence have little or no opportunity to develop. A mother who is dissatisfied with her married life may transfer to her child the love which she once felt for her husband and which she believes is no longer welcomed by him. This is especially true if the child is a boy. An only girl in a family of boys (especially if she is the youngest child) may become the apple of her father's eye and the center of his life.

The overprotected child does not lead a normal child's life. Usually his activities and his companions are hand-picked. He may be sheltered from any normal childhood difficulties, and granted all of his whims or wishes. The household revolves around the child. Such parental attitudes not only affect the "spoiled" child unfavorably but also may arouse resentment and jealousy among other children in the family. Overprotected children tend to display infantile, withdrawing types of behavior and to need assistance from others in meeting school or social situations.

Parental domination or submission. Related to the difficulties in family life that result from overindulgence or rejection of the child are those which arise from overdomination by or oversubmission of parents in relation to their children. Overdominance or oversubmissiveness of a parent may result from unadjusted marital relations, from the early training of the parent, or from the possession of a generally dominant or submissive nature. Such parents usually display similar attitudes toward other members of the family.

Parental domination tends to develop apparently desirable social attitudes in children. As a result of their home training they are able to adjust successfully to their school responsibilities. Because of their lack of freedom in the home, however, they may exhibit inability to express themselves, shyness, self-consciousness, seclusiveness, and general submission to authority.

In general, the characteristics of children of submissive parents are the opposite of those displayed by children of dominant parents. Children who enjoy great freedom in the family exhibit tendencies toward disobedience, irresponsibility, and uncooperativeness. They may lack the power of concentrated and systematic work, and be careless, lazy, unpunctual, and stubborn. Yet they usually are well poised, and possess adequate powers of expression. They are generally untractable and defiant of authority.

Conflicting ideals.   If parental attitudes differ greatly as a result of early childhood training, educational advantages, intellectual ability, religious affiliation, or recreational interests, resulting conflicts may be the causes of family disharmony and disruption. The husband or wife who is mentally superior to the mate is likely, after the first thrill of the marital relationship, to find that he or she is bored by the other. The fact that the children themselves may inherit the intelligence level of one or the other of the parents may lead to further difficulties. Parental ambitions may be thwarted, or the less able parent may tend to protect the less able child from the ire of the other parent, resulting in resentments and possible family cleavage.

As a result of their own early experiences, parents may disagree concerning the training of their children. One parent may favor a strict upbringing; the other may desire a more lenient treatment. Young children soon recognize this difference in parental philosophy and learn to capitalize upon it, if assured of the ready sympathy and protection of the less strict parent. Family deceits are practiced, habits of "getting out" of expected duties or responsibilities are common, and family loyalties are strained.

Whether or not persons of different religious affiliations should marry is a much-discussed question. Many examples can be cited of instances in which such marriages have been very successful, and the children have made desirable religious adjustments. Unless the couple have given the matter serious consideration before marriage and have agreed upon a policy for the religious training of their children, however, a marriage of this kind often results in the development of an indifferent or non-religious life for the family.

Golf widows and bridge or canasta widowers have been the subjects of much good-natured and humorous sympathy. Extremes of difference between husband and wife in their recreational interests subtract from the kind of companionship that is vital to family well-being. There is likely to be some resentment against the mate's interest in an activity which takes him away from the home and the family circle during leisure time. The neglected mate tends to exhibit an antagonistic attitude toward the other's absorbing interest. He is bound to reflect this attitude in his relations with his mate, his children, and other close associates of the family. Again, family loyalties may center around the apparently neglected mate.

Very serious are the effects of conflicts between the traditional ideals of parents and those which their children meet in their associations with other families. This situation is especially difficult for adolescents. If the parents have certain Old World attitudes toward the social activities of their children, it is difficult for both them and the young people to have the latter denied privileges which are accepted as a matter of course in other homes.

Anyone who has been closely associated with these rebellious adolescents cannot refrain from sympathizing with them when they raise questions similar to the following: "Why must I be home before eleven o'clock at night?" "Why am I not allowed to go out with boys?" "Is it wrong for a girl to smoke an occasional cigarette?" These questions usually are followed by the statement that other nice young people are allowed to do these things. Resentment toward the parents for their "intolerant" attitude often is accompanied by a lack of respect for the parents' judgment and, in many instances, the practice of the forbidden activity without parental knowledge. This struggle between the urge for individual freedom and respect for authority may result in an apparent victory for the latter, but the attitude of thwarting or the sense of guilt which may accompany defiance of authority interferes with the young person's normal social development.

Family relatives. The presence of relatives in the home is a well-known source of family conflict. Temporary or more permanent misunderstanding of feelings of hostility may arise between husband and wife or between parents and children that are caused by the presence in the home or close to the home of the domineering mother-in-law, the fussy father-in-law, the indulgent or critical grandparent, the hanger-on brother of a mate, and the self-sacrificing sister or aunt. Any one of these can damage the feelings of security among the members of a family unit which help family life become a welcome relaxation from more formal social relationships. Interference with parental rearing of children can lead to a display of bad manners and a lack of proper restraint and reticence on the part of the offending relatives, the parents, and the children.

Relatives may take it for granted that their kinship gives them special privileges. They seem to feel that they are justified in interfering with matters which are no concern of theirs. In fact, they appear to believe that it is their responsibility not only to give advice but also to insist that their counsel be accepted and followed. These persons would hesitate to attempt to control the behavior of persons not related to them or to ask special consideration from them; but the tie of kinship seems to absolve such relatives from all restriction in their demands. Here we find the conflict between the desire for individual freedom and the drive for power.

The working mother. The changed occupational status of woman brings with it a changed family relationship. If the mother's income is needed in the family, the father often develops a feeling of incompetence. In such instances, the children are likely to defer to the mother as the more stable parent. For a wife to earn more than her husband intensifies this family attitude. Sometimes the mother resents the fact that she must help in the provision of family needs. This fact combined with work fatigue causes her to shift the responsibility of the home care to an older child or to the father.

Tired, resentful parents and overburdened children are unable to develop the spirit of companionable home life. During the mother's absence from home, the children, as a result of their freedom from parental observation, may engage in activities that are socially unacceptable. In the evenings, the various members of the family may tend to drift away from the home for entertainment, since the family atmosphere is not conducive to pleasant relaxation.

If the mother is a career woman, the husband's attitude may be one of pride in his wife's achievements or of discontent because he and their children have not been able to stimulate in her the same interest and enthusiasm as has her outside activity. Here again parental attitude is reflected in the attitudes of the children. There are many homes, however, in which the mother's accomplishments in her profession or business are a source of pride and interest to her children, especially if the latter are old enough to appreciate her work and if she provides for their proper care during her absence. The very fact that she has this outside interest makes of her a *person* as well as a *mother*. Contrariwise, if the mother's interest in her career is so strong that she leaves the care of her family to strangers, her husband and children may experience an attitude of resentfulness toward her work and herself and feel themselves to be neglected and unloved.

Crowded city living.   As has been said earlier, many families of the past enjoyed free country life; cooperative effort in the production of family needs; self-made recreational activities; plenty of space, light, and air; and relatively regular and similar working hours which provided for communal leisure-time activities, and the general self-sufficiency of the family as a social unit. All of this gradually has changed to an almost complete dependence upon outside agencies for the supplying of life necessities as well as of recreational opportunities. We have moved to a mode of life in which the working hours of the various members of the family differ greatly, and to a general dependence of the family upon the community for its survival.

Because of their differing occupational and recreational interests, it is possible for the members of a family not to see one another for several days. A woman of the writers' acquaintance laughingly remarked one day that, during the week, she communicates with her sister by way of notes. Week ends are regarded as times for family reunions. However, the popularity of out-of-town week-end parties may interfere with this opportunity for family unity of activity and interests.

Apartment-house children are sadly limited in their activity. Frequently the modern child supposedly may be seen, but should never be heard by critical neighbors. Natural energy must be expended in city playgrounds rather than in the home. Parents desire their children to live a normal child's life but they also wish to be proper tenants. Hence they attempt to satisfy their children and their landlord by training their young people to enjoy quiet recreational activities. Many intelligent parents, rebelling against these restrictions, become interested in suburban living that has the advantage of providing for the children more freedom of activity. Such a move penalizes the wage earners of the family by increasing the number of hours consumed in traveling between their job and their home.

Broken homes. Homes that are broken as a result of the desertion of the family by a parent, or by the separation or divorce of the parents, give rise to one or more of the family maladjustments that have been discussed. To these types of broken homes may be added those which have been disrupted by the death of a parent. In all cases the family unity is interfered with; new adjustments must be made; financial worries may be experienced; and, especially in the homes broken as a result of the separation of the parents, loyalties are divided.

It is difficult to conclude that a broken home has a more serious maladjusting effect upon children than does a home in which there is dissension, nagging, and resentment. It is a fact, however, that a disrupted home, for any reason whatever, has been found to be one of the significant factors of adolescent and adult social maladjustment. Often the remaining parent may attempt through remarriage to re-establish family unity. This may cause greater friction and discord in the family, unless the new member is able to recognize possible difficulties of adjustment and is slow to demand family loyalty from the young members.

Educating for Marital and Family Adjustment

S O M E researchers in the field of social interrelationships and personal and social adjustment tend to regard inadequate home and family life to be a major causative factor of childhood misdemeanors, adolescent delinquency, and adult crime, as well as of serious mental and emotional disorder at any age.

The need for education. We have said earlier that much public emphasis has been placed upon the social patterns of home relationships. This trend has led to a minimizing of the fact that in the majority of the American homes are developed youthful attitudes of emotional control, constructive behavior, and home and social adaptation. It is important, however, to keep in mind that the exhibition by an increasing minority of young people of maladjusted behavior is a matter of serious social concern.

Undesirable conditions outside the home may become strong motivators of individual maladjustment. Disintegrating factors in the home are significant, even though they do not constitute the prime or only cause of maladaptation. We have discussed some of the maladjusting factors of family life. Vaughan presents a summarized list of family needs and difficulties. He suggests possible means of improving family relationships.

Research in mental hygiene has demonstrated that children need the emotional security provided by a home in which the parents love each other and their offspring. The parents need a sense of stability, too. Our high divorce rate is evidence that people lack the emotional maturity necessary to make a go of marriage and family life. Mates who cannot live together peaceably demonstrate to their youngsters a pattern of conflict that offers little recommendation to them for establishing homes of their own. Many homes were broken by separation or death during the recent war. Housing shortages are fostering friction and chronic worry. Family life is affected adversely by the fact that so many women work in business and industry. Women who have jobs are not inclined to bear children or to care for them properly. Childlessness, promiscuity, and sexual frustration contribute to the instability of marriage. The younger generation is not likely to achieve emotional adulthood under such untoward conditions; later they will get married and perpetuate the same unpropitious kind of home life. It is a vicious circle. We can extricate ourselves only by learning how to become mature persons in spite of the unfavorable social climate. Progress can be made through training in mental hygiene and through education for marriage and family living.[2]

The functions of education. **Problems** of adjustment associated with marriage and family living can be classified roughly as (1) premarital adjustment, (2) husband-wife adjustment, (3) child care and rearing, and (4) parent-child adjustment. In the past these problem situations were more or less neglected areas of formal education.

Any assistance that young people receive in preparation for meeting marriage and family responsibilities was incidental. To the extent that their mentors were mature, well-adjusted married men and women, considerable help was afforded. Preachments, warnings, or prejudiced advice, offered by embittered, frustrated, and maritally unsuccessful relatives or associates, sometimes caused the young people to experience fear of marriage and feelings of insecurity about assuming family responsibility.

One of the outcomes of increased public interest in the preventive aspect of the mental-hygiene movement has been greater concern with ways of improving family disintegration and of preserving physically and mentally healthy family units. The principles of good physical and mental hygiene are being applied in a practical fashion through the organization of planned programs of education and of guidance for young people as a preparation for marriage, and for parents as a preparation for child rearing.

The first regular course on the family was taught at Boston University, in 1922, by Ernest E. Groves. Since that time an increasing number of similar courses have come to be offered by high schools and colleges throughout the country. Effort in this direction has been encouraged by national organizations, which recognize the seriousness of the problems that grow out of ignorance concerning our unwholesome attitudes toward matters dealing with the sex life of an individual. (See Chapter 12.) Significant progress toward the development of programs of sex education or education for home and family living has been made by these agencies: Amer-

2 W. F. Vaughan, *Personal and Social Adjustment* (New York: The Odyssey Press, 1952), pp. 170–71.

ican Association of Marriage Counselors, American Social Hygiene
Association, Family Welfare Association, National Committee for
Mental Hygiene, and National Conference on Family Relations.

As a result of the efforts of these organizations, especially the
ASHA, some form of education for home and family living is required by state law in the schools of Oregon and Michigan. In
several other states educational programs in this area are permissive.
Other states are in the process of having similar programs approved
by legislative action.

There appears to be a rapidly growing interest in acquainting
young people with correct factual material concerning their sexual
functions and in helping them develop wholesome attitudes and
behavior in their relationships with members of the opposite sex.
There still are state and city school systems, however, which are
reluctant to introduce this area of study into their schools. Moreover, in those schools which do not hesitate to include in their
curriculums some preparation for marriage adjustment there is
indecision as to whether a well-planned program of study should
be presented in the form of a single course or whether the material
of study should be divided, with as little overlapping as is possible
among various curricular areas: physical education, physiology
and hygiene, general science, biology, home economics, English,
and the social studies.

Group and individual counseling services are available in many
communities. Young people who are contemplating marriage, or
married couples who are experiencing adjustment difficulties receive information and counsel at a counseling agency that is associated with a local church, a mental- or social-hygiene agency, or
one of the Y's. In addition, various national and state organizations
periodically conduct open meetings and group discussions for the
purpose of further stimulating public interest in the maintenance of
healthful marriage and family conditions.

For example, the annual conference of the ASHA, held in
New York City in December, 1954, dealt with the theme "A
Broader Base for Education for Personal and Family Living." The
conference in which the authors participated as group leaders was
attended by men and women from all parts of the country, including young unmarried men and women. The general meeting and
the panel discussions dealt with every phase of premarital, marital,

and family adjustment, and included consideration of problems encountered by individuals from the preadolescent years upward. Attention also was given to the specific problems of men and women preparing to enter or now serving in the Armed Forces. In addition, plans were discussed for the expansion of community educational offerings and for the pre-service and in-service training of community lay leaders. The serious interest and wholesome attitudes displayed by participants in this and similar conferences represent encouraging indications of the recognition by the general public of the need of providing sound, intelligent programs of education in marriage and family living.

Scientific research concerning the physical welfare of young adolescents accompanied by education for parents in the rearing of children preceded the present great concern over the basic principles of sexual and marital adjustment. The lowered infant mortality rate is evidence of the success achieved in dealing with the prebirth and postbirth care of mother and child. Progress has not been so satisfactory, however, in attempted education of parents toward providing for their children a home climate in which the latter's mental health is preserved and emotional disturbances prevented.

There are encouraging indications of increasing parental interest in child rearing. Parent and parent-teacher associations are struggling with the problem. Child-study groups, under expert leadership, are thriving. Young mothers and mothers-to-be, as well as some young fathers, are trying to become good parents. They are attending group and individual conferences, and are reading books and magazine and newspaper articles that deal with meeting the home problems of children and adolescents. Because of general interest in the movement, however, the leaders of education in child rearing are encountering several difficulties. Motivated by a strong desire to rear their children properly, some parents read *one* book on the subject. Their enthusiasm is greater than their ability to apply intelligently the precepts presented, however. Hence these parents not only attempt to follow slavishly the book's recommendations but also consider themselves to have become experts in the field as a result of their limited reading. There are other parents who are experiencing serious difficulties that are caused by the willful and tantrum behavior of their preadolescent or adolescent children. These parents take their problems to the "experts" in whom they have so great faith that they expect to be given a quickly working prescription through the application of which can be effected an almost overnight rehabilitation of their wayward children.

Another difficulty that is causing educational leaders considerable concern grows out of the fact that, for the most part, the parents and parents-to-be who seek help in rearing their children are emotionally stable and well-adjusted men and women who are meeting their parental responsibilities with intelligent understanding, but who are eager to improve their approaches. Too often the men and women whose need is great for education in home and family living are completely disinterested. They do not attend parent-teacher meetings, they do not read books and articles on the subject, and they rarely can be persuaded to seek help or counsel.

Finally, special emphasis is being given to the close relationship that exists between an individual's power to achieve satisfactory sexual, marital, and parental adjustment and all the other areas of his personal and social adjustment. Fundamentally, education aimed at the development of sexual control and marital adaptation begins in the cradle. Studies have shown that adolescents and adults who engage in sexual aberrations, delinquency, and crime usually have a history of childhood display of uncontrolled and tantrum behavior, home- and school-experienced frustrations and conflicts that provoked socially disapproved activities even during their early years. For this reason major educational stress is placed upon the development of stable personalities during the early maturing years, although reconditioning of maladjusted home and family attitudes and behavior is not neglected.

▶ **Questions and Problems for Discussion**

1. To what extent has your social or emotional adjustment been affected by the following: national background, economic status, educational and cultural level of your family?

2. What do you consider to be the optimal economic status for adjusted family living in your community?

3. Trace the effects upon your own social and emotional adjustment of your age place among the children of your family; the fact that you were a "wanted" or a "rejected" child.

4. Who was or is the dominant member of your family? Why? How were (are) you affected by this dominance?

5. How did your adolescent leisure-time activities differ from those of your parents? Explain any difference.

6. Describe the qualities which you would like the mother (or father) of your child to possess.

7. Describe your interpretation of the ideal mate.

8. Which do you consider the most desirable home environment: large city, small town, suburb to a large city, or rural area? Defend your opinion.

9. How would you meet the "in-law" problem?

10. Which do you consider less serious (and why) for a child—a home in which parents are not compatible, or divorce of the parents?

11. To what extent should parents control decisions of their children concerning vocational choice, friendships, leisure-time activities, or choice of mate?

12. Name factors of modern civilization that can be expected to counteract possible family disintegration.

13. What is your attitude toward mixed marriages?

14. What opportunities have you had for participation in courses or discussions dealing with education for marriage or parenthood? List the topics which you would like to have included in a course of this kind.

CHAPTER Fourteen

Earning Occupational Success

A N individual in his occupational life is motivated by the same drives and urges that control other phases of his inter-human relations. A normal individual feels the urge to create, to accomplish, to recognize personal or social value in his achievement, and to carry his activity to a successful conclusion. He also is motivated in his work by a desire for personal gain. He desires social benefits to accrue as a result of his labor. Self-interest, self-approval, and the approval of others are essential if he is to appreciate the full value of his accomplishments.

The Individual as a Worker

THE WORKER is not and cannot be looked upon as a mechanical robot. He must understand the purpose and goal of his performance; this driving curiosity to know and to understand must be satisfied if he is to be a well-adjusted worker. His urge for mastery must find expression in intelligent control of his job and of other phases of the work situation that properly are his responsibility. To the extent that he subordinates his own ideas, interests, or desire for mastery to another person, he recognizes that the authority to which he is subject is just and right and that he will not lose his own self-respect by submitting to the will of another. Hence, in order to be a satisfied worker, he knows and appreciates levels of authority and his own proper place in relation to them.

Human drives related to work.   The young child's tendency to refer to objects in his immediate environment as "my dish," "my sunshine," or "my" anything finds its counterpart in the worker's attachment to his work environment. The business or factory is often referred to as "mine." Tools or equipment become so much a part of himself that he may become annoyed if they are used by another person, even when he himself does not need them. A typist may hesitate to give up a typewriter which she has used for a long time even though she is given a better one in its stead. For many years a man had been using an old desk. The drawers stuck, the wood was splintered, and its general appearance was disreputable. When it finally was replaced by a large modern desk, this man remarked that he felt like a stranger in his office and that he could not concentrate on his work at this desk as he could at his *own* desk.

A few workers are content to be isolated in their work, but many of them need the presence of their kind in order to be satisfied. A newcomer added to the group may break the morale of the workers until they are willing and able to accept him as one of them. Many a man is torn between the satisfaction of promotion to another department and the pull of wanting to remain with his former associates. The greater his loyalty to his old group, the harder it may be for him to adjust to the new workers or to be accepted by them. He is then, for a while, a man without a group, since his former associates no longer consider him to be a member of their group and he feels himself to be unwanted by the new.

These are some of the drives of the worker. Adjustment to his occupational activities depends upon the extent to which he is able to achieve satisfying realization of these motivating urges.

The total personality.   The worker does not bring to his job a mere part of himself. There are few, if any, workers who are able to separate their work lives from their other experiences. An individual's health, his ability to evaluate his job in terms of social and personal usefulness, his relations with his family, his social interests —in fact, his whole philosophy of life is reflected in his success and satisfaction or his failure and lack of satisfaction in his occupational life.

Causes of maladjustment in work. The maladjusted worker is the fearful worker who has failed in one way or another to find complete satisfaction in his job. The sources of this dissatisfaction may lie within or without the individual. Psychologists and mental hygienists interested in business and industry are attempting to discover the bases of occupational maladjustment and, by amelioration or removal of them, to help individual workers toward better work adjustment.

A worker may become dissatisfied with his job for one or more of a number of reasons. His work may be too fatiguing; he may experience a feeling of personal inadequacy in meeting the demands of his work. Various occupational fears may assail him, such as possible loss of his job, wage cut, incapacity through ill health, unfair supervision, failure to achieve a personal ambition, lack of cooperation among his fellow workers, and old-age dependency. Industrial psychology is aimed at the removal for workers of as many as possible of these sources of discontent or feelings of frustration through the improvement of placement, plant organization, supervision, wage scales, and working conditions.

Work relationships. An individual's relationship to his job includes much more than the momentary relationship that exists between him and the task he performs at any one time. The purpose and function of the work, his ability to perform it, the attitude of his employer toward him and of himself toward his employer, the permanency and the social status of the job, the attitude of his family toward the work, and the kind and amount of effort that the job demands of him are potent factors in his adjustment or maladjustment.

Problems of Pre-Job Adjustment

M O S T persons spend the greater part of their waking day in work that is aimed at the meeting of their life needs. As has been said earlier, life adjustments are influenced to a great extent by the satisfactions that are experienced on the job as well as by the money that is earned.

Determination of suitable work.   Some individuals continue in an occupation, earning reasonable success in their work, without ever being certain that they are in the kind of work for which they are best suited. In fact, there are people who do a good job for ten or more years in one kind of work. They then, either by accident or design, prepare themselves for another field in which they believe they will be happier, and more successful economically.

In order to be outstanding in fields such as art, music, and dramatics, a person probably needs certain specific talents that are not possessed by the majority of people. There are tests of musical and artistic aptitude that may give some indication of the degree of talent that a person possesses in one or the other of these two fields. The possession of a special talent usually shows itself early, if the individual is given an opportunity during his school days to exhibit the beginnings of good achievement in the field, if he himself is interested, and if a teacher or parent is quick enough to recognize the special talent and provides further training for the young person. Even though the student shows a definite aptitude in a field, however, everyone concerned needs to be realistic about the extent to which the talented young person shall be encouraged to continue his studies.

Opportunities in the field, financial ability to achieve a high degree of performance, and the person's own willingness to sacrifice time and energy to perfect his skill are important considerations. Too often, young people who possess no more than a fair degree of talent are encouraged to look forward to a vocational career in a field where no more than average or less than average occupational success can be achieved. Such a person had better turn to another vocation for his lifework, and use his special talent as an avocation.

There are parents who regard participation in the arts as an insecure way of earning a living, e.g., a boy who gives evidence of unusual talent in one or another form of art is not permitted to develop his talent but is forced by his parents to prepare instead for a *solid* vocation, such as business, mechanics, or a profession. Many an adult who, as a boy, was denied by his parents the right to follow his own vocational interest, has failed to earn success in the field that was chosen for him. He either dabbles at the same time (on the side) in the field of his own choice or, later in life, gives up the undesired vocation and devotes all of his time and energies to the other, sometimes at great monetary sacrifice.

Barring fields that require special talent, the choice of the vocational course to be followed by an intelligent student may be any one of many. His choice depends upon the opportunities available in one or another of them, if the personal qualities that lead to success in one hold for the others. A young woman, for example, who is interested in and able to work with people may be equally successful as a nurse when the demand for nurses is great, or as a teacher in times of teacher shortage and oversupply of nurses. The specific training for the two vocations differs. Therefore, before her graduation from high school, she decides which vocation she wishes to enter.

Although there are batteries of aptitude and personality tests that can be utilized for the purpose of discovering an individual's fitness for entrance into any one of many vocations, the final choice usually should be made in terms of available openings and the individual's well-considered interest in one field rather than in another. Whatever the choice may be, an important consideration is that, after a person enters a field for which he appears to be qualified and in which he sees opportunities for advancement, he stays in it rather than dissipate his energies by flitting from one field to another.

Individual potential and job analysis. This is a problem that faces all young people and, to a lesser extent, those adults who for one reason or another are forced to change their vocation. In order to choose a vocation intelligently and profitably, an individual needs to familiarize himself with three factors: (1) his own abilities, interests, and personal characteristics, (2) available fields of work and their requirements, and (3) the extent to which his potentialities meet the requirements of the respective occupations.

A complete analysis of any one of these three factors is a serious project and must be undertaken in a businesslike and objective fashion. Opportunities for self-analysis are improving and yielding some reliable data. Many studies are being conducted of the specific and detailed activities of various types of work. It is almost impossible to evolve a complete list of all the minute details of movement and of activity needed for every one of the thousands of specific jobs in which an individual may engage. However, studies made to date have resulted in the compilation of the major requirements of many work fields. Besides a knowledge of the requirements of a vocation and his own fitness for it, the individual needs, while on the job, to gain increased efficiency and to earn advancement. A young man or woman who is really interested in achieving success in his work activities usually is eager to perfect his skills. In his discussion concerning the training of industrial workers, Berrien makes the following comments:

> Happily, the task of motivating young workers to learn a new job is less difficult than motivating many students in academic study. The rewards for success are usually much more immediate in the industrial situation than in college or university life. A study of the wages of learners in 410 representative American manufacturing concerns showed that a little less than one-fifth of the companies paid either the standard wages or the minimum wages of the job to novices. It is consequently safe to say that most learners in industry are motivated to attain skill in their jobs by the desire for higher wages—a very immediate and effective reward.
>
> Related to the question of precise objectives in training is the importance of providing the learner with information relative to his progress. Knowledge of one's progress is an important force motivating the individual to eliminate his errors and consolidate his improvement—provided he knows exactly what his errors are and what parts of the task he is performing correctly.[1]

The training situation is different for the young person who is planning to enter an occupational field that requires long and intensive training. Concern about immediate study difficulties may cause him to lose interest in his long-range goal. He may become discouraged by an occasional failure in his courses. He may doubt his capacity to prepare adequately for his chosen field.

Granted that the individual is qualified for such training as

[1] F. K. Berrien, *Practical Psychology* (New York: The Macmillan Company, 1952), revised ed. p. 216. Used with the permission of The Macmillan Company.

will make him an efficient worker in a chosen vocation, he still has two factors to consider: (1) possible opportunities for the training needed and (2) financial ability to meet the cost of the training. If either of these two factors is unavailable, the individual is forced into preparation for an allied activity, the training for which is within the realm of possibility.

Public and private agencies are fast meeting the first of these needs. Vocational "scouts" are studying professional, business, and industrial trends. On the basis of their findings, they are predicting the vocational needs of the future, and are aiding in the establishment of proper training facilities and in the encouragement of students for them. Mistakes are made, such as the school that set up an elaborate home-economics program for an expected need five years hence only to discover that not home-economics experts but stenographers and typists represented the new need of their community.

Many vocational-training courses are expensive and therefore prohibitive for some qualified candidates. Scholarships in privately endowed schools and community support of vocational schools are attempting to meet this need. If an individual shows a special ability in a particular field, it is becoming increasingly possible for him to obtain the required training.

The point at which a man or woman may stop his training and enter into active work on the job varies with the kind of work in which he plans to engage. Usually, for the so-called professions—medicine, law, teaching, engineering or nursing—the worker in the field needs fairly complete pretraining, including supervised practice, before he enters into the field. The young physician spends several years as an intern at a hospital, the teacher goes out into a school and observes an experienced teacher and does some practice teaching under supervision. The lawyer-to-be spends a period of time with a well-established law firm before he hangs out his shingle. This practical experience is needed; most people are hesitant to employ the services of these professional people until they have learned on the job, as well as from books and demonstrations.

In some fields, such as business, it is possible for a person to master the rudiments of his work during his regular schooling and then to engage in the more simple phases of the work. He assumes greater responsibility as he gains greater practical experience in it and continues his studying as he works.

There is a growing educational trend to combine study with work practice. The cooperative study-work plan is used in some colleges such as Antioch, and in an increasing number of high schools. No matter how thorough a person's preliminary preparation for his work life has been, it probably is to his benefit to continue his studying after he has started to work. In most vocational fields, newer methods and improved procedures require that workers in these occupations constantly attempt to become informed about such changes, if they desire to develop greater skill or earn promotion in their work.

In order to meet workers' demands for continued study, evening courses are increasing in number; business and industrial organizations are offering in-service training to their employees, or are allowing their workers to take leaves of absence for continued study. Such continued study is valuable to the employer and to the employees to the extent that through it the efficiency of the worker is increased. If, however, the study is too far removed from the kind of work that is being done on the job the worker may be distracted from his best job achievement. Berrien has this to say about on-the-job training:

> The most general form of training in American industry is to place the new employee with a skilled workman as a learner or helper. In some instances the foreman takes the responsibility of "breaking in" the new man and then turns him over to an experienced worker who continues to guide his learning.
>
> The chief advantages of this system are its simplicity and alleged economy. Certainly the known costs of on-the-job training are small, partly because the trainee is contributing to the total output while he is learning and no special instructors or equipment are necessary. On the other hand, the hidden costs of the system may be quite sizable if consideration is given to the total time lost from production by foremen and others who must instruct the trainees. There is the further possibility that the emphasis on speed, which regular production work is bound to exert, will ultimately result in poorly trained men. When new men are assigned to experienced workers

there is less possibility of standardized instruction than in the vestibule school. Perhaps offsetting some of these disadvantages is the fact that whatever the candidate learns will very likely be immediately related to his job. In addition, his adjustment to fellow workers and the supervisory personnel is not delayed but develops along with his job skill. In small plants where only a few novices are introduced at a time, on-the-job training is probably the only economical procedure to follow. However, possibly several such enterprises might pool their training resources in a central vestibule school for their mutual benefit.

It is significant in evaluating these two methods of training that a number of defense-industry companies like Pratt & Whitney used the "watch-the-man-who-knows-how" method in the early days of World War II, but discarded it because trainees hesitated to interrupt production men to ask questions and then rarely reached normal production speed because they were afraid they might spoil materials. This company found that a course lasting 325 hours, consisting of classroom and shop training under the direction of full-time teachers, provided both faster and more thorough training than the previous methods.[2]

The value of training on the job is dependent upon several factors. The workday may need to be lengthened to include both work production and training. As part of the training, the worker may be required to engage in home study. In either case, sufficient time may be denied the worker to engage in relaxing recreational and social activities. If the program of work and study is too strenuous, the worker's health may be affected and the extra study will then interfere with the progress of both the employer and the employee. Study while on the job must be adjusted to the job needs and to the health of the worker. A balanced program, intelligently carried out, motivates interested and successful achievement and results in a high degree of occupational adjustment.

[2] Berrien, op. cit., pp. 227–28.

Factors of Adjustment of the Worker to the Job

THE RELATIONSHIPS which grow out of his work are certain to influence all of an individual's other relationships. If it is true that as a man is, so will his work be, it is equally true that as his work relationships are, so will he be. A study of occupational adjustment, then, cannot be divorced, except in particulars, from a study of life adjustment in general.

General personality adjustment. Individuals differ in their physical structure and vigor, their mental ability, their special aptitudes, and their degree of emotional stability. In like manner, different types of occupational work differ in their physical, mental, aptitudinal, and emotional requirements. There are certain personality traits, however, the possession of which predisposes toward success, no matter what the specific character of the work may be.

Employers are becoming increasingly aware of the value to them of employees who possess such traits as punctuality, industry, honesty, and sincerity, emotional control in difficult situations, loyalty to their employer, neatness and cleanliness, and appreciation of their own position in and relationship to the function and organization of the entire personnel. These qualities are no different from those that affect adjustment in any social relationship. The "spoiled" child, the lazy child, the irresponsible child, the sulky child, or the emotionally uncontrolled child is in danger of becoming the uncooperative, lazy, irritable, and unstable worker.

If the job is unsuitable or if the working conditions are undesirable, the worker's unfavorable characteristics will be intensified; serious job maladjustment may result. The individual who has developed wholesome personality qualities is unlikely to suffer too greatly from job dissatisfaction. If the worker's choice of vocation has not been wise or if working conditions are intolerable, however, even good behavior patterns break down and the worker may become maladjusted.

Personal fitness for entrance into one or another occupational field constitutes a major factor of vocational selection. High-school counselors are faced with the problem of helping young people determine the degree to which they possess those personal characteristics that predispose toward successful participation in a desired occupational field. Although the display of industry, conscientiousness, integrity, and cooperation is effective in any occupational field, various areas of vocational activity, by the nature of their demands, set ability limitations.

Physical endurance, strength, and health status are important. For example, a young woman who is intensely interested in teaching is barred from entering the profession because of her diabetic condition. A man who aspires to be a pilot is subjected to rigid examination of his physical and mental status: sight, heart condition, muscular coordination, quickness of response, and physical endurance.

Jobs have intellectual levels. There are forms of work which are peculiarly adapted to superior, average, and subnormal levels of intelligence, respectively. Comparisons of vocational success with mental ability seem to indicate that, on the average, the occupational hierarchy from unskilled labor through semi-skilled, skilled, and technical to professional levels of work is accompanied by a corresponding rise in the levels of mental ability.

Many studies have been conducted, for example, to discover the relationship that appears to exist between degree of mental alertness and specific occupational requirements. An extensive study of this kind was conducted with the members of the Armed Services during World War II. Army General Classification Tests (AGCT) were administered to selectees from various civilian occupations. The purpose of the testing program was to discover what relationship might exist between intelligence and occupational activities. The results of the study are presented graphically in Figure 6.

As presented, the data for the occupations studied indicate that, within limits, one can find in them persons who range from relatively low to very high intelligence. Since the average or mean intelligence decreases from lawyer to farmer, however, it can be concluded that chances of success in the professions and the alertness-demanding business fields are greater for those persons who give evidence of above-average intelligence.

The more intelligent are found in the professions, not only because they have won in competition with less able individuals, but also because they themselves would be less successful in a work field which required less mental challenge. An exceedingly intelli-

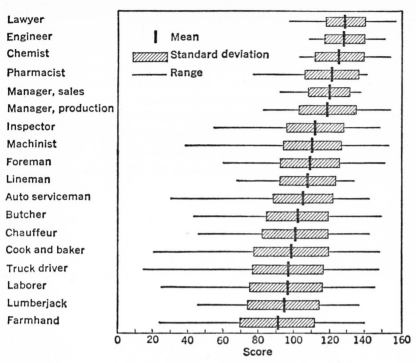

Fig. 6. Intelligence and Occupation

This figure shows the mean, dispersion, and range of intelligence in various occupations as determined from selectees in World War II. Note that the average score (indicated by the cross mark on the bar) increases with the level of the occupation, and that the dispersion (indicated by the bar) is greater at the bottom than at the top of the chart. Nevertheless, it is clear that in virtually every occupation there are persons of high intellectual capacity, as indicated by the range (the line). (Drawn by permission from data selected from Harrell, T. W., and Harrell, M. S., "Army General Classification Tests, Scores for Various Occupations." Educational and Psychological Measurements, 5:229–39, 1945. Table I.) [3]

gent young man of definite creative ability accepted a position in a newspaper office which required that much of his time be given to routine work with files. He soon discovered a way of organizing the files that would reduce the tediousness of the job. Unfortu-

[3] J. E. Anderson, *The Psychology of Development and Personal Adjustment* (New York: Henry Holt and Company, 1949), p. 551.

nately for him, the management was not interested in the reorganization of the files, but wanted a man who would do a satisfactory job of working with the files in their existing condition. He lost his job because he was too intelligent for the routine work expected of him. Many persons who are mentally slow are competent and satisfied workers in routine types of work that would be unbearably monotonous for and inaccurately done by the mentally above average person who obtains his satisfaction from the challenge of changed activity or problem solving.

Similar to intelligence as a work selector is the personality factor usually referred to as temperament. Work which involves human contacts requires a different type of emotional response than does the work which involves contact mainly with inanimate objects. The tact, the frankness of approach, and the alertness to human reactions required of the physician, the lawyer, the teacher, the nurse, the salesman, or the social worker are not needed to the same degree by the accountant, the mechanic, or the scientific research worker.

Successful adjustment to occupational work, then, can be measured in terms of the individual's personal fitness for the work in which he is engaged. The first step in this adjustment should be the selection of an occupation for which he is adapted and in which, under favorable working conditions, he will be able to develop those of his traits that are conducive to success in the chosen work.

Workers' attitudes. Attitudes of workers vary from extreme discontent and bitterness to almost complete happiness, satisfaction, and loyalty. Many factors contribute to this variation in feeling. A worker rarely displays one general attitude toward all phases of his work experiences and environment. Rather is it true that a worker exhibits varying attitudes in his work relationship. He tends to have an accepting or a rejecting attitude toward the job itself. Seldom is he totally indifferent to it.

The individual who is engaged in work of his own choice and for which he is adequately prepared usually evinces interest in it and often is enthusiastic about it, in spite of other undesirable elements in the situation. Contrariwise, the worker whose job represents nothing more to him than his salary or pay check, who has no real aptitude for or interest in it, or who recognizes in himself the lack of proper training, tends, in spite of other favorable conditions, to dislike the work, often finding it so intolerable that he quits it.

In his relations with his immediate superior, an individual is affected by his own ability to adjust to other persons, by the supervisor's attitude toward his workers, or by the worker's degree of skill. A feeling that the supervisor or employer is favoring other workers rather than himself, lack of expressed approval from the supervisor, or the worker's consciousness of his own ineffectiveness (that the supervisor should recognize even though he may not) may develop in the worker an antagonistic attitude that is difficult to overcome.

A worker is seldom neutral in his attitude toward his fellow workers. Appreciation of his own success and of similar effectiveness on the part of his associates develops in the worker a feeling of friendliness and cooperation that usually is reciprocated. Dislike, jealousy, and uncooperativeness grow out of feelings of personal ineffectualness as compared with the other workers and unequal treatment of the workers by the supervisors, or an appreciation by the worker of himself as superior in one way or another to the others.

The worker's attitude toward the organization is closely related to its community status, to the efforts made by the organization to improve working conditions, or to the worker's appreciation of the purpose of the work and his part in it. A respected establishment, providing desirable working conditions and engaging in worth-while production in which the worker has a significant place, tends to develop a feeling of pride, loyalty, and oneness. A worker cannot tolerate being ashamed of his job or of his employer. If economic necessity forces him to remain in his position, his attitude tends to be one of bitterness both toward the organization and toward an unkind fate.

A worker's attitude toward his job, his supervisor, his fellow workers, or the organization itself, affects the success and value of his work. The worker whose attitude toward all phases of his work life is favorable is a contented and effective worker. Any form of antagonism is sure to affect the quality of his work and to decrease his value to his employer.

Monetary returns versus job satisfaction.   The average person probably does his best work when he enjoys his vocational activities and feels that he is receiving adequate remuneration for his endeavors. There are people who are so much interested in service to others or in a particular field of work that they are unwilling to change from it to a more lucrative position, however. Many country doctors and small-town ministers earn barely enough to meet their expenses. The enjoyment that they receive from their activities and their mode of life more than compensates for the financial rewards which are denied them. Librarians and teachers in some areas experience a similar situation. Sometimes, when the going becomes particularly difficult, they may consider themselves foolish for remaining in their chosen field. Rarely do they change their occupation, however, unless they are tempted to do so by the promise of a much larger income. One case in point was the serious exodus of men and women from the teaching profession during and after World War II. Teachers, especially in small school systems, were notoriously underpaid. As a result of the teacher shortage of the 1950's, citizen groups and school leaders joined in a campaign to increase teachers' salaries in order to attract and keep able people in the profession.

There are men who find themselves becoming discontented in an occupational field that pays well but does not offer the stimulating challenge which they desire. Opportunities may be open to a man in this situation for a change to a more interesting but poorer paying field for which he is trained, or even to the starting of a business of his own that may necessitate the investment of the savings that he has accumulated during his years of work. A decision as to what to do in a situation of this kind depends chiefly upon the man's home responsibilities and the attitude of his family.

If a change in occupation were to necessitate the sacrificing by his children of their educational or career interests, the average man would hesitate to decrease the family income in spite of his worker dissatisfaction. It may be that his wife and children are willing to sacrifice temporarily in order that the breadwinner may engage in an activity which is more interesting to him and which later may be expected to yield financial returns that are equal to or exceed what he is earning at present. There can be no objection then to his starting a new venture. The man himself must be certain, however, that his desire for change is not a temporary whim or fancy, or that he is not being influenced in his decision by well-meaning but mistaken friends or business associates.

A man may fail to find himself vocationally until he is middle-aged or older. His own interests or occupational considerations may bring about a change of work that proves highly satisfactory from the personal point of view, as well as financially. In general, though, most satisfying work experiences are achieved by the person who is guided early into a field for which he is personally suited and for which he has been adequately trained.

Although a worker's attitude is partially the result of his own ability to adjust to his work situation, the conditions under which he works exercise a potent influence upon his attitude and his efficiency. Therefore, in order to ensure for the worker an adjusted work life, factors outside the control of the worker must be considered.

Factors of Adjustment of the Job to the Worker

THE RELATIONSHIP between supply and demand in the field of employment has an important influence upon the morale of a worker. If an individual is fitted for a type of work in which there is a reasonable demand for well-trained persons, and if then the individual has the opportunities for adequate training with assurance of placement, he views the future with hope and enthusiasm. His attitude toward his training and his subsequent employment favors a desirable adjustment to the job and further study toward advancement.

Adjustment and employment conditions. Because of a scarcity of available openings, a person may be barred from entrance into an occupational field for which he is qualified and for which he may have adequate training. A resulting attitude of discouragement and futility will develop. Moreover, if the individual discovers that placement in the coveted field has been made as a result of political or social favoritism, bitterness and social antagonism may result. Economic need may force the individual into another occupational field, but rarely is he able to bring to the new job the enthusiasm and interest that are conducive to happiness and efficiency. If he is intelligent and emotionally stable, he will endeavor honestly to fulfill his obligations in this job but he also will be on the alert to obtain an opportunity in his chosen field. If the latter is too late in coming, he may have lost his original adequacy for the work by the time he reaches his goal, with the result that neither can he gain from it the satisfaction that he had expected nor can he fulfill his early promise of success in it.

In times of business and industrial depression, workers who have jobs are afraid to lose them. They may tolerate undesirable working conditions because they fear that complaints may jeopardize their position. The fear of being "laid off" may interfere with their efficiency. They are unable to bring to the job success in achievement which would be possible if their work were accompanied by a realization of relative security or of advancement. They may be afraid that any sign of decreased efficiency may place them among the first to be discharged. Hence their efficiency is lessened by the worry that they may not be "kept on." They may believe that discharges are made unfairly and that, if they do not have a "drag" with the administration, they may lose out. This attitude may result either in attempts to gain favor or in an attitude of bitterness toward the organization. On the other hand, if job supply is below job demand, the employed worker may feel that the employer is at his mercy, since workers are hard to obtain. Consequently, he may become overbearing, careless in his work, and make demands upon his employer that may be difficult for the latter to meet.

As the worker grows older, unless his work has been such that skilled workmanship and experience have won for him personal recognition, a fear of the loss of his present employment and of his inability to obtain new employment becomes a menace to job adjustment. Unemployment insurance and old-age pension systems are doing much to relieve workers of this worry.

Effect of wages and hours upon adjustment. If the average worker is underpaid and is forced to work for too long hours, he is a dissatisfied worker. Labor organizations, labor-relations boards, and labor-management committees have striven for and are continuing to fight for better wage adjustment. Employers are recognizing the value of rest and relaxation as stimulators of increased and improved production. The eight-hour (and shorter) working day, the five-day working week, and the two-week or longer vacation are helping the worker gain renewed energy for his work hours. Short rest periods during the day are becoming popular. Yet long periods of leisure between work periods distract from concentrated attention to work and may lead to lax or indifferent work habits. Experiments with desirable work and rest ratios help discover, for the different forms of occupational work, the optimum relationship between work and relaxation.

The value of any form of work as represented by the amount of financial reward attached to it has not yet been determined satisfactorily. Such factors as length and amount of training needed for the work, traditional attitudes toward the form of work and years of service, and the demand for the service have been generally accepted as criteria for wage standards. Much worker dissatisfaction is caused by the belief that discriminations in wage scales are based upon factors that are superficial and unworthy. An individual who recognizes himself as a conscientious, able, and hard worker easily may learn to resent his own relatively small wage as compared with that of other persons who with similar training and work experience, less work effort, and shorter hours, receive much higher wages than he does.

Effects of the physical conditions of the job.   Certain physiological, psychological, and esthetic needs of the worker require attention. Improper lighting, insufficient or badly regulated heating and ventilation, unsanitary lavatory facilities, and/or distracting noise in an office or other work room interfere with a worker's health, contentment, and work efficiency. Modern methods of meeting these needs are providing for the worker comfortable furniture and other work equipment, attractive rest-rooms, libraries, company cafeterias, and other healthful conditions. Attractiveness as well as utility in building construction, decoration, furnishings, and landscaping of the grounds satisfy the worker's inherent love for the beautiful, and do much to encourage in him pride of possession and improvement of morale.

Although individual workers vary in their susceptibility to fatigue and the recognition of their work as monotonous, there are factors in the work itself that may arouse fatigue in the worker or cause the work to become uninteresting. A balanced work-and-rest program can reduce materially the fatigue element of a specific kind of work. An arrangement whereby a worker is permitted, within his abilities and training, to vary his work units from one type of activity to another not only reduces the strain of repeating the same operation to the point of complete boredom, but aids also in encouraging the worker's desire to envision his part in the completed product by allowing him to follow the steps of its production.

Work accidents are caused partly by the individual's own carelessness or lack of knowledge or skill and partly by insufficient or inadequate safety devices. The tired worker, the bored worker, and the sick worker tend to have more accidents than do healthy, alert, and interested workers. Anything, then, that the management can do to preserve the health, interest, and alertness of the worker will tend to reduce the incidence of accident. If machinery and equipment are fitted with the best-known safety devices and if precautions are taken by the management to reduce the exposure of their workers to certain occupational diseases, the confidence with which the worker attacks the job increases. The knowledge that his wellbeing is cared for and that, if an unavoidable accident should occur, he and his family are protected by accident and health insurance, will insure the employee's adjustment and his value to his employer.

Supervision and worker adjustment. Important to a worker are supervisory recognition of his successful achievement, constructive and unemotional treatment of his mistakes, appreciation of the value of his contribution to the progress of the organization, and available opportunities to take part in group conferences dealing with improved techniques. In fact, any evidence on the part of the supervisor or employer of his realization that the worker is a living, thinking, and feeling human being rather than an inanimate machine will call forth from the average worker a spirit of loyalty, cooperation, and unity of purpose.

The human factor cannot be divorced from occupational work. No matter how humble the worker's position is nor how routine his work may be, he still needs to maintain his self-respect in the group. If this is gained as a result of intelligent leadership, other things being equal, an adjusted work life will result. If the leadership takes the form of an attempted domination of an inferior, the worker's struggle to maintain his own self-respect and the respect of his fellow workers will show itself in bitter denunciation, disloyalty, and rebellion, with consequent reduced and inferior production.

Job Relations
A Supervisor Gets Results through People

Foundations for Good Relations

Let each worker know how he is getting along.
    Figure out what you expect of him
    Point out ways to improve.
Give credit when due.
    Look for extra or unusual performance
    Tell him while "it's hot."
Tell people in advance about changes that will affect them.
    Tell them WHY if possible.
    Get them to accept the change.
Make best use of each person's ability.
    Look for ability not now being used.
    Never stand in a man's way.
People Must Be Treated As Individuals.

The unadjusted worker. Some workers who seem unable to adjust to their job can be found in every form of business and industry. Some persons are definitely unemployable because of their personality lacks and unfortunate habits and attitudes. There are others who, although they can obtain employment, appear to lack the stability and perseverance necessary for efficient job continuance. Examples of such persons are known to all of us.

A young man who had found it difficult to follow high-school routine was placed in a routine job. Since he seemed to be a pleasant person he was at first liked by his employer. He soon began to make slight errors, however. When these were brought to his attention, he convinced his employer that if he were given another type of work in the factory, for which he considered himself particularly fitted, there would be no further reason for such errors. This was done, but after a while the same carelessness was evidenced. Because of his likable disposition, his employer was persuaded to try him in still another type of activity; but this young man was unable to continue in any form of work satisfactorily for more than a month or two. He has many good qualities, but his inability to persevere has resulted in constant change of position. He does not recognize this lack in himself and constantly complains about the unfairness of employers. Employment agencies are familiar with the type of worker who seems able to secure a job but unable to hold it.

There are jobs and job conditions that seem to militate against successful achievement on the part of even well-qualified workers. Unhealthful physical environment and unintelligent supervision make it impossible for the average worker long to remain adjusted to his job. Business and industrial research, psychology and mental hygiene, intelligent business and industrial leadership, careful selection of workers, and hygienic working conditions are needed in order to insure desirable job adjustment for American workers.

Guidance and Occupational Adjustment

S C H O O L S and other social agencies are beginning to recognize their function in the preparation of American youth for occupational life. In the schools, especially on the secondary level, attempts are being made to ascertain the individual aptitudes, abilities, and interests of their students. Personality and vocational tests are administered, and a careful study is made of classroom and extra-classroom activities. Further, by means of courses in occupational surveys, reading materials, visits to industry, lectures, and conferences with business and industrial leaders, the schools are acquainting their students with work possibilities. Young people are encouraged to make their vocational choices early enough in high school to insure for themselves adequate and thorough training for their chosen vocation. School systems are enlarging their educational facilities in order to include many of these preparatory training experiences. This is especially true of junior colleges and other post high-school institutions.

When the young people are ready to enter upon their occupational work, school authorities attempt to place their students. This is done either through their own placement departments or in cooperation with local, state, federal, or private employment agencies. Programs of "follow up" of their working graduates or drop outs are then used for the purpose of helping their former students toward better job adjustment. Follow up also can serve the purpose of obtaining data concerning working conditions and requirements that will help school counselors in the guidance of their present students toward occupational adjustment.

A comprehensive program of vocational guidance as outlined above is at present an ideal rather than an actual accomplishment. Few communities or school systems are sufficiently well organized, or have the money, building facilities, or trained corps necessary for the complete achievement of these guidance objectives. In an increasing number of communities good beginnings have been made; a greater interest is being exhibited in this direction in all sections of the country.

Guidance on the job.   Apart from major reforms in such matters as wages, hours, supervision, and general working conditions, individual workers need personal help and guidance toward good personal adjustment. A well-organized business or industrial plant includes a personnel department. To preserve the physical and mental health of individual workers, the services of a physician and a nurse, a psychologist, a psychiatrist, and a psychiatric social worker are provided.

Medical assistance and advice are available for the worker who needs it. One insurance company not only provides a large and competent medical staff for its employees but also maintains a completely equipped sanatorium in a healthful and beautiful country environment. To this rest home, employees are sent for recuperation from illness or for rest, either at a very small expense to the employee or without cost to him.

The psychologist's function is to test an applicant for employment and placement, or an employee for promotion or transfer. In a few companies, it is the policy not to discharge an employee if he fails in one department. With the help of the psychologist, he is transferred to other departments until he finds the one in which he is successful. No employee is discharged unless he has shown inability to succeed in any department.

The psychiatrist deals with the individual peculiarities, grievances, emotional disturbances, and personal problems of the workers. He also recommends hygienic improvements in the organization or in general business policies. He is responsible for the individual adjustment of the workers and for the building up of healthy morale and loyalty to the company.

The work of the psychiatric social worker takes her into the home and social life of the maladjusted worker. She gathers data concerning the out-of-work habits and relationships of the worker, for use by the physician, psychologist, or psychiatrist who may be working with an individual's problem of adjustment. She then co-operates in the carrying out of suggestions for the worker's read-justment. Her help sometimes continues with an individual after he has been discharged from or has left the company.

It is unfortunate that a guidance program of this type is possible for only large business houses or industrial plants. The small employer cannot afford these services for his workers. There is needed a cooperating agency in each community to which these employers may refer their maladjusted workers. A few such experiments have been started.

Another form of guidance needed by the occupational worker is help toward rehabilitation when and if, through illness, business depression, war experience, or any other cause, he loses the opportunity to continue his present work. The federal government has been working on this problem, and some private agencies have been meeting the situation more or less adequately.

Adjustment of the Professional Worker

THE OCCUPATIONAL adjustment of the professional worker differs somewhat from that of other workers. The professions demand from those persons who desire to enter them a general ability level above the average, certain specific aptitudes, long and intense training that usually includes apprenticeship practice during the training. Required also are personal qualities that are basic to the worker's willingness to persevere in his work and to attend punctiliously to details, and ability to work without the direction and supervision of others.

His long and thorough training tends to develop in the professional worker a mastery of, an appreciation of, and an interest in his work that are not found to so great an extent among other workers. The professional worker views his vocation as a life calling and continues to be a student as well as a worker. Most professions demand that those engaging in them recognize the humane and social functions of their work. Hence the public expects the professional worker to give freely of his time, energy, and skill or knowledge, to the improvement of human welfare, with or without financial reward.

The scientist, the artist, the lawyer, the physician, the nurse, the teacher, and the religious or social worker may be so absorbed in their work, they may be so filled with the urge for creation or service, and their work may have become so much a part of their life interest that the financial returns beyond what they need for simple existence are of minor importance to them. Moreover, since their work is their life, they are willing and eager to devote long hours to it.

Instead of working under the supervision of another person, the professional worker is working more or less in cooperation with others of his kind toward the realization of a common goal. The members of a profession usually are bound by a group code of ethics. A well-known example is the ancient Hippocratic oath which still is administered to those persons who are about to enter upon the practice of medicine. A professional code of ethics, combined with a government licensing of some professional workers, has developed among these workers an attitude of personal responsibility for successful achievement that motivates their entire life pattern.

Because of his absorbing interest in his work and the demands made upon his time, the professional worker often finds it difficult to achieve a hygienic balance between his occupational work and his other responsibilities. As a result, he may experience inadequate adjustment in areas of health, of family relations, and of social and leisure-time relationships.

Since the professions still represent an enviable social status, many individuals, unfitted by general ability, specific aptitude, or emotional constitution, desire to enter them. For these persons there are unsatisfying consequences, either in their attempts to prepare for the profession of their choice, or, if they succeed in passing this hurdle, in their later opportunities of successful achievement. For the well-qualified and well-trained professional man or woman a sane program of efficient and self-sacrificing service, combined with relaxing and enjoyable family and social relationships with his peers, offers a full and complete life of self-realization and social value.

The Well-Adjusted Worker

THE WELL-ADJUSTED worker is the man or woman who is healthy; who is engaged in work that he enjoys, for which he has adequate and progressive training, and in which he is able to utilize to its fullest extent whatever capacity he possesses for creative expression. He is receiving a financial reward commensurate with his work, his needs, and his interests. He has sufficient leisure time to devote to relaxing social and avocational activities. He respects, admires, and is loyal to administrators and supervisors who are tolerant of unavoidable failure and generous with deserved approval, concerned with the general and individual welfare of the worker, and actuated by a belief in the value of cooperation on the part of both the employer and employee in the achievement of worthy products or service for social benefit.

A well-adjusted worker is a well-adjusted person in all of his relationships—work, home, and social. He enjoys a pleasant and stimulating home life and relaxing social activities. He is liked and respected in his community and is as actively engaged in civic projects as his leisure time and income permit. The well-adjusted worker is a well-adjusted citizen. In America, in all types of vocational work, there is an encouragingly large number of such workers.

A period of war and its aftermath tend to create certain worker problems of adjustment that are more severe than those that are experienced during peacetime occupational activity. World War II and the Korean episode were no exceptions to this. During the period of world conflict worker shortage was so extreme that labor conditions deviated sharply from their accustomed pattern. Wages rose rapidly. Hygienic hours of work were disregarded almost completely. Competency on the job was not always possible. Laws governing the employment of women and of minors were relaxed. In spite of some minor tragedies in the work world, a stupendous job of production was accomplished with a minimum of friction between management and labor.

The immediate postwar period was accompanied by occupational difficulties. Sudden cessation of war production and consequent labor layoffs, anticipation of reduced earning power, job competition resulting from the return of war veterans, shortage of materials needed for peacetime production, and an increase in cost of living were among the factors that resulted in a topsy-turvy labor situation. At the time of this writing the work situation appears to be in the process of stabilization. Consumer difficulties engendered by high living costs are being ameliorated somewhat by rising wage scales. Although labor still is seeking a more equitable balance between income and outgo, employment is at an all-time high, and labor-management relations are showing an encouraging trend toward effective cooperation.

VOCATIONAL ADJUSTMENT TEST [4]

In the appropriate test below, read each question carefully and encircle the number at the right of the page that most nearly corresponds with your attitudes and behavior.

For Employees:

	No	?	Yes
1. Did you seek vocational guidance before you entered upon your occupational career?	1	2	3
2. Did you, rather than your parents, select your vocation?	1	2	3
3. Do you believe that you are suited for your job?	1	2	3
4. Do you consider your present job to be dignified?	1	2	3
5. Did you prepare for your vocation through part-time work experience while you still were in school?	1	2	3
6. Did you choose your vocation because you like it?	1	2	3
7. Do you have adequate training for your job?	1	2	3
8. Are you well groomed when you apply for a job?	1	2	3
9. Do you dress correctly for your work?	1	2	3
10. Do you fear an interview for a new job?	3	2	1
11. Do you get along well with your coworkers?	1	2	3
12. Can you take criticism from your supervisor?	1	2	3
13. Do you put in an honest day's work?	1	2	3
14. Do you have ample time for recreation?	1	2	3
15. Are your working conditions healthful?	1	2	3

[4] L. D. Crow and A. Crow, *Eighteen to Eighty, Adjustment Problems of Adults,* The Christopher Publishing House, Boston, 1949, pp. 113–14. Copyrighted by the authors and used with their permission.

16. Does your job allow for a vacation of at least two weeks each year? 1 2 3
17. Are you working toward advancement in your organization? 1 2 3
18. Do you tend to brag about your job success? 3 2 1
19. Do you receive proper appreciation for work well done? 1 2 3
20. Do you spend much of your time in faultfinding and bickering? 3 2 1
21. Do you arrive at work on time? 1 2 3
22. Do you respect the opinions of others? 1 2 3
23. Do you talk too much on the job? 3 2 1
24. Do family troubles interfere with your work efficiency? 3 2 1
25. Do you fear your boss? 3 2 1

Total Score.......

If your score exceeds 65 you may consider yourself a well-adjusted and successful worker.

For Employers:

No ? Yes

1. Are you courteous to all applicants for a position in your organization? 1 2 3
2. Do you expect accurate personal data from all applicants? 1 2 3
3. Do you or a qualified executive interview personally all applicants? 1 2 3
4. Do you try to make an applicant feel at ease during an interview? 1 2 3
5. Are you successful in selecting employees who will fit well into your organization? 1 2 3
6. Do you try to maintain friendly but dignified relations with your employees? 1 2 3
7. Are you equally friendly with male and female employees? 1 2 3
8. Are you certain that your younger employees are of legal age for work? 1 2 3
9. Do you encourage friendliness among your employees? 1 2 3
10. Do you expect your employees to be generally well groomed? 1 2 3
11. Do you help your employees to advance on the job? 1 2 3
12. Do your employees fear you as a supervisor? 3 2 1

13. Do you commend the work of your deserving employees?   1   2   3
14. Do you discourage bickering and faultfinding among your employees?   1   2   3
15. Do you expect your employees to arrive at work on time?   1   2   3
16. Do you give deserving employees who wish to leave your organization a favorable recommendation?   1   2   3
17. Do you give consideration to the opinions of your employees?   1   2   3
18. Do you give proper credit to an employee who offers a valuable suggestion?   1   2   3
19. Do you keep working quarters well lighted and well heated?   1   2   3
20. Do you provide sanitary conditions for your employees?   1   2   3
21. Do you allow adequate time for lunch?   1   2   3
22. Do you provide suitable rest periods during the day?   1   2   3
23. Do you allow your employees to engage in a reasonable amount of conversation on the job?   1   2   3
24. Do you provide sufficient and attractive rest and recreational facilities for your employees?   1   2   3
25. Do your employees have a chance to advance in your organization?   1   2   3

Total Score.......

If your score exceeds 65 you may consider yourself to be meeting employer responsibilities successfully.

▶ **Questions and Problems for Discussion**

1. To what extent do you think an employee should shield an incompetent fellow employee? List the factors that may influence the employee's attitude.

2. Should an employee ask for promotion or raise in salary, or should he leave such matters to his employer? Suggest an equitable solution.

3. What should be the attitude of an employee during business hours toward a supervisor who is a personal friend? Suggest difficulties that may arise.

4. What, in your opinion, is a fair distribution of sick leaves?

5. To what extent should a worker offer suggestions to an employer concerning desirable improvements in work methods?

6. Upon what basis should "layoffs" be made?

7. What should be a worker's attitude concerning a fellow worker who is a slacker?

8. How far should the personal initiative of a worker be allowed to function?

9. Should there be any restriction of the voluntary output of a worker? Discuss.

10. What should be the attitude of an experienced worker toward a new employee?

11. Give examples of the influence of home life upon worker efficiency.

12. How should a woman worker respond to advances of a man employer? Of a male fellow worker?

13. What should a worker do if a fellow worker takes credit for the work done by the former?

14. List placement agencies in your community. Evaluate their efficiency.

15. Suggest ways of helping a maladjusted worker.

16. List opportunities in your community for continued study on the job. Illustrate from your own experience or that of other workers the relative efficiency of these agencies.

CHAPTER Fifteen

Using Leisure Time Effectively

A WELL-ADJUSTED man or woman gains satisfaction from participation in a reasonable amount of daily activity that is directed toward the achievement of economic security. The attitude of self-realization resulting from these efforts continues the adjustment process and provides for the individual the motive power to become a better citizen. Interesting as his work may be, however, a normal man or woman does and should desire to engage in activities that are more or less unrelated to his work. Such activities offer opportunities for relaxation, socialization, or participation in avocational, civic, or educational programs and projects. No matter what his age may be, an individual needs to experience a balanced program of work and play.

The Relationship between Work and Play

THE EXTENT to which a specific activity is work or play has been the subject of much discussion. It would seem that in order to differentiate between the two there is required the use of certain criteria such as the *goal* or purpose of the activity, the *attitude* or interest of the person at the moment, and the *individual* himself in relation to the activity.

Work versus play.   When a project is undertaken in order to attain a goal that lies beyond the activity itself or when the attitude is such that the activity is being engaged in for a reason that is external to the doing, the activity falls into the category of *work*. Whether or not monetary compensation is received for the activity is a negligible factor. It is important, however, to know something about the attitude of the person toward the activity. The individual concerned determines what that attitude is. He alone can classify the activity as work or play.

Although it is difficult to formulate an exact definition of play, certain distinctive characteristics can be detected in all activities that are considered to be recreational. The criteria for classifying an activity as play are the same as those for work—the *goal*, the *attitude*, and the *individual*. If the activity is engaged in for the sake of the activity itself and for no other purpose, and if the attitude is one of pleasure that results from a felt interest in the activity at the moment, it can be classified for the individual as *play* or relaxing activity.

In leisure-time activity, relaxation and spontaneous pleasurable expression are the chief concerns of the individual. The relief from muscle and nerve tension derived from such activity results in mental and physical exhilaration. However, if an individual pursues the supposedly recreational activity because of the interest of another person rather than as the result of a genuine interest of his own, the activity which until that time may have been play for him suddenly passes over into the category of work.

Functions of recreational activities.   Since play is one of the most valuable means of relieving muscle and nerve tension, it is a health-preserving activity for the child, the adolescent, and the adult. To be mentally healthy, an individual needs to learn how to relax during his leisure time. Recreational activities also provide an opportunity for social development, since the social drives can be satisfied through these media. The great desire to play brings people together; they create opportunities for play and they organize their life so that they have time and a place for it.

The extended leisure time that is available to most workers

gives them a chance for the relief of tensions connected with their occupational activities. The values gained could be multiplied many times if recreational facilities were made available for individuals within easy reach of their homes. Thereby, they might avoid the exhaustion that accompanies tiring travel after participation in recuperative activities. The automobile affords some relief to the city worker; but holiday jams on the highways introduce annoying factors that offset the health values of wholesome recreational activity.

The Provision of Recreational Facilities

RECREATIONAL activities may be organized or unorganized. Such leisure-time activities as listening to radio or phonograph recordings, watching television or motion-picture programs, or singing around the piano in the home; gathering with friends in a game room or in the back yard; gardening; fishing; meeting associates at soda fountains; reading light fiction or popular magazines; window shopping (especially in small towns on Saturday night); tinkering around the home, and short automobile trips are common experiences in the lives of most Americans. These forms of recreation are relatively unorganized and are engaged in more or less at will, usually with little preparatory planning.

Other forms of recreation are more highly organized and require the cooperation of outside agencies. Among such leisure-time activities can be included long automobile trips; airplane flights; musical and dramatic presentations, or lectures; participation in organized games or attendance at them; skating, skiing, boating, and similar activities.

Recreational agencies. These agencies may be either publicly organized and controlled or commercial enterprises. Most communities realize that some of the commercial agencies are socially undesirable. They represent unhygienic physical conditions or unhealthful media of influence. Consequently, there appears to be a concerted drive on the part of community leaders throughout the country not only to provide recreational facilities for their people but also to improve and regulate commercially run projects.

In many cities and towns schools and other public buildings are thrown open to the public for recreational activities that are suitable for all ages and both sexes. Public lectures, musical programs, motion pictures, plays, and other forms of entertainment are presented in the auditorium. Physical activities, such as basketball, indoor baseball, handball, softball, table tennis, bowling, and dancing are made available in the gymnasium. Individual rooms are given over to small discussion groups; clubs, and chess, checkers, and card games. For outdoor recreation playgrounds, beaches, recreation parks, golf courses, and baseball diamonds are provided.

Semi-private and philanthropic organizations—national, state, and local—have devised well-organized programs of leisure-time activities. The "Y's," the Knights of Columbus, settlement houses, and various socio-civic organizations, such as Rotary, Kiwanis, and Lions clubs as well as community women's clubs, share in this activity.

Many business organizations are providing recreational opportunities for their employees. Religious and other community organizations now offer to teen-agers and to adults of any age many opportunities for participation in interesting activities. No one needs to be without a means of filling his leisure hours.

Publicly supported or semi-private projects are limited, however, by the great financial cost of construction and maintenance, and by the lack of space for adequate facilities. In large cities it often is difficult to find space for recreation in overcrowded areas where the need for it is greatest. Traveling to those areas where space is available may be a long and tiring journey which reduces the benefits that may have been gained from participation in recreational activities. Crowded streetcars, buses, and subways on Sunday nights cause one to question the value of the activity which takes people so far from home and which returns them to their home hot, tired, and generally disgruntled.

If commercially controlled facilities for recreation are organized and regulated by civic-minded owners they can supplement the work done by public agents. Annual flower shows of community botanical gardens may be supplemented by private showings. Musical organizations and choral societies offer fine entertainment at reasonable price. Youth hostels; organized tours by bus, plane, or train; many excellently run summer camps; swimming pools; golf courses, and tennis courts are some of the recreational facilities that are available in most communities for the average citizen.

In many communities there are certain commercial agencies that are unwholesome. Among these are cellar clubs, some night clubs, poolrooms, gambling establishments, race tracks, unrealistic motion-picture programs, overexciting radio or television programs, trashy or sensational magazines and books, and inartistic comic strips. Even though such media of entertainment may not be definitely harmful to the physical and mental health of those who "enjoy" them, they have little value as adequate and healthful relaxers.

Many communities have attempted legal restrictions of socially disapproved recreation and have appointed officials to carry out their regulations. This is a difficult task. There are people who appear to believe that any regulation or supervision of their leisure-time activities limits their enjoyment. Commercial interests cater to the tastes of their patrons and offer them what they seem to want. Perhaps regulated recreational facilities offer their patrons what the leaders *think* the people should want. Besides regulation and supervision of recreation there is also needed an education of the tastes of the users of such agencies.

Educational Opportunities for Adults

AN INCREASING number of men and women recognize the value of continuing their education beyond the period of their formal school training. As a result of the desire of adults to devote some part of their leisure time to organized study, many types of educational programs are being made available for their use.

Although there has been a steady growth of adult education, the past twenty-five years have given a decided impetus to its advancement. Today all forms of social and civic organizations and institutions include in their programs certain educational facilities for their members.

Types of adult education. Religious organizations have widened their function to include not only religious education but also parent education, health education, forum discussions of public questions, dramatics, training classes for volunteer leaders, radio sermons, and similar projects. Religious organizations for young people, such as the Christian Endeavor Society and the Jewish Centers, combine social activities with educational programs. This work is encouraged and extended by organizations such as the International Council of Religious Education, the Federal Council of Churches, the National Conference of Christians and Jews, and the National Catholic Welfare Council.

The United Parents' Association sponsors a comprehensive program of parent education. Men's and women's clubs are not limited in their activities to purely social purposes, but have developed programs of general culture, civic, and practical home education. Universities have established centers to meet the educational needs of persons far removed from the university campus. Correspondence courses sponsored by reliable (and sometimes unreliable) organizations are becoming increasingly popular.

Professional, business, and industrial associations and organizations offer advanced training to their workers. These projects are additions to general and specialized, publicly supported, and privately endowed schools and classes for further education. They are developing a citizenry, the members of which devote their days to gainful occupation and their evenings to further self-improvement.

General cultural education is provided for the masses of the population by programs conducted in libraries, museums, and art galleries; by national parks, public exhibits, expositions, planned tours, and by organizations similar to the School for Social Research in New York City and the Denver Opportunity School. There is no lack of cultural and educational opportunities for all people.

Education for civic and political responsibility is fostered by such organizations throughout the country as non-partisan groups, women's political groups, and conferences for first voters. Radio forums and round-table discussions are becoming increasingly popular as means of developing an attitude of awareness concerning social and civic institutions and problems. The various occupational groups, as a part of their educational program, are encouraging periodic conventions, conferences, and general meetings, in order to give their members an opportunity to pool experiences and to become acquainted with the current trends and practices of their respective types of work.

Millions of dollars are spent annually by public and private organizations for the education of the American adult population. Who can say what the ultimate benefits may be? A democratically run government cannot succeed unless all of its citizens are alert and intelligent concerning their social institutions, and are developing themselves to the limit of their potentialities. Adjustment implies knowledge and wise use of this knowledge. Any money spent for the achievement of these objectives and any time devoted to it can be repaid many times in terms of the intelligent and constructive behavior of the people who participate in such programs.

Indirect and subtle factors of education. An individual constantly is surrounded by forces that consciously or unconsciously affect him for good or ill. Public opinion shapes the pattern of indirect education and is molded by the varying forces for which it is responsible. The public demands certain types of stimulation. It is only through the more direct influence of educational leadership that any pronounced change can be effected. This general situation applies to the educational influence of newspapers, magazines, radio programs, dramatic productions, and motion pictures.

The newspaper is one of the most powerful organs of informal education. The educational value of this medium of education depends upon the leadership potentialities of any particular newspaper and the type of readers for which it is intended. A well-organized, fact-respecting, and liberal but honest newspaper can wield a tremendous educational power. News items; advertising material; editorials; special features; book, musical, and dramatic reviews; the woman's page, and sport and financial sections offer daily opportunities for up-to-the-minute education. Moreover, if the newspaper is well written, readers receive daily experience in the correct use of the English language.

The influence of the radio is similar to that of the newspaper. Radio programs originally were intended to be a source of entertainment. Although much of radio time still is devoted to entertainment and advertising, there is a growing utilization of the radio as an instrument of directed education.

Interested groups are aware of the influencing power of radio and television. They vie with one another in offering stimulating and worth-while programs. Safety, health, history, cooking, buying and general household information, political and social world issues, fine musical and dramatic programs, and town meetings of the air find their place on most radio and television schedules.

Another powerful agency of education is the motion picture. Its influence reaches all ages and all classes of people. Since "screen" life is a relatively inexpensive means of escape from unsatisfying reality, habitual motion-picture "fans" tend to be persons who have failed to make completely satisfying life adjustments. The busy, well-adjusted individual probably devotes relatively little of his time to attendance at motion pictures. Hence he is likely to choose his pictures carefully so that he is assured of experiencing only the best in the way of motion-picture entertainment. To the extent that the directors or producers of motion pictures aim to present pictures that represent basically sound scripts and that are technically artistic, attendance at motion-picture programs can be educationally valuable.

Value of Leisure-Time Programs

N O T only does an individual plan for his working day and the work that he expects to do, but he also attempts to allot time for adequate periods for recreation. His program varies with the type of work in which the individual is engaged, the neighborhood in which he lives, his age, and his physical vigor. Recreational activities cannot be left to chance; they represent the outcomes of careful planning and supervision for adults as well as for young people.

Need for recreational activities. No matter how much a person enjoys his regular work he needs an occasional period of relief from it. The arranging of a daily or a weekly program in such way that it will present a healthful balance between productive work and relaxing, interesting social activity, is an art. Not all people can achieve this balance. Too many of us either allow our social interests to interfere with our work life or carry into our supposedly leisure time too much worry about our responsibilities and duties.

The problem of the average adult is not that of finding ways in which to have fun or places to which to go. Rather does an individual's difficulty arise in his inability to choose wisely among the many opportunities that are available. He may wonder how much time he should devote to these activities, or whether he can attract to himself the kind of people with whom he would like to participate in social activities. He may be in doubt as to the amount of time that he should give to one rather than to another kind of recreational interest. He may feel a lack of knowledge concerning the recreational opportunities that are available in his community, his participation in which would be welcomed by the group, and which he could afford.

Recreational programs receive attention when consideration is given to the solution of the delinquency problem. While recreation can be no cure-all for juvenile delinquency it can contribute to both prevention and treatment. In his discussion concerning "The Community and the Delinquents," Kvaraceus outlines ways in which communities fall short in establishing programs for the benefit of youth during their leisure hours. He suggests:

> There are a number of ways in which personal and community recreation programs fall far short of attaining the full benefits that can come from the worthy use of leisure time.
>
> 1. Many, if not most, recreational activities tend in the direction of monied activity. Unless the child has a quarter in his pocket with which to buy a comic book, attend a movie, or pay his dues to a club (for which his parents have already bought a uniform and a camping kit), he is likely to remain idle. In spite of the fact that much money is poured down the recreational funnel by the average family, an adequate base for financing community recreation has not yet been worked out; nor has the public fully accepted the idea of community responsibility for financial support in this area.
>
> 2. Recreation tends toward spectator and passive activity for many youths.
>
> 3. If the child takes part in a recreational program, this usually means that he is engaged in some sports program that calls for a specialized skill possessed by only a few children.
>
> 4. The heavy dependence upon sports as the core recreational activity in many communities leaves seasonal gaps when little or nothing is offered.
>
> 5. There is much duplication in membership and participation by a few children, with complete neglect of a

large portion of the community's youth. Frequently it is the latter group that is in the greatest need of recreational services.

6. Family recreation is either sporadic or nonexistent.

7. Children and youth are ordinarily given very little real opportunity to participate in the planning or the conduct of their leisure-time activities.

8. Leadership in planning and carrying out public and private recreational programs is largely on an amateur basis.

9. There is exploitation of children and youths in those recreational activities that are chiefly useful to tickle the vanities of fond fathers and mothers.

10. The emphasis in the community's recreational program is too frequently skewed in the direction of boy activities, leaving little opportunity for girl participation.

11. Despite the fact that nearly every educational policies commission set up in recent years has emphasized the "worthy use of leisure time" as one of the major objectives of the schools' program, the systematic development of recreational skills and attitudes has received scant attention in the classroom, gymnasium, or on the playground.

12. There is little or no attempt at evaluation of the recreation program, either within specific organizations or on a community-wide basis.

These are the twelve cardinal defects that must be overcome if the community recreational program is to serve the needs of all boys and girls and thus function as a preventive of delinquency.[1]

Time to be devoted to purely social activity.   Industry, business, and organized professions recognize the fact that men and women need time off for relaxation. Yearly vacations are granted by most occupational organizations that range in length from two weeks to several months. The five-day working week and shorter daily working hours are becoming increasingly popular. Although

[1] W. C. Kvaraceus, *The Community and the Delinquent* (Yonkers-on-Hudson: World Book Company, 1954), pp. 320-21.

during a period of occupational emergency workers may be encouraged to extend their periods of work, most organizations disapprove of their workers' holding dual jobs or of devoting an undue amount of time to purely work activities.

The utilization of mechanical aids in industry, business, and the home is doing much to lighten the burden of production as well as of housekeeping. The American people are enjoying an amount of leisure time that was undreamed of by their forefathers. At the same time, one often hears comments to the effect that we have lost some of the genial friendliness and participation in gracious social living that were characteristic of the past. There may be some truth in this statement. We often waste much of our increased leisure in aimless bustling around and concern with trifling bits of "busyness."

If a person is sincerely interested in meeting his work responsibilities adequately, he needs sufficient sleep so that he goes to his work the next day refreshed and clearheaded. For the person whose associates live nearby, an informal get-together, a few rubbers of bridge, an evening of canasta, or a few hours of participation in community projects can be a form of relaxation that is engaged in several evenings during the week. Any of these activities benefit rather than harm the individual.

The city dweller may be forced to spend two or three hours in travel if he wishes to engage in social activities at the homes of his special friends. As a result, an evening of social activity may mean that the person does not retire until the wee hours of the morning. Hence he is too tired to do a good day's work. For the city man and woman, social activities usually need to be crowded into week ends, holidays, and vacations. Even then they cannot be too strenuous if they are to be of value to a person. Too often a man or woman who has returned from a vacation needs to rest before he starts to work again.

Recreational activities as life interests. Among recreational interests that are common to all ages are: reading good books; participating in religious and community projects such as leadership in children's and young people's groups, and cooperation in worthwhile "special projects"; attending musical and dramatic performances and motion pictures; engaging with one's friends in indoor games such as table tennis, card games, musical programs on the part of those who can play a musical instrument for the fun of it, or just interesting conversation, or engaging in out-of-doors sports such as golf, swimming or boating, and attending professional sports of various types.

There are many recreational activities which a person can begin during his youth and enjoy throughout his life. The difficulties often arise during the middle years. During this period a man or woman may become so engrossed with his business or home responsibilities and duties that he neglects to continue the recreational activities of his earlier years. He gradually drops out of the groups which at one time meant so much to him. As the members of such groups become scattered, he often is too busy to make new friends or to find new activities that are purely social. Everything he does must have a purpose. He often meets and works with others in commendable projects of one kind or another, but he seldom develops intimate friendships. He acquires a host of acquaintances but gains few friends. He is likely to lose most of those with whom he had been accustomed to engage in social activities unless he spends much of his leisure time with them.

Value of becoming a sports fan.   It is better to be an active participant in sports than it is to sit on the bench and cheer the team. Attendance at a big-league or intercollegiate game does have health and social value, however. To watch an outdoor game is to benefit by breathing fresh air. To join a large group of persons in the fun of cheering or "booing" a player, an umpire, or a manager gives one a feeling of belonging. Sometimes a widespread interest in a particular group of players may do much to develop community feeling and cooperation.

Loyalties developed along these lines are good if they are not carried too far. For a game to upset the routines of a large number of persons—especially children—is not good training in emotional control. Moderation in an individual's interests in sports as well as in all his life interests is necessary, if attendance at games is to relax rather than to excite the individual.

Value of membership in a club.   There is probably no more pathetic individual than the perennial "joiner"—the man or woman who becomes a member of every new club in his community and a follower of every cult. This person's difficulty is either that he has not enough constructive work activity to keep him busy, or that his own personality characteristics are such that he cannot achieve security in any one group. A man (or a woman) who attempts to affiliate himself with too many social or community groups usually does not remain long in any of them. Like the butterfly, he flits from one to another trying to extract from each something that is satisfying. Usually he is disappointed.

The extreme opposite of the joiner is the individual who refuses to become a member of any organized group. He believes that he has more important things to do. He is likely to assert that all the club wants is a large membership so that a few can benefit from the collected dues. He also may claim that the supposed purposes of an organization do not always present accurately the actual function of the group which may be participating in activities other than those for which it is organized.

Much can be gained by a person of any age from membership in a few well-organized groups, the members of which are bound together by similar and worth-while interests. A group of this kind can become a powerful influence in a community. Furthermore, the individual members experience desirable privileges and responsibilities that are important in any form of group living. A cooperative member of a good club usually can be counted on to be a good citizen.

Every young person can aim to affiliate himself with a club that has a good reputation in the community. It may be a religious, business, political, community, or purely social organization. The individual is given an opportunity to become acquainted with others of his kind. Many men and women maintain their membership throughout their lifetime in an organization of which they had become active members during their adolescence or early adulthood. Also, the attaining of a position of leadership in a club may prepare a person for leadership in other areas—business or industry, community or national.

Unfortunately, there are undesirable clubs that have been organized by groups of malcontents or of inhibited young people. Hence, before a person joins a club, it is his duty to evaluate the ideals of the group and his own ability to make a worth-while contribution to its activities. If the general conduct of club projects appears to be nonconstructive, membership in the group can be avoided and another group sought that is more promising of desirable activities.

Effect of leisure upon the individual.   Available leisure time which is coordinated with successful and pleasant work-filled time does not present serious problems. However, if leisure time results from unemployment in gainful or in satisfying work, the adjustments needed are significant. If during his leisure time the individual is unable to look forward to the challenge of a period of work, leisure time no longer is a period of relaxation but becomes an avenue to boredom and discontent.

The individual who is financially able to refrain from gainful work activity must plan to fill his leisure time with activities that will take on a similitude of work. Welfare or church work, participation in civic projects, playing with inventions, collecting, a planned course in reading, or a program of study in terms of the individual's interest are needed if the individual is to be happy and contented in his extended leisure. For the unemployed individual who needs to work for a living, enforced leisure, instead of being devoted to idle activities or to the nursing of real or imagined worries, might include a program aimed at the improvement of the individual's fitness for work, and directed toward further study and preparation for occupational placement.

Personality development through leisure-time activities.   The play of the growing child contributes fundamentally to his physical, mental, and social development. The child can be given the kind of toys that stimulate him and give him a chance for physical and mental activity through their operation and manipulation. Not only his playthings but also the types of games in which he engages and the character of his associates are important.

As an individual grows older, an interest outside his work has hygienic value. To be willing to follow this interest in the form of a hobby requires persistence and personal denials, and is a character builder. A hobby may become so absorbing an interest, however, that the individual is forced either to give up his hobby or to leave his present occupational work. Thus an avocational interest may develop into a vocational pursuit and bring financial gain to the person engaging in it. If this hobby becomes too engrossing, the individual may need to turn to other play activities in order to maintain hygienic balance.

Leisure is used to maintain personal integrity. The individual's leisure-time reading and study activities; his attendance at motion-picture houses, theaters, lectures, museums, dances, musical programs; his participation in formal or informal social gatherings, physical sports, or civic projects, and all other activities in which he engages for recreational purposes, not only reflect his personal attitudes but also affect them.

As the individual's recreational activities may be affected by economic or social changes, so is his personality influenced by his changed leisure-time activities. Play is a normal human activity. Healthy individuals are active either mentally or physically during all their waking hours. Therefore, desirable opportunities and equipment for socially approved recreational activities ought to be made available for everyone. Social and individual benefits accrue to the community that is foresighted enough to provide interesting and worth-while recreational opportunities for persons of all ages.

▶ Questions and Problems for Discussion

1. Make a survey of your local community in order to determine the space facilities and opportunities available for recreation.
2. What are some of the values to be derived from play?
3. Discuss the socializing influence of clubs and other forms of group activity.
4. How do you spend your leisure time?
5. Evaluate the play program that is found in the elementary school, the high school, and the college.
6. Describe the mental-health values of work.
7. What is the relationship between world peace and satisfied workers?
8. Plan a sound program of leisure-time activities.
9. What are the problems that result from extended leisure time?
10. Indicate specific ways in which the *play attitude* can be introduced into or connected with your vocational activity.
11. What is the significance of play in personality development?
12. Name some of the therapeutic values of work.
13. Outline your play and work program for the next month.
14. Name your favorite outdoor sport; your favorite indoor game. Give reasons for the selections.

15. What is your favorite recreational activity? To what extent do you participate in it?

16. To what extent should education on the adult level become a public responsibility?

17. Discuss the educational values of newspapers, and of radio, television, and motion-picture programs.

CHAPTER Sixteen

Toward Better Personal-Social Adjustment

PROFESSIONAL as well as thoughtful lay persons are devoting considerable attention to the problems of human adjustment. Popular interest has been awakened concerning the connotation of the term; the possible bases of "good" adjustment, and of inadequate adjustment or maladjustment; the ways in which positive adjustment can be preserved, inadequate adjustment prevented, and maladjustment cured. Most writers and discussants tend to differentiate between personal adjustment and social adjustment, however.

This dichotomy probably can be explained in terms of differing emphases. The psychologist is interested primarily in personal adjustment; the sociologist stresses the societal aspect of adjustment. Actually, individual development and adjustment take place in a social frame of reference. Societal adjustment reflects the impact upon group attitude and activity of the adjustment status of the individuals that comprise a society. Hence any distinction between the two is largely academic rather than real.

In our discussion of the basic factors that underlie adjustment in various life areas we have attempted to direct the reader's attention to the significance, in the life of an individual or of a group, of interpersonal and intersocial relationships as these relationships are affected by psychological and cultural factors. In this chapter are considered some of the values that are inherent in culturally positive adjustment, the significance of basic human needs and wants, and a consideration of the various aspects of personal-social adjustment status.

Effects of Relative Values

A s applied to personal and social adjustment, the terms poor, inadequate, adequate, good, and better may seem to have relative rather than absolute meaning. Adjustment is adequate or inadequate for what? Improved adjustment is better than what? Implicit in any attempt to evaluate personal or group attitudes, behavior, conditions, or situations is an agreement concerning the ideal standard to be used as a basis of comparison.

Significance of accepted ideals. From a study of personal and cultural development from prehistoric times to the present, it can be recognized that individual and societal conduct motivators have undergone many changes. As you know, the modern psychologist and social scientist are concerned primarily with cause-and-effect relationships. When we speak of personal and social values we are applying to scientific findings the ethical ideals or success-achieving standards that are peculiar to a specific cultural group's traditional background and that may differ from culture to culture and from generation to generation.

An individual's evaluation of material objects and conditions usually is understood and accepted. It is recognized that one is expressing his likes and dislikes or the satisfaction of his needs when he says that his watch has been adjusted, the soup is tasty, his suit fits him, the cards dealt him in a card game are fine, or this year's crop of wheat is good. It is much more difficult to reach general agreement concerning what is meant by a "good" person, a "good" society, a "good" life, or "good" personal or social adjustment.

The interpretation given to the term "good" or "adjusted" as applied to individual or group behavior is determined by the relation of that behavior to existing situational ideals, standards, or needs. There usually is a "best" thief in a gang of thieves; among the pariahs of India probably could be found one individual who was the best adjusted member of his low-caste group, regardless of whether his caste were considered to constitute a good society in comparison with other societies and different standards of adjustment.

Interdependence of values. Personal and social values are not mutually independent. Since society represents an interacting group of individuals, *"values are relative to the nature of man as this nature is revealed in social action."* [1] Through the ages the display of certain personal characteristics has been recognized as contributing to the well-being of society. These personal qualities include honesty, honor, integrity, sincerity, fidelity, self-control, and concern for the welfare of others. To the extent that the individual members of a group give evidence of the possession of these qualities in their group interactions, they constitute good or well-adjusted members of a good society. However, the form in which these characteristics show themselves varies with the needs, customs, and structure of the particular society in which they function.

If a society establishes certain society-benefiting criteria by which individual attitudes and behavior are evaluated, a member of the group who deviates in any way from society-accepted standards thereby gains social disapproval. Group rejection may intensify the already deviated behavior; adjustment to the requirements of group life is inadequate. If the individual remains in the group, he may become badly maladjusted. Removal to a societal situation in which evaluating criteria are less rigid and in which greater permissiveness of self-ordering behavior is customary may result in the former deviate's acceptance as a well-adjusted member of the new group.

If the existing status of a society is regarded as representative of the inevitable effects upon it of certain non-controllable factors of influence, it cannot be evaluated as *good* or *bad*. From the point of view of the extent to which and the ways in which a society meets the fundamental needs of its members, it can be evaluated in comparison with other societies as relatively good or bad. According to Dewey and Humber:

[1] R. Dewey, and W. J. Humber, *The Development of Human Behavior* (New York: The Macmillan Company, 1951), p. 714. Used with the permission of The Macmillan Company.

The good society is one in which the basic biogenic and sociogenic needs of man are fulfilled. Even though in extreme instances of deprivation, such biogenic impulses as hunger and thirst usually assume priority over others, in the good society all of the needs must be satisfied in a balanced fashion. Provision for one in excess will not satisfy the others. Because of man's extremely modifiable nature, there are many combinations of culture patterns which are equally good or bad. It is perhaps this fact that gave rise to the belief that *any* society is a good society, that there is no basis of objective judgment of man's behavior or his works. However, man's nature sets limits to the variation which societies can exhibit and still qualify as "good societies." [2]

The Significance of Basic Human Needs

A L L living organisms exhibit characteristic behavior responses to changes in their environment. Certain fundamental responses are made for the satisfaction of organic needs. In the simple organism, changes in response follow a simple pattern, are more or less automatic, and are directed toward immediate satisfaction of wants and toward protection from danger. The farther up in the animal scale the organism finds its place, the more complex become felt needs.

The human being finds that his wants and interests extend beyond the fulfillment of his organic needs. He needs to adapt himself to his environment and to adjust the environment to his interests. He faces the serious problem of adapting to the presence, behavior, and interests of his associates. He develops positive behavior traits and, at the same time, changes any ineffective behavior patterns that he already has developed.

Fundamental life needs. For an individual, a generation, or a series of generations, the basis of good adjustment is considered to be the fulfillment of inherent needs and wants that include many interests and activity areas. In a good society, every individual is afforded an opportunity to satisfy those fundamental desires that, as listed by Thorndike, include:

[2] Ibid., p. 729.

1. Maintenance of the inner causes of the joy of living at or above their present average.
2. Food when hungry, and drink when thirsty.
3. A diet that is physiologically adequate.
4. Protection against pain-causing animals.
5. Protection against disease-causing organisms, poisons, and other causes of disease.
6. Protection or insurance against accidents and disasters, such as floods, earthquakes, wars, for which the person is not responsible.
7. Protection against extreme shocks, fear, and strains.
8. Some room or place where he can rest undisturbed, protected from the elements and from bad or uncongenial men.
9. Enjoyable bodily activity, especially when young.
10. Enjoyable mental activity, including aesthetic pleasures.
11. Opportunity for human society.
12. Opportunity for courtship, love, and life with one's mate.
13. Opportunity to care for children and to be kind to human beings and animals.
14. The approval of one's community, or at least the absence of scorn or contempt.
15. The approval of one's self, self-respect, the absence of shame and remorse.
16. Opportunity to have friends and affection, if deserving of them.
17. Opportunity to be a friend and give affection.
18a. Opportunity to exercise power over some person, animals, things, or ideas, making them do one's will.
18b. Opportunity to serve a worthy master.
19. Membership in organized groups, and the right to participate in activities or ceremonies which are (or at least are thought to be) important.
20. Opportunity to compete with one's peers, winning in about 50 per cent of the trials.
21. Opportunity to compete with one's own past record,

and, if deserving, to have the pleasures of achievement and success.

22. Occasional opportunities for adventure, risk, and
danger.

23. Something to be angry at and attack.

24. Protection by society (via customs, laws, and government) in what is regarded by the existing moral
code as a good life.

25. Freedom to discover and publish verifiable truth.

26. Enjoyment of the happiness of others.[3]

Thorndike's listed urges touch every phase of human interest
and activity. They include the physical and psychological satisfactions that represent the bases of human strivings toward life
adjustment. Individuals differ in their felt need to satisfy a particular urge; it probably would be difficult for any individual to
fulfill all of his felt needs, without the help of others. When personal and social values are in accord, society can help each individual achieve positive and wholesome satisfaction of his basic
physical and psychological needs, wants, and interests. In so far as
each member of society is impelled to satisfy his desires, through
socially accepted behavior, he becomes a well-adjusted, "good"
citizen of a "good" society.

Aspects of Personal-Social Adjustment

THROUGHOUT the discussion we have stressed the interrelations that exist between an individual and the group or groups
of which he is a member. At each age level he brings to his societal
relationships whatever personal qualities he has developed as the
result of the influence upon his inherited potentialities of his experiences in previous group situations. Every boy and man, and
every girl and woman reflect in their personal and social reactions
the effect upon them of parental strengths and weaknesses, and of
parental and marital home, educational, occupational, and recrea-

[3] E. L. Thorndike, *Human Nature and the Social Order* (New York: The
Macmillan Company, 1940), pp. 404-5. Used with the permission of Robert Thorndike.

tional influences. At the same time, the individual himself, through his displayed attitudes and his behavior, exercises a more or less potent influence upon his physical and social environment. Hence personal-social adjustment represents a continuous two-way process.

The continuity of the adjustment process.   Adjustments vary with people and situations. They are influenced by the number and quality of environmental stimuli. Some persons adjust easily and successfully; others are motivated toward behavior which hinders their subsequent efforts at adaptation. Each new environment presents many adjustment problems. Variation to be found among people in meeting new situations is not a mere matter of chance. An individual constantly is acquiring new behavior patterns and attitudes; his adjustments are based upon specific and definite factors within and outside his own developing personality. This is true whether the adjustments are satisfying, or whether individual or social problems arise.

The strains and stresses of modern life are making it increasingly difficult for the average individual to maintain a consistently stable attitude of acceptance. Many persons who experience conflicts and difficulties, however, are able to meet such disturbances by changing their customary activities, their habitual attitudes, or their former points of view. They are flexible; they can adapt themselves to changing conditions and still maintain their self-esteem and the respect of their associates.

The maintenance of good physical health is dependent upon the exercise of sound principles of physical hygiene. The application of the principles of mental hygiene can help in the preservation of good mental health. One visit to a physician or one month of watching one's diet cannot insure continued good health; neither can a quickly broken resolution to "mend one's ways" bring about permanent control of behavior. Healthful results can be achieved only through continued adherence to the principles of physical and mental hygiene.

The mental-hygiene approach.   The achieving of emotional stability may be a slow process, especially if in the physical and social environment one is exposed to many conflict-arousing situations. Serious problems of personal-social adjustment have been experienced by people during every stage of civilization; they are not the concomitants only of our modern fast pace of living and confused state of world affairs. Approaches to attempted solution of problem situations vary, however.

To prevent physical or mental illness, primitive peoples employed magic; later, superstitions exercised a strong influence upon individual and group behavior. Today, emphasis is placed upon scientific methods of research and the development of various theories of cause-effect relationships. The history of the mental-hygiene movement exemplifies twentieth-century interest in mental and emotional health. Increased understanding of the causes of mental and emotional breakdown has resulted in the development of functional approaches toward the maintenance of sound mental health.

A significant factor in homeostasis or organic equilibrium that is associated with an individual's personal and social adjustment is his appreciation of those values that seem to him to be most worthwhile. These values are the resultants of his learning experiences; they set the goals toward which he strives in every area of his life adjustment.

An individual's developing values affect his childhood relationships with his parents, other relatives, peer associates, teachers, and other adults. During later adolescence and adulthood, his established set of values influences his attitudes and behavior in his various situational relationships, such as courtship, marriage, family rearing, occupational activities, leisure-time and recreational pursuits. At any period of his existence a person's philosophy of life constitutes the interplay of his developing set of values and his relational experiences.

To be emotionally secure, a human being needs to experience self-esteem and self-confidence. It is unlikely that he never will encounter self-reproaching and self-defensive conditions or experiences. If his attitudes in situations provocative of the loss of self-esteem is directed by positive life values, however, he is enabled to meet his problem with an insightful understanding of the basic causes of the problem. Either unaided or with the help of others, he can solve his problem and regain confidence in himself and the power to avoid or to adjust satisfactorily to similar situations.

In an earlier chapter we referred to the value of parents' encouraging a child to engage in simple decision making. The child or adolescent who is given appropriate opportunity to manage his own affairs thereby is being prepared to accept and to meet adult responsibilities. Modern educational philosophy emphasizes the importance of this phase of school training. The function of guidance and counseling services is placing increasing stress upon helping young people help themselves. The development of emotional maturity is closely related to the achievement of self-direction.

The emotionally insecure or immature person lacks self-confidence; he is suggestible, and is prone to follow the dictates or advice of others rather than to make his own decisions. His submission to the wishes or demands of others is both a symptom of existing instability and a stimulator of frustration arousal. He resents that to which he submits as well as his own submissiveness. He may become completely helpless in situations that call for immediate action; his opinions concerning and evaluations of conditions and situations are not his own but mirror the expressed attitudes of other persons. Some immature individuals seem able to continue to perform on a low plane of personal endeavor, overshadowed by their more confident associates. Their inner dissatisfactions come to the surface, however, in self-defensive querulousness, bickering, faultfinding, and expressions of self-pity or self-abnegation. Other insecure and submissive individuals retreat from their experienced anxieties and feelings of incompetence into a dream world of which they are the powerful and aggressive leaders.

The emotionally mature, self-directing individual is able to cope with difficult situations and annoying conditions. He is not fearful for himself or afraid of others. His judgments or decisions may not always be valid but he is able and willing to admit his inadequacy and to learn from his mistakes. He is able to solve his own problem conflicts. In a crisis situation, he exhibits self-control; he becomes a source of strength for the less mature members of the group; if necessary, he takes leadership responsibility.

The mature, self-directing person commands the respect and admiration of his associates. To the extent that he is outgoing and interested in the welfare and activities of other people, he is tolerant in his attitude toward them; he attempts to understand and accept them, even though he may disapprove some of their actions or attitudes. In return, his associates are likely to display a similar willingness to overlook his mistakes; he appreciates their faith in him, without displaying attitudes of exaggerated self-importance. Concerning the emotionally well-organized person, Lindgren says:

> Because the mature person is aware of his own pattern of motivation and has insight into the motives of others, he is less anxious about what others might do to him. He does not see the acts of others as threats, unless he has some realistic reason to do so. If something makes him angry or afraid, he accepts his fear or his anger as a reasonable thing. The mature person assumes that it is legitimate to express feelings and that they should be expressed in a manner as socially acceptable as possible, out of respect for the feelings of others. Sometimes this means sublimation into some form of symbolic behavior; sometimes it means commenting humorously on one's irritation; and sometimes it means standing up for one's rights frankly and honestly. At the same time the mature person also realizes that strong emotions may be aroused not so much by what others may be doing to him as by his own more or less neurotic needs, for no person is so mature as to be entirely free from immature lapses." [4]

It is not an easy task to determine and to aid an individual to develop all of the subtle qualities that comprise mental and emotional good health. The criteria of personal and social acceptance are rooted in personal inheritance and cultural background. Emotional immaturity and inadequate asocial adjustment may incite the committing of major asocial behavior such as overaggression or boorishness, violation of community-enacted rules and regulations, felony, delinquent acts, and crime. The mentally and emotionally inadequate person may disregard ethical codes and moral standards; he may sin and experience consequent guilt feelings. Any departure from group accepted standards of good behavior affects adversely the attitude of the group toward the offender and may result in his being penalized by the group.

An individual usually is made aware of his major areas of asocial activity. He may offend the group in minor matters, and

[4] H. C. Lindgren, *Psychology of Personal and Social Adjustment* (New York: American Book Company, 1953), p. 463.

thereby earn social disapproval. He may recognize the fact that he is not accepted, but he is unaware of the underlying reason for this non-acceptance. For example, there is a tendency among some moderns to ridicule an Emily Post emphasis upon correct etiquette. Yet, certain deviations from what is considered by most people to be good social usage may be extremely offensive to the majority of the group. A person, unwittingly, may experience maladjustment in his social relations because his language patterns are grammatically incorrect, or he habitually expresses himself in obscene or profane language; according to group standards, his choice of clothes is inappropriate, his eating and drinking habits are offensive; he monopolizes the conversation, or he displays in other ways lack of consideration for the standards or interests of his associates.

The confident, outgoing, and controlled person usually is alert to the social factors of a situation. If he is guilty of a minor infringement of group custom or standards, he recognizes his fault, admits it, and refrains from repeating it. If he displays an attitude of willingness to learn what is expected of him by the group, the latter gives evidence of a willingness to accept him and help him fit into their social pattern.

Compared to serious conflict-arousing situational factors these minor elements of social adjustment may seem to be unimportant. Inadequacy to meet them may constitute continuously experienced barriers, however, to the achieving of satisfying security in the good opinion of one's associates. Eventually, inadequate adjustment may become serious maladjustment with all the behavior abberrations which were discussed in an earlier chapter.

The application of the principles of mental hygiene has begun to permeate the home, school, business, and industry, and other social agencies. In our discussions of the various aspects of development and adjustment we have followed the mental-hygiene approach. Much can be done for an individual to help him achieve adequate patterns of adjustment. Fundamentally, however, the individual himself is responsible for his attitudes and behavior. Shaffer emphasizes this point when he says:

> Persons may legitimately demand of psychologists if
> there are not some principles of mental hygiene by which
> individuals may help themselves to attain fuller, happier,

and better-adjusted lives. The answer is affirmative. In fact, there is no kind of improvement in behavior and adjustment except self-improvement. Clinicians, teachers and parents can only assist in the prevention or cure of adjustive difficulties; the real changes must be made by the individual himself. It must be emphasized, however, that there is no royal road to the attainment of good adjustment or of desirable traits of personality. Any gain must rest on a well-formulated desire for improvement and on conscientious and continued effort.[5]

Shaffer asserts further:

> To formulate the general principles of positive mental hygiene is an ambitious task, but not an impossible one. With our present degree of knowledge of human nature any such list must be tentative and approximate. Only when all of the causes of deviations of behavior are thoroughly understood will the principles of good adjustment take the form of incontrovertible laws. In spite of this objection, it is desirable for urgent practical purposes to make the best statement that present knowledge affords. At least we are able to set forth some generalizations that are better than none at all. It is difficult to state the conditions of good mental health; it is admittedly still more difficult to apply these concepts and to live according to them. The principles of positive mental hygiene, however, contain within themselves the germ of their own accomplishment, for following the simpler and easier ones makes it possible to achieve the others.[6]

Shaffer then lists the more obvious and essential conditions of effective living to be:

1. Maintenance of good physical health.
2. An objective attitude.
3. Insight into one's own conduct.
4. A confidential relationship with some other person.

[5] L. F. Shaffer, *The Psychology of Adjustment* (Boston: Houghton Mifflin Company, 1936), pp. 533–34.
[6] Ibid., pp. 535–36.

5. Attention to the present situation.
6. A sense of the ridiculous.
7. Planned activity.
8. Satisfying work.
9. Rest and recreation.
10. Normal social participation.[7]

Individual responsibility for adjustment. As you already know, each individual possesses specific traits and characteristics, abilities, drives, thoughts, and actions that are peculiar to himself. He experiences environmental stimulations and opportunities that differ from the life experiences of every other individual. Within the individual a constant battle rages between the urge to do and the urge to leave undone, the satisfaction of achieving personal desires and consideration for the needs of others, the drive for freedom and the habit of restraint, the desire for approval and the dread of disapproval. The individual continuously experiences the emotional strains and stresses of his loves, his fears, his dominations, his submissions, his drives toward self-glorification or self-abasement, and, finally, those innumerable behavior responses through which he strives to attain the satisfaction of his physical, emotional, and social needs.

Since the total personality is more than the complex of specific traits, the essence of personality is intangible, subtle, and undefinable. Hence it is difficult to predict with certainty the kind of adult a child eventually will become. Results of studies seem to indicate that the physical and mental health of the parents and the kind of environment in which a child develops are predicating factors of the adequacy of his personal and social adjustment. Yet, in some instances, the expected outcomes are not evidenced. Specific influences of which the significance is not recognized are the bases of deviations from what normally might be anticipated. There are certain cause-effect relationships, however, that seem to function for most individuals as adjustive or maladjustive factors.

Much of family discord can be attributed to the insistence by one or more of its members upon the fulfillment of personal wants and preconceived notions of individual rights and responsibilities. Many occupational difficulties seem to stem from personal struggles

[7] Adapted from Shaffer, ibid., pp. 535–39.

to gain money, prestige, and power. Social maladjustment is rooted in selfish interest and in competition for personal distinction or control. Political, economic, national, or international conflict can result from an overemphasis upon individual or group superiority.

Emotionally mature men or women participate to the limit of their abilities in family, occupational, social, and civic projects and activities. At the same time, they develop an inner attitude of personal sufficiency. They can appreciate the beauty and worth of natural, scientific, and artistic phenomena. They are imbued with the power of self-direction. Fundamentally, they are relatively untouched by destructive forces outside themselves.

In general, a full and rich life cannot be developed in a meager and uninspiring environment. Hence everyone needs to be stimulated by whatever is best in the way of home conditions, educational advantages, occupational opportunities, and social and civic adjustment. Mental hygiene succeeds in its function as it progressively makes possible, for every individual, equality of opportunity within personal limitations for constructive adjustment to fundamental human wants and urges. Beyond that the "good" life can be attained by an individual only through his conscious striving to achieve socially acceptable and personally satisfying attitudes and behavior patterns.

▶ **Questions and Problems for Discussion**

1. Discuss the importance of a sense of humor in individual adjustment.

2. Show how the application of mental-hygiene principles can be a positive force of adjustment.

3. Explain the mental-hygiene values to an individual of having "a task, a plan, and freedom."

4. To what extent should all personal wants be fulfilled at any one time?

5. List what you consider to be important life values.

6. How do you interpret the term *adjusted living?*

7. Justify the statement that we are the products of the past.

8. What are your present personal problems and worries? What are you doing to alleviate them?

9. List adjustment problems that you seem to have in your social life. What plans do you have for their solution?

10. What adjustment problems do you have in your student life or in your vocational activities? Indicate what you are doing to meet them satisfactorily.

11. Explain some of the strains and stresses in modern living that were not experienced fifty years ago.

12. Who do you believe is to blame for the widespread maladjustment among adolescents? What can be done to help them toward better adjusted patterns of living?

13. Evaluate the impact of the high divorce rate on adjustment in family life.

14. Good adjustment concerns an individual's total personality. Explain.

Selected Films,

Selected Readings,

and Index

List of Selected Films

MANY TOPICS in this book can receive further clarification through the use of excellent audio-visual aids that are available. It is recommended that the films listed here be previewed by the instructor before class showing in order that attention may be directed to the various phases of adjustment that are presented in them.

All the films included in the list are 16mm. sound films. The running time is given in minutes for each film. The addresses as well as full names of producers and distributers are given in the Directory of Film Sources that follows the List. Some of the films can be obtained from local film libraries.

Part I. *Films Concerned with Personal and Social Adjustment*

A Job for Bob (RFA, 30 min.). The story of an ambitious young man who was helped by guidance to find and adjust to a job.

Act Your Age (Emotional Maturity (C, 14 min.). Presents common types of infantile reactions such as temper tantrums and weeping.

Age of Turmoil (McGraw, 20 min.). Presents sketches of boys and girls in their early teens.

Alice Adams (NYU, 15 min.). Includes excerpts from the play which shows the adjustment difficulties of a young girl with friends who have more money than she has.

Am I Trustworthy? (C, 11 min.). Examples of trustworthiness are presented in this film.

Aptitudes and Occupations (C, 16 min.). Shows the extent to which an individual possesses ability in various fields.

Are You Popular? (C, 11 min.). Shows the behavior of a boy and a girl who are liked by others.

Attitudes and Health (C, 11 min.). Shows how self-confidence and right attitudes are vital to good health.

Baby Meets his Parents (EBF, 11 min.). Shows parental influence on personality development during infancy.

Better Use of Leisure Time (C, 11 min.). A guide to development of attitudes toward leisure-time activities.

Careers for Girls (MOT, 18 min.). Presents types of work open to women.

Children Growing up with Others (UWF, 30 min.). Shows the development of self-reliance.

Children Learn by Experience (UWF, 40 min.). A detailed consideration of children's learning interests and activities.

Children's Emotions (McGraw, 22 min.). The important emotions of childhood are described, and the methods of dealing with them are explained.

Choosing Your Occupation (C, 11 min.). Includes occupational possibilities and the preparation and guidance needed.

Condition Improved (NFBCan–McGraw–30 min.). Presents the value of occupational therapy in rehabilitation of the handicapped.

Control Your Emotions (C, 14 min.). Includes the application of psychological concepts to the practical work of emotional control.

Counseling—Its Tools and Techniques (Mahnke, 22 min.). Presents the techniques that can be used by the guidance counselor.

Date Etiquette (C, 11 min.). Presents ways of being socially comfortable during the dating experience.

Dating: Do's and Don'ts (C, 13 min.). Raises questions concerning dating and presents partial answers as guides for discussion.

Developing Friendships (C, 11 min.). Helps young people understand the meaning of friendships.

Developing Responsibility (C, 11 min.). Presents the difficulties encountered and the rewards of persistent endeavor.

Developing Self-reliance (C, 11 min.). Shows how necessary self-reliance is to all successful endeavor and happiness.

Developing Your Character (C, 11 min.). Portrays what good character is and how it can be achieved.

Diagnosis and Planning Adjustments in Counseling (McGraw, 18 min.). Presents various counseling situations.

Early Social Behavior (EBF, 11 min.). Presents the behavior of young children in various social situations.

Effective Criticism (C, 11 min.). Concerns the skills involved in taking and in giving criticism.

Emotional Health (McGraw, 20 min.). Presents problems of emotional disturbance and therapy in severe cases.

Employing Disabled Workers in Industry (Castle, 20 min.). Shows how handicapped persons have made good adjustment on the job.

Exercise and Health (C, 11 min.). Shows how physical and mental health depend upon proper physical exercise.

Experimental Studies in Social Climates of Groups (Iowa, 30 min.). Presents the effects of various forms of group organization upon the behavior of boys.

Family Circles (McGraw, 31 min.). Shows the extensions of the family circle into other agencies of the community.

Family Life (C, 11 min.). Shows the happiness that can be gained from a well-managed home.

Family Teamwork (Frith, 18 min.). Shows family cooperation and adjustment.

Farewell to Childhood (IFB, 20 min.). Presents a teen-age girl who longs for adulthood but fears the privileges associated with it.

Finding the Right Job (C, 11 min.). Emphasizes some of the crucial stages in obtaining a job.

Finding Your Life Work (Mahnke, 22 min.). Shows the thinking and planning of a boy in relation to his vocational choice.

Friendship Begins at Home (C, 16 min.). Presents the value of friendship in the home.

Frustration Play Techniques (NYU, 35 min.). Demonstrates special play techniques for diagnosing personality.

Fun of Making Friends (C, 11 min.). Presents many points about how to make and keep friends.

Gangs Raid the Orchard (NYU, 11 min.). Presents a situation in gang life.

Going Steady (C, 11 min.). Problems of teen agers when they "go steady."

Grief (NYU, 45 min.). Shows the effect upon an infant of his mother's prolonged absence.

Growth: A Study of Johnny and Jimmy (IFB, 43 min.). Presents the developmental pattern of each twin to the age of eight.

Growth of Adaptive Behavior (EBF, 15 min.). Presents the finer motor coordinations during a child's first five years.

Guidance Problems of School and Home (TC, 18 min.). Presents causes of a child's poor home and social adjustment.

He Acts His Age (McGraw, 13 min.). Presents the development of children at various ages.

Heredity and Environment (C, 11 min.). Presents a sound understanding of the influences that shape the lives of individuals.

How Behavior Grows (EBF, 14 min.). Shows both the physical and the mental growth of the very young child.

How Honest Are You? (C, 13 min.). The viewer is given an opportunity to draw certain conclusions concerning his own honesty.

How to Develop Interest (C, 11 min.). Consideration is given to three fundamental questions concerning interest.

How to Investigate Vocations (C, 11 min.). Concerns the investigation of vocations with the aim of selecting the kind of work best suited to the individual.

How to Keep a Job (C, 11 min.). Shows what should be done to perform successfully on the job.

How to Say No (Moral Maturity) (C, 11 min.). Shows how to say "No" and keep your friends.

Human Growth (U of Oregon, 19 min.). Concerns human growth and development and a discussion of some of the problems.

Human Reproduction (McGraw, 20 min.). Includes information concerning human reproduction and the process of birth.

Individual Differences (McGraw, 23 min.). Presents two approaches in meeting the problems of pupils.

Improve Your Personality (C, 11 min.). Presents a frank discussion of personality that is basic to self-analysis.

Know Your Baby (NFBCan, 11 min.). Shows the psychological care to be given to a newborn infant.

Learning to Understand Children, Part 1—A Diagnostic Approach (McGraw, 21 min.). Techniques used by a teacher to discover the causes of social maladjustment of Ada Adams.

Learning to Understand Children, Part 2—A Remedial Program (McGraw, 23 min.). Describes the remedial techniques used by the teacher to help Ada in her adjustment.

Life with Baby (MOT, 18 min.). Aids parents and adolescents gain a better understanding of the mental and physical growth patterns of children.

Life with Junior (MOT, 18 min.). Presents the happenings of an average day in the life of a school-age child.

Maintaining Classroom Discipline (McGraw, 14 min.). Presents various classroom situations and emphasizes correct methods of developing desirable behavior.

Making the Most of School (C, 11 min.). Reveals the value of school beyond day-by-day assignments.

Make Your Own Decisions (C, 11 min.). Presents a series of five questions and shows how each contributes to the development of self-reliance.

Marriage Films:

    Are You Ready for Marriage (C, 16 min.)

    Choosing for Happiness (McGraw, 14 min.)

    Choosing Your Marriage Partner (C, 13 min.)

    It Takes all Kinds (McGraw, 20 min.)

    Jealousy (McGraw, 18 min.)

    Marriage and Divorce (MOT, 15 min.)

    Marriage Is a Partnership (C, 16 min.)

    Marriage Today (McGraw, 22 min.)

    This Charming Couple (McGraw, 19 min.)

    Who's Boss (McGraw, 18 min.)

    Who's Right (McGraw, 18 min.)

Meaning of Adolescence (McGraw, 16 min.). Presents present-day adolescent development.

Meaning of Engagement (C, 13 min.). Presents the engagement period as one of preparation for successful marriage.

Mechanical Aptitudes (C, 11 min.). Sound guidance practices are demonstrated in a variety of situations.

Meeting Emotional Needs of Children (NYU, 33 min.). Shows the interdependence of the child and his parents and other adults in his environment.

Meeting the Needs of Adolescents (McGraw, 19 min.). Presents the experiences of a fourteen-year-old boy and his seventeen-year-old sister during their growing up.

Overcoming Fear (C, 13 min.). Shows the value of courage in meeting problems in everyday living.

Overcoming Worry (C, 11 min.). Shows ways to overcome worry.

Personal Qualities for Job Success (C, 11 min.). Shows that personal qualities for job success can be developed in high school.

Physical Aspects of Puberty (McGraw, 19 min.). Emphasizes the physiological aspects of puberty.

Picture in Your Mind (IFF, 16 min.). Presents causes of prejudice and attempts to indoctrinate the viewer toward a better attitude toward others.

Playtown, USA (AssnFlm, 23 min.). Presents community interest in providing recreational facilities for youth.

Preface to a Life (Castle, 28 min.). Shows the possible impact of several types of environmental influences upon an individual.

Prejudice (AssnFlm, 60 min.). Provides for personal examination of prejudices and stimulates discussion of intercultural relations.

Problem of Pupil Adjustment, Part 1—The Drop-Out: A Case Study (Mc-Graw, 20 min.). Presents a drop-out and the guidance given for his adjustment.

Problem of Pupil Adjustment, Part 2—The Stay-In: A School Study (Mc-Graw, 19 min.). Shows what can be done to keep pupils in school.

Right or Wrong? (Making Moral Decisions) (C, 11 min.). Presents the problem of what to do when a gang of boys break a warehouse window.

Search for Happiness (MOT, 17 min.). Presents the problems of modern living and suggestions for meeting them.

Self-Conscious Guy (C, 11 min.). Presents Marty who suddenly becomes aware of his feelings of self-consciousness.

Shy Guy (C, 13 min.). Presents the value of friendliness as a means of improving an adolescent's social adjustment.

Shyness (NFBCan, McGraw, 23 min.). Concerns excessive shyness in children and what can be done to help them.

Snap Out of It (C, 13 min.). Shows how emotional balance can be developed once it has been upset.

Social Courtesy (C, 11 min.). Reveals that social effectiveness requires a natural, easy form of behavior that includes the use of courtesy.

Social Development (McGraw, 16 min.). Presents the social behavior patterns of children at various stages of development.

Social-Sex Attitudes in Adolescence (McGraw, 22 min.). Shows the early experiences of a boy and a girl in their dating, falling in love, and marriage.

Testing Intelligence with the Stanford-Binet (PaStaCol, 18 min.). Two six-year-olds and two ten-year-olds are tested.

The Teacher as Observer and Guide (TC, 20 min.). Shows the importance of the teacher in the classroom.

The Terrible Twos and the Trusting Threes (McGraw, 20 min.). Presents the social behavior of the child at two years and at three years of age under the same conditions.

This Is Robert (NYU, 80 min.). Traces the development of Robert from his arrival in nursery school at two through his first year in a public school at seven.

Toward Emotional Maturity (McGraw, 11 min.). Presents ways in which adolescents can be prepared to understand and control their emotions.

Understanding Children's Play (NYU, 10 min.). Shows adults how to understand and help children in their use of toys and play materials.

Understanding Your Emotions (C, 13 min.). Shows different emotional responses to the same stimulus.

Understanding Your Ideals (C, 13 min.). Emphasizes the importance of ideals to an individual's well-being and happiness.

You and Your Family (AssnFlm, 10 min.). Presents typical family problems illustrating the relationships that should prevail between parents and their children.

You and Your Parents (C, 13 min.). Describes the process of growing away from parents as a normal course of events.

You and Your Work (C, 11 min.). Shows job failure and how rehabilitation helped an individual to succeed.

Your Children and You (BIS, 31 min.). Shows the care given to young children from the first few months to the age of four or five.

Part II. *Films Concerned with Maladjustment, Mental Illness, and Therapy*

A Criminal Is Born (TFC, 21 min.). Presents the stories of three boys who develop criminal tendencies because of inadequacies of home life.

Activity for Schizophrenia (Castle, 23 min.). Presents behavior characteristic of this psychosis.

Behavior in Hypnotic Regression (Bucknell, 17 min.). Shows extreme regressive behavior.

Boy in Court (NatPro, 12 min.). Presents the procedures used by the juvenile court in dealing with a delinquent.

Breakdown (NFBCan, 41 min.). The story of a young woman's schizophrenic breakdown and her recovery in a mental hospital.

Children of the City (BIS, 30 min.). Shows how a Scottish town handles the adolescent problem.

Children on Trial (IFB, 62 min.). Presents the experiences in approved schools of juvenile delinquents who eventually make satisfactory adjustments.

Children's Village (McGraw, 19 min.). Presents a clear picture of modern methods of treating juvenile delinquents.

Crime Lab. (McGraw, 14 min.). Surveys the techniques in modern crime detection.

Frustration Play Techniques (NYU, 35 min.). Demonstrates special techniques for diagnosing personality.

High Wall (McGraw, 32 min.). Presents problems associated with prejudice.

Instructing the Disabled on the Job (Castle, 14 min.). Shows the importance of a supervisor's attitude toward disabled workers.

Mental Mechanisms Series (NFBCan, Distributed by McGraw):
Feeling of Rejection (23 min.)
Feeling of Hostility (27 min.)
Overdependency (32 min.)
Feelings of Depression (30 min.)

Mental Symptoms Series (NFBCan, Distributed by McGraw):
  Schizophrenia: Simple-type Deteriorated (11 min.)
  Schizophrenia: Catatonic Type (12 min.)
  Schizophrenia: Hebephrenic Type (13 min.)
  Paranoid Conditions (13 min.)
  Organic Reaction-type: Senile (10 min.)
  Depressive States: I (12 min.)
  Depressive States: II (11 min.)
  Manic State (15 min.)
Nation's Mental Health (McGraw, 18 min.). Shows facilities for therapies
  applied.
New Prisons—New Men (McGraw, 11 min.). Shows the treatment of con-
  victs at a state prison.
Nurse's Day with the Mentally Ill (PaStaCol, 28 min.). Presents the work
  of a psychiatric nurse.
Out of True (IFB, 41 min.). Deals with factors that cause mental illness and
  therapy that aids in recovery.
Problem Children (NYU, 20 min.). Suggests ways to handle aggressive and
  passive child behavior.
Psychiatry in Action (BIS, 62 min.). Shows the treatment of war-induced
  neuroses.
Psychoneuroses (NYU, 23 min.). Presents evidence of psychogenic symptoms as well as of symptoms of organic disease.
Recreational and Occupational Therapy (Castle, 13 min.). Presents the
  work done in occupational therapy by hospitals and community agencies.
Return to Action (BIS, 19 min.). Shows techniques of rehabilitation of the
  disabled.
The Feebleminded (PaStaCol, 41 min.). Presents the magnitude of the
  problem of the feeble-minded.
The Quiet One (Athena, 67 min.). Presents the experiences of a mentally
  disturbed boy and shows how he is rehabilitated in a school for delinquent boys.
Ways to Settle Disputes (C. 11 min.). Demonstrates that the settlement of
  disputes must involve give and take and settlement must be desired if
  it is to be achieved.
What's on Your Mind (NFBCan, 10 min.). Shows the disadvantages of
  attempts to use quacks and the advantages of trained psychiatrists in
  the treatment of mental disturbance.
Who's Delinquent? (McGraw, 16 min.). Indicates how a newspaper editor
  attempts to discover the causes of juvenile delinquency and presents a
  program for improvement of conditions.

AssnFlm: Association Films, Inc., 35 West 45th St., New York 19, N.Y.

Athena: Athena Films, Inc., 165 W. 46th St., New York 19, N.Y.

BIS: British Information Services, 30 Rockefeller Plaza, New York 20, N.Y.

Bucknell: Bucknell University, Lewistown, Pa.

C: Coronet Instructional Films, 65 E. South Water St., Chicago 1, Ill.

Castle: United World Films, 1445 Park Ave., New York 29, N.Y.

EBF: Encyclopedia Britannica Films, Inc., 1150 Wilmette Ave., Wilmette, Ill.

Frith: Frith Films, 840 Seward St., Hollywood 38, Calif.

IBF: International Film Bureau, Suite 1500, 6 N. Michigan Ave., Chicago 2, Ill.

IFF: International Film Foundation, Inc., 1600 Broadway, New York 19, N.Y.

Io: University of Iowa, Bureau of Audio-Visual Instruction, Extension Division, Iowa City, Iowa.

Mahnke: Carl F. Mahnke Productions, 215 E. 3 St., Des Moines, Iowa.

McGraw: McGraw-Hill Book Company, Inc., Text-Film Department, 330 West 42nd St., New York 36, N.Y.

MOT: March of Time Films, 369 Lexington Ave., New York 17, N.Y.

NFBCan: National Film Board of Canada (Films distributed by McGraw-Hill)

NatPro: National Probation and Parole Association, 1790 Broadway, New York 19, N.Y.

NYU: New York University Film Library, 26 Washington Pl., New York 3, N.Y.

PaStaCol: Pennsylvania State University, Audio-Visual Library, State College, Pa.

RFA: Religious Film Association, Inc., 45 Astor Pl., New York 3, N.Y.

TC: Teachers College, Columbia University, Bureau of Publications, 525 West 120 St., New York 27, N.Y.

TFC: Teaching Film Custodians, Inc., 25 West 43 St., New York 36, N.Y.

U of Oregon: University of Oregon, Portland 4, Ore.

UWF: United World Films, Inc., 1445 Park Ave., New York 29, N.Y.

Selected Readings

Abt, L. E., and Bellak, L. *Projective Psychology*. New York: Alfred A. Knopf, Inc., 1950.

Alexander, F. G., and Ross, H. (eds.) *Dynamic Psychiatry*. Chicago: The University of Chicago Press, 1952.

Alvarez, W. *The Neuroses*. Philadelphia: W. B. Saunders Co., 1951.

Anastasi, Anne: *Psychological Testing*. New York: The Macmillan Co., 1954.

———, and Foley, J. P. *Differential Psychology*. New York: The Macmillan Co., 1949.

Anderson, C. M. *Emotional Hygiene* (4th ed.). Philadelphia: J. B. Lippincott Co., 1948.

Anderson, J. E. *The Psychology of Development and Personal Adjustment*. New York: Henry Holt & Co., 1949.

Arnold, M. B. *The Human Person: An Approach to an Integral Theory of Personality*. New York: The Ronald Press Co., 1954.

Asch, S. E. *Social Psychology*. New York: Prentice-Hall, Inc., 1952.

Austin, M. C., and Thompson, G. G. "Children's Friendships: A Study of the Bases upon Which Children Select and Reject Their Best Friends," *Journal of Educational Psychology*, 39 (1948): 101–16.

Ausubel, D. P. *Theory and Problems of Adolescent Development*. New York: Grune and Stratton, 1954.

Baber, R. F. *Marriage and Family* (2nd ed.). New York: McGraw-Hill Book Co., 1954.

Bach, G. R. *Intensive Group Psychotherapy*. New York: The Ronald Press Co., 1954.

Backus, O., and Beasley, J. *Speech Therapy with Children*. Boston: Houghton Mifflin Co., 1951.

Baker, H. J. *Introduction to Exceptional Children* (2nd ed.). New York: The Macmillan Co., 1953.

Baldwin, A. L. *Psychological Development in Childhood*. New York: The Dryden Press, 1954.

Barker, R. G., *et al. Child Behavior and Development* (2nd ed.). New York: McGraw-Hill Book Co., 1953.

Barr, A. S. (Chairman). "Special Issue on Classroom Dynamics," *Journal of Educational Research*, 45 (1951): October, 81–160; November, 161–204.

Barron, M. L. *The Juvenile in Delinquent Society*. New York: Alfred A. Knopf, Inc., 1954.

Baruch, D. W. *New Ways in Discipline*. New York: McGraw-Hill Book Co., 1949.

Beach, F. A. *Hormones and Behavior*. New York: Hoeber, 1948.

Beaumont, H., and Macomber, F. G. *Psychological Factors in Education*. McGraw-Hill Book Co., 1949.

Bell, J. E. *Projective Techniques*. New York: Longmans, Green and Co., 1948.

Bergler, E. *Conflict in Marriage*. New York: Harper & Brothers, 1949.

Bernard, H. W. *Toward Better Personal Adjustment*. New York: McGraw-Hill Book Co., 1951.

———. *Mental Hygiene for Classroom Teachers*. New York: McGraw-Hill Book Co., 1952.

Bernard, J. *American Community Behavior*. New York: The Dryden Press, 1949.

Berrien, F. K. *Practical Psychology*. New York: The Macmillan Co., 1952.

Blair, G. M., Jones, R. S., and Simpson, R. H.: *Educational Psychology*. New York: The Macmillan Co., 1954.

Blake, R. R. *et al. Perception—An Approach to Personality*. New York: The Ronald Press Co., 1951.

Blos, P. *The Adolescent Personality*. New York: Appleton-Century-Crofts, 1941.

Blum, M. L., and Balinsky, B. *Counseling and Psychology*. New York: Prentice-Hall, Inc., 1951.

Boardman, R., and Hildreth, G. "Adjustment Problems of the Gifted," *Understanding the Child*. 17 (1948): 41–44, 51.

Bonner, H. *Social Psychology*. New York: American Book Co., 1953.

Bordeaux, J. *How to Talk More Effectively* (3rd ed.). Chicago: American Technical Society, 1952.

Bossard, J. H. S. *The Sociology of Child Development.* New York: Harper & Brothers, 1954.

——, and Ball, E. S. *Family Situations: An Introduction to the Study of Child Behavior.* Philadelphia: University of Pennsylvania Press, 1943.

Bosselman, B. C. *The Troubled Mind—A Psychiatric Study of Success and Failure in Human Adaptation.* New York: The Ronald Press Co., 1953.

Bowman, H. A. *Marriage for Moderns* (3rd ed.). New York: McGraw-Hill Book Co., 1954.

Bradley, C. "Early Evidences of Psychosis in Children," *Journal of Pediatrics,* 30 (1947): 529–40.

Bradley, D. *Your Problems Can Be Solved.* New York: The Macmillan Co., 1945.

Buhler, C., *et al. Childhood Problems and the Teacher.* New York: Henry Holt & Co., 1952.

Burgess, E. W., and Locke, H. J. *The Family* (2nd ed.). New York: American Book Co., 1953.

Burton, W. H. *The Guidance of Learning Activities* (2nd ed.). New York: Appleton-Century-Crofts, 1952.

Cameron, N. *The Psychology of Behavior Disorders.* Boston: Houghton Mifflin Co., 1947.

Cantor, N. *The Teaching-Learning Process.* New York: The Dryden Press, 1953.

——. *Dynamics of Learning,* (2nd ed.). Buffalo: Foster and Stewart, 1950.

Cantril, H. *The "Why" of Man's Experience.* New York: The Macmillan Co., 1950.

Carmichael, L. (ed.). *Manual of Child Psychology* (2nd ed.). New York: John Wiley & Sons, 1954.

Carroll, H. A. *Mental Hygiene* (2nd ed.). New York: Prentice-Hall, Inc., 1951.

Cartwright, D., and Zander, A. (ed.). *Group Dynamics.* Evanston: Row, Peterson and Co., 1953.

Cattell, R. B. *Personality.* New York: McGraw-Hill Book Co., 1950.

——. *Description and Measurement of Personality.* Yonkers: World Book Co., 1946.

Chevigny, H., and Braverman, S. *The Adjustment of the Blind.* New Haven: Yale University Press, 1950.

Children in Focus. 1954 Yearbook of the American Association for Health, Physical Education and Recreation. Washington: National Education Association, 1954.

Chrisholm, L. L. *Guiding Youth in the Secondary School* (rev. ed.). New York: American Book Co., 1950.

Christenson, H. T. "Students' Views on Mate Selection," *Marriage and Family Living.* 9 (1947): 85–88.

Clawson, J. *Psychology in Action.* New York: The Macmillan Co., 1945.

Cobb, K. *Problem Behavior and Adjustment in Children.* Boston: Houghton Mifflin Co., 1953.

Colby, K. M. *A Primer for Psychotherapists.* New York: The Ronald Press Co., 1951.

Cole, L. *Psychology of Adolescence* (4th ed.). New York: Rinehart & Co., 1954.

Commins, W. D., and Fagin, B. *Principles of Educational Psychology.* The Ronald Press Co., 1954.

Crider, B. "Phobias: Their Nature and Treatment," *Journal of Psychology.* 27 (1949): 217–229.

Cronbach, L. J. *Essentials of Psychological Testing.* New York: Harper & Brothers, 1949.

———. *Educational Psychology.* New York: Harcourt, Brace & Co., 1954.

Crow, A. "Parental Attitudes toward Boy-Girl Relations," *The Journal of Educational Sociology* (November, 1955), 126–133.

Crow, L. D. "Attitude Development for International Understanding," *The American School Board Journal* (December, 1953), 25–26.

———. "The Role of the Teacher in the Development of International Understanding," *Educational Administration and Supervision,* 39 (1953): 375–77.

——— and Crow, A. *Adolescent Development and Adjustment.* New York: McGraw-Hill Book Co., 1956.

———, *Child Psychology.* New York: Barnes and Noble, Inc., 1953.

———. *Educational Psychology* (rev. ed.). New York: American Book Company, 1954.

———. *Human Development and Learning.* New York: American Book Co. 1956.

———. *Introduction to Guidance.* New York: American Book Co., 1951.

———. *Mental Hygiene* (2nd ed.). New York: McGraw-Hill Book Co., 1951.

———. *Our Teen Age Boys and Girls.* New York: McGraw-Hill Book Co., 1945.

———. *Readings in Psychology.* New York: Barnes and Noble, Inc., 1954.

———, and Skinner, C. E. *Psychology in Nursing Practice.* New York: The Macmillan Co., 1954.

Cruze, W. W. *Adolescent Psychology and Development.* New York: The Ronald Press Co., 1953.

Deese, J. E. *The Psychology of Learning.* New York: McGraw-Hill Book Co., 1952.

Dennis, W. *Readings in Child Psychology.* New York: Prentice-Hall, Inc., 1951.

Deutsch, A. *The Mentally Ill in America* (2nd ed.). New York: Columbia University Press, 1949.

Dewey, R., and Humber, W. J. *The Development of Human Behavior.* New York: The Macmillan Co., 1951.

Dollard, J., *et al. Frustration and Aggression.* New Haven: Yale University Press, 1939.

———, and Miller, N. E. *Personality and Psychotherapy.* New York: McGraw-Hill Book Co., 1950.

Donahue, W. T. *The Measurement of Student Adjustment and Achievement.* Ann Arbor: University of Michigan Press, 1949.

Douglass, H. R. (ed.). *Education for Life Adjustment.* New York: The Ronald Press Co., 1950.

Dublin, L. I., and Spiegelman, M. *The Facts of Life.* New York: The Macmillan Co., 1951.

Dunlap, K. *Personal Adjustment.* New York: McGraw-Hill Book Co., 1945.

Eckenrode, C. J. "Their Achievement Is Delinquency," *Journal of Educational Research,* 43 (1950): 554–60.

Eissler, K. R. (ed.). *Searchlight on Delinquency.* New York: International University Press, 1949.

English, H. B., and Rainy, V. *Studying the Individual Child.* New York: Henry Holt & Co., 1950.

English, O. S., and Finch, S. M. *Emotional Problems of Growing Up.* New York: W. W. Norton & Co., 1951.

Eysenck, G. *Dimensions of Personality.* New York: The Macmillan Co., 1949.

Faris, R. E. L. *Social Psychology.* New York: The Ronald Press Co., 1952.

Ferguson, L. W. *Personality Measurement.* New York: McGraw-Hill Book Co., 1952.

Fidler, G. S., and Fidler, J. W. *Introduction to Psychiatric Occupational Therapy.* New York: The Macmillan Co., 1954.

Fiedler, M. F. *Deaf Children in a Hearing World.* New York: The Ronald Press Co., 1952.

Fields, M. R., Goldberg, T. A., and Kilander, H. S. *Youth Grows into Adulthood.* New York: Chartwell House, 1950.

Finlay, W. W., *et al. Human Behavior in Industry.* New York: McGraw-Hill Book Co., 1954.

Fisher, V. E. *The Meaning and Practice of Psychotherapy*. New York: The Macmillan Co., 1950.

Fleck, H. *How to Evaluate Students*. Bloomington: McKnight and McKnight, 1953.

Forest, I. *Child Development*. New York: McGraw-Hill Book Co., 1954.

Foshay, A. W. "The Teacher and Children's Social Attitudes," *Teachers College Record*, 52 (February, 1951): 281–96.

Foster, R. G. *Marriage and Family Relationships*. New York: The Macmillan Co., 1944.

Frank, L. K. *Individual Development*. New York: Doubleday & Co., 1954.

——. *Projective Methods*. Springfield, Ill.: Charles C. Thomas Publisher, 1948.

——. *Feelings and Emotions*. New York: Doubleday & Co., 1954.

Freeman, F. S. *Theory and Practice of Psychological Testing*. New York: Henry Holt and Co., 1950.

Freud, S. *An Outline of Psychoanalysis*. New York: W. W. Norton & Co., 1949.

Garrison, K. C. *Growth and Development*. New York: The Ronald Press Co., 1951.

——. *Psychology of Adolescence* (4th ed.). New York: Prentice-Hall, Inc., 1950.

Gatling, F. P. "Frustration Reaction of Delinquents," *Journal of Abnormal and Social Psychology*. 45 (1950): 749–52.

Geddes, D. P. (ed.). *An Analysis of the Kinsey Reports of Sexual Behavior in the Human Male and Female*. New York: E. P. Dutton, 1954.

Gibson, J. J. *The Perception of the Visual World*. Boston: Houghton Mifflin Co., 1950.

Glueck, S. S., and Glueck, E. T. *Unraveling Juvenile Delinquency*. Boston: Harvard University Press for the Commonwealth Fund, 1950.

Gondor, E. I. *Art and Play Therapy*. New York: Doubleday & Co., 1954.

Gray, J. S. *Psychology in Industry*. New York: McGraw-Hill Book Co., 1953.

——. (ed.). *Psychology in Use* (2nd ed.). New York: American Book Co., 1951.

Greene, E. B. *Measurement of Human Behavior*. New York: The Odyssey Press, 1952.

Guilford, J. P. *Psychometric Methods* (2nd ed.). New York: McGraw-Hill Book Co., 1954.

Guthrie, E. R. *The Psychology of Human Conflict*. New York: Harper & Brothers, 1938.

——. *Psychology of Learning* (rev. ed.). New York: Harper & Brothers, 1952.

—————, and Edwards, A. L. *Psychology: A First Course in Human Behavior.* New York: Harper & Brothers, 1949.

Hadfield, J. A. *Psychology and Mental Health.* New York: The Macmillan Co., 1950.

Harmon, M. "Television and the Leisure Time Activities of Children," *Education,* 71 (1950): 126–28.

Harsh, C. M., and Schrickel, H. G. *Personality Development and Assessment.* New York: The Ronald Press Co., 1950.

Hartley, R. E., Frank, L. K., and Goldenson, R. M. *Understanding Children's Play.* New York: Columbia University Press, 1952.

Hartwell, S. W. *Practical Psychology and Mental Hygiene.* New York: McGraw-Hill Book Co., 1947.

Havinghurst, R. J. *Human Development and Education.* New York: Longmans, Green and Co., 1953.

—————, and Breeze, F. H. "Relation Between Ability and Social Status in a Midwestern Community, III. Primary Mental Abilities," *Journal of Educational Psychology,* 38 (1947): 241–47.

Heck, A. O. *The Education of Exceptional Children* (2nd ed.). New York: McGraw-Hill Book Co., 1953.

Heffernan, H. (ed.). *Guiding the Young Child.* Boston: D. C. Heath & Co., 1951.

Hepner, H. W. *Psychology Applied to Life and Work* (2nd ed.). New York: Prentice-Hall, Inc., 1950.

Hilgard, E. R. *Introduction to Psychology.* New York: Harcourt, Brace and Co., 1953.

Hollingshead, A. B. *Elmtown's Youth.* New York: John Wiley & Sons, 1949.

Horney, K. *Neurosis and Human Growth.* New York: W. W. Norton & Co., 1950.

—————. *The Neurotic Personality of Our Time.* New York: W. W. Norton & Co., 1937.

Hume, E. G. *Learning and Teaching in the Infants Schools.* New York: Longmans, Green and Co., 1953.

Hunt, J. McV. (ed.). *Personality and the Behavior Disorders,* 2 vols. New York: The Ronald Press Co., 1944.

Hurlock, E. B. *Developmental Psychology.* New York: McGraw-Hill Book Co., 1953.

—————. *Adolescent Development.* New York: McGraw-Hill Book Co., 1955.

Hymes, J. L. *Effective Home-School Relations,* New York: Prentice-Hall, Inc., 1953.

—————. *Understanding Your Child.* New York: Prentice-Hall, Inc., 1952.

Ingram, C. P. *Education of the Slow-Learning Child.* New York: The Ronald Press Co., 1953.

Irwin, F. W. "Motivation," in Helson, H. *Theoretical Foundations of Psychology*. New York: D. Van Nostrand Co., 1951.

Jackson, L., and Todd, K. M. *Child Treatment and the Therapy of Play* (2nd ed.). New York: The Ronald Press Co., 1950.

Jenkins, G. G., and Newman, J. *How to Live with Parents*. Chicago: Science Research Associates, 1950.

Jennings, H. H. *Sociometry in Group Relations: A Work Guide for Teachers*. Washington: American Council on Education, 1948.

——. *Leadership and Isolation*. New York: Longmans, Green & Co., 1950.

Jersild, A. T. *Child Psychology* (4th ed.). New York: Prentice-Hall, Inc., 1953.

——, and Tasch, R. J. *Children's Interests and What They Suggest for Education*. New York: Columbia University Press, 1949.

Jones, A. J. *Principles of Guidance* (4th ed.). New York: McGraw-Hill Book Co., 1951.

Jones, H. "Group Sentiment and Delinquency," *Mental Health*, 8 (1948): 41–44.

Jung, C. G. *The Practice of Psychotherapy*. Vol. 16 in Jung's Collected Works. New York: distributed by Pantheon Books, 1954.

Kanner, L. *Child Psychiatry* (2nd ed.). Springfield, Ill.: C. C. Thomas Publisher, 1949.

Kaplan, L., and Baron, D. *Mental Hygiene and Life*. New York: Harper & Brothers, 1952.

Katz, B. *How to Be a Better Parent*. New York: The Ronald Press Co., 1953.

——, and Lehner, G. F. *Mental Hygiene in Modern Living*. New York: The Ronald Press Co., 1953.

Keller, F. J. *Principles of Vocational Education*. Boston: D. C. Heath & Co., 1952.

Keyes, K. S. *How to Develop Your Thinking Ability*. New York: McGraw-Hill Book Co., 1950.

Kilpatrick, W. H., and Van Til, W. (eds.). *Intercultural Attitudes in the Making*. New York: Harper & Brothers, 1947.

Kinsey, A. C., *et al. Sexual Behavior in the Human Female*. Philadelphia: W. B. Saunders Co., 1953.

——. *Sexual Behavior in the Human Male*. Philadelphia: W. B. Saunders Co., 1948.

Kirkendall, L. A. *Understanding Sex*. Chicago: Science Research Associates, 1948.

Kitson, H. D. *Helping People Find Jobs*. New York: Harper & Brothers, 1950.

Kuhlen, R. G. *The Psychology of Adolescent Development.* New York: Harper & Brothers, 1952.

———, and Thompson, G. G. *Psychological Studies of Human Development.* Appleton-Century-Crofts, 1952.

Kvaraceus, W. C. *The Community and the Delinquent.* Yonkers: World Book Co., 1954.

Landis, J. T., and Landis, M. G. *Personal Adjustment, Marriage and Family Living.* New York: Prentice-Hall, Inc., 1950.

Landis, P. H. *Adolescence and Youth* (2nd ed.). New York: McGraw-Hill Book Co., 1952.

Langdon, G., and Stout, I. W., *Teacher-Parent Interviews.* New York: Prentice-Hall, Inc., 1954.

Lawshe, C. H. *The Psychology of Industrial Relations.* New York: McGraw-Hill Book Co., 1953.

Le Cron, L. M., and Bordeaux, J. *Hypnotism Today* (3rd ed.). New York: Grune & Stratton, Inc., 1952.

Lemkau, P. V. *Mental Hygiene in Public Health.* New York: McGraw-Hill Book Co., 1949.

Lewin, K. *Resolving Social Conflicts.* New York: Harper & Brothers, 1948.

Lightfoot, C. *Characteristics of Bright and Dull Children.* New York: Bureau of Publications, Teachers College, Columbia University, 1951.

Lindgren, H. C. *Psychology of Personal and Social Adjustment.* New York: American Book Co., 1953.

———. *Mental Health in Education.* New York: Henry Holt & Co., 1954.

Lippitt, R. "Group Dynamics and Personality Dynamics," *American Journal of Orthopsychiatry,* 21 (January, 1951): 18–31.

Little, W., and Chapman, A. L. *Developmental Guidance in Secondary School.* New York: McGraw-Hill Book Co., 1954.

Longerich, M. C., and Bordeaux, J. *Aphasia Therapeutics.* New York: The Macmillan Co., 1954.

Louttit, C. M. *Clinical Psychology of Children's Behavior* (rev. ed.). New York: Harper & Brothers, 1947.

Lowenfeld, V. *Creative and Mental Health* (rev. ed.). New York: The Macmillan Co., 1952.

Lund, F. H. *Emotions.* New York: The Ronald Press Co., 1939.

Machover, K. *Personality Projection in the Drawing of the Human Figure.* Springfield, Ill.: C. C. Thomas Publisher, 1949.

Maier, N. R. F. *A Study of Behavior without a Goal.* New York: McGraw-Hill Book Co., 1949.

Maslow, A. H., and Mittelmann, B. *Principles of Abnormal Psychology* (rev. ed). New York: Harper & Brothers, 1951.

McClelland, D. C., *et al. The Achievement Motive*. New York: Appleton-Century-Crofts, 1953.

McDaniel, H. B. *Guidance Services in the Modern School*. New York: The Dryden Press, 1954.

McGeoch, J. A., and Irion, A. L. *The Psychology of Human Learning*. New York: Longmans, Green & Co., 1952.

McKay, H. D. "The Neighborhood and Child Conduct," *Annals of the American Academy of Political and Social Science*, 261 (1949): 32–41.

McKinney, F. *The Psychology of Personal Adjustment*. New York: John Wiley & Sons, 1949.

Malm, M., and Jamison, O. G. *Adolescence*. New York: McGraw-Hill Book Co., 1952.

May, R. *The Meaning of Anxiety*. New York: The Ronald Press Co., 1950.

Mays, A. B. *Essentials of Industrial Education*. New York: McGraw-Hill Book Co., 1952.

Menninger, W. C. *Psychiatry in a Troubled World*. New York: The Macmillan Co., 1948.

Merrill, M. A. *Problems of Child Delinquency*. Boston: Houghton Mifflin Co., 1947.

Merry, F. K., and Merry, R. V. *The First Two Decades of Life*. New York: Harper & Brothers, 1950.

Mikesell, W. H., and Hanson, G. C. *Psychology of Adjustment*. New York: D. Van Nostrand Co., 1952.

Mitchell, E. D., and Mason, B. S. *The Theory of Play*. New York: A. S. Barnes Co., 1948.

Monachesi, B. D. "Personal Characteristics and Socio-Economic Status of Delinquents and Non-Delinquents," *Journal of Criminal Law & Criminology*, 40 (1950): 570–83.

Moore, C. H., and Cole, W. E.: *Sociology in Educational Practice*. Boston: Houghton Mifflin Co., 1952.

Moore, T. V. *Personal Mental Hygiene*. New York: Grune & Stratton, 1945.

Morgan, J. J. B. *Keeping a Sound Mind*. New York: The Macmillan Co., 1946.

Moser, C. G. *Understanding Boys: Through Infancy, Childhood and Adolescence*. New York: Association Press, 1953.

Moustakas, C. E. *Children in Play Therapy*. New York: McGraw-Hill Book Co., 1953.

Murphy, G. *Personality: A Biosocial Approach to Orgins and Structure*. New York: Harper & Brothers, 1947.

———, and Ladd, H. *Emotional Factors in Learning*. New York: Columbia University Press, 1945.

Neisser, E. G. *Children in the Family: Rivals and Friends*. New York: Bureau of Publications, Teachers College, 1951.

Neumeyer, M. H. *Juvenile Delinquency in Modern Society*. New York: D. Van Nostrand Co., 1949.

Newcomb, T. M. *Personality and Social Change*. New York: The Dryden Press, 1943.

Norvell, G. W. *Reading Interests of Young People*. Boston: D. C. Heath & Co., 1950.

O'Brien, P. V. *Emotions and Morals*. New York: Grune & Stratton, 1950.

Olson, W. C. *Child Development*. Boston: D. C. Heath & Co., 1949.

Osborn, L. A. *Psychiatry and Medicine*. New York: McGraw-Hill Book Co., 1952.

Overstreet, H. A. *The Mature Mind*. New York: W. W. Norton & Co., 1949.

Patty, W. L., and Johnson, L. S. *Personality and Adjustment*. New York: McGraw-Hill Book Co., 1953.

Peck, L. *Child Psychology*. Boston: D. C. Heath & Co., 1953.

Pepinsky, H. B., and Pepinsky, P. N. *Counseling: Theory and Practice*. New York: The Ronald Press Co., 1954.

Phillips, L., and Smith, J. G. *Rorschach Interpretation: Advanced Technique*. New York: Grune & Stratton, 1953.

Prescott, D. A. *Emotion and the Educative Process*. Washington: American Council on Education, 1938.

Redl, F., and Wattenberg, W. W. *Mental Hygiene*. New York: Harcourt, Brace & Co., 1951.

Remmers, H. H. *Introduction to Opinion and Attitude Measurement*. New York: Harper & Brothers, 1954.

Remmers, H. H., Ryder, E. R., and Morgan, C. L. *Introduction to Educational Psychology*. New York: Harper & Brothers, 1954

Rennie, T. A. C., and Woodward, L. E. *Mental Health in Modern Society*. New York: The Commonwealth Fund, 1948.

Review of Educational Research. "Guidance Counseling and Pupil Personnel." Entire issue, 24 (April, 1954): 107–90.

Reymert, M. L. *Feelings and Emotions: The Mooseheart Symposium*. New York: McGraw-Hill Book Co., 1950.

Reynolds, M. M. *Children from Seed to Saplings* (2nd ed). New York: McGraw-Hill Book Company, 1951.

Rivlin, H. *Educating for Adjustment*. New York: Appleton-Century-Crofts, 1936.

Rockwood, L. T., and Ford, M. E. *Youth, Marriage and Parenthood*. New York: John Wiley & Sons, 1945.

Rogers, C. R. *Client-Centered Therapy*. Boston: Houghton Mifflin Co., 1950.

Ross, H. *Fears in Children*. Chicago: Science Research Associates, 1951.

Rothney, J. W. M., and Roems, B. A. *Counseling the Individual Student*. New York: The Dryden Press, 1949.

Ruch, F. L. *Psychology and Life* (4th ed.). Chicago: Scott, Foresman and Co., 1953.

Rumney, J., and Murphy, J. P. *Probation and Social Adjustment*. New Brunswick: Rutgers University Press, 1952.

Rusk, H., and Taylor, E. *Living with a Disability*. New York: Doubleday & Co., 1953.

Ryan, T. A., and Smith, P. C. *Principles of Industrial Psychology*. New York: The Ronald Press Co., 1954.

Sarason, S. B. *Psychological Problems in Mental Deficiency*. New York: Harper & Brothers, 1953.

Saul, L. J. *Emotional Maturity*. Philadelphia: J. B. Lippincott Co., 1948.

Schacter, H. *How Personalities Grow*. Bloomington: McKnight & McKnight, 1949.

Shaffer, L. *Psychology of Adjustment*. Boston: Houghton Mifflin Co., 1936.

Shaw, F. J., and Ort, R. S. *Personal Adjustment in the American Culture*. New York: Harper & Brothers, 1954.

Sherman, M. *Basic Problems of Behavior*. New York: Longmans, Green and Co., 1941.

———. *Intelligence and Its Deviations*. New York: The Ronald Press Co., 1945.

Skinner, B. F. *Science and Human Behavior*. New York: The Macmillan Co., 1953.

Smart, M., and Smart, R. *An Introduction to Family Relationships*. Philadelphia: W. B. Saunders Co., 1953.

Smith, F. V. *The Explanation of Human Behavior*. New York: The Macmillan Co., 1952.

Smith, H. P. *Psychology in Teaching*. New York: Prentice-Hall, Inc., 1954.

Snygg, D. *Motivation*. New York: Doubleday & Co., 1954.

———, and Combs, A. W. *Individual Behavior*. New York: Harper & Brothers, 1949.

Sorenson, H. *Psychology in Education* (3rd ed.). New York: McGraw-Hill Book Co., 1954.

Stagner, R. *Psychology of Personality* (2nd ed.). New York: McGraw-Hill Book Co., 1948.

Steckle, L. C. *Problems of Human Adjustment*. New York: Harper & Brothers, 1949.

Strang, R. *An Introduction to Child Study* (3rd ed.). New York: The Macmillan Co., 1951.

Strecker, E. A., *et al. Discovering Ourselves.* New York: The Macmillan Co., 1945.

Strong, E. K. "The Role of Interests in Guidance," *Occupations,* 27 (1949): 517–22.

Super, D. E. *Appraising Vocational Fitness by Means of Psychological Test.* New York: Harper & Brothers, 1949.

Symonds, P. M. *The Dynamics of Human Adjustment.* New York: Appleton-Century-Crofts, 1946.

——. *Dynamic Psychology.* New York: Appleton-Century-Crofts, 1949.

——. *The Ego and the Self.* New York: Appleton-Century-Crofts, 1951.

Taba, H., and Elkins, D. *With Focus on Human Relations.* Washington: American Council on Education, 1950.

Tappan, P. W. *Juvenile Delinquency.* New York: McGraw-Hill Book Co., 1949.

Taylor, W. S. *Dynamic and Abnormal Psychology.* New York: American Book Co., 1954.

Telford, C. W. "A Study of Religious Attitudes." *Journal of Social Psychology,* 31 (1950): 217–30.

Terman, L. M., and Oder, M. H. *The Gifted Child Grows Up.* Stanford University: Stanford University Press, 1947.

——, and Merrill, M. A. *Measuring Intelligence.* Boston: Houghton Mifflin Co., 1937.

Thomas, R. M. *Judging Student Progress.* New York: Longmans, Green & Co., 1954.

Thompson, G. C. *Child Psychology.* Boston: Houghton Mifflin Co., 1952.

Thorndike, E. L. *Human Nature and the Social Order.* New York: The Macmillan Co., 1940.

Thorpe, L. P. *The Psychology of Mental Health.* New York: The Ronald Press Co., 1950.

——. *Psychological Foundations of Personality.* New York: McGraw-Hill Book Co., 1938.

——, and Katz, B. *The Psychology of Abnormal Behavior.* New York: The Ronald Press Co., 1948.

Thurstone, L. L., and Thurstone, T. G. *Primary Mental Abilities.* Chicago: Science Research Associates, 1951.

Tiffin, J. *Industrial Psychology* (3rd ed.). New York: Prentice-Hall, Inc., 1952.

Tompkins, S. *The TAT: The Theory and Technique of Interpretation.* New York: Grune & Stratton, 1947.

Travis, L. E., and Baruch, B. *Personal Problems of Everyday Life.* New York: Appleton-Century-Crofts, 1941.

Traxler, A. E. *Techniques of Guidance.* New York: Harper & Brothers, 1945.

Tyler, L. E. *The Psychology of Human Differences.* New York: Appleton-Century-Crofts, 1947.

Vaughan, W. *Personal and Social Adjustment.* New York: The Odyssey Press, 1952.

Vinacke, W. E. *The Psychology of Thinking.* New York: McGraw-Hill Book Co., 1952.

Wallin, J. E. W. *Children with Mental and Physical Handicaps.* New York: Prentice-Hall, Inc., 1945.

Warters, J. *Achieving Maturity* (2nd ed.). New York: McGraw-Hill Book Co., 1949.

———. "Guidance through Groups," *Rev. of Ed. Research,* 21 (1951): 140–48.

———. *Techniques of Counseling.* New York: McGraw-Hill Book Co., 1948.

Weiss, E. *Principles of Psychodynamics.* New York: Grune & Stratton, 1950.

Wells, F. L. "Adjustment Problems at the Upper Extremities of Test Intelligence: Cases 39–54," *Journal Genetic Psychology,* 76 (1950): 3–37.

White, R. W. *The Abnormal Personality.* New York: The Ronald Press Co., 1948.

Wilkinson, B. *Understanding Fear in Ourselves and Others.* New York: Harper & Brothers, 1951.

Williams, E. G. *Counseling Adolescents* (rev. ed.). New York: McGraw-Hill Book Co., 1950.

Witkin, H. A., *et al. Personality Through Perception: An Experimental and Clinical Study.* New York: Harper & Brothers, 1954.

Witmer, H. L., and Kotinsky, R. (eds.). *Personality in the Making.* New York: Harper & Brothers, 1952.

Witty, P. *The Gifted Child.* Boston: D. C. Heath & Co., 1951.

Wrenn, C. G. *Student Personnel Work in College.* New York: The Ronald Press Co., 1951.

———, and Dugan, W. E. *Guidance Procedures in High School.* Minneapolis: University of Minnesota Press, 1950.

Young, P. T. *Emotion in Man and Animal.* New York: John Wiley & Sons, 1943.

———. *Social Treatment in Probation and Delinquency.* New York: McGraw-Hill Book Co., 1952.

Zachry, C. B., and Lighty, M. *Emotion and Conduct in Adolescence.* Appleton-Century-Crofts, 1940.

Zeran, F. R. (ed.). *Life Adjustment Education in Action: A Symposium.* New York: Chartwell House, Inc., 1953.

Index

Abulia, 194
Accidents, of workers, 280
Acculturation, 242
Acrophobia, 189
Action: compromise, 151–3; direct, 151–3
Adience: adient-avoidant, 142–3; convergent, 143, 144; divergent, 144; double-adient, 143–4
Adjustment: achieving good job, 286–7; areas of, 6–9; aspects of personal-social, 312–20; continuing process of, 313; dynamics of, 14; educating for marital, 255–60; emotions as related to, 314–16; and financial security, 278–9; guidance and occupational, 282–4; inadequate personality, 30–1; individual responsibility for, 319–20; of job to worker, 177–182; mechanisms of, 155–79; mental ability and, 25–7; mental hygiene approach to, 313–19; patterns of, 154–5; personal habits and, 29; physical factors of, 24–5; prejob problems of, 264–70; of professional worker, 284–6; process of human, 4–6; tests of vocational, 287–9; theories of, 9–10; wholesome, 29–30; of worker, 264, 271–84, 288–93; of worker to supervisor, 280–2
Adolescent, attitudes of, 93–4
Adult, types of education for, 295–8
Adventure, urge for, 65–6
Affection, urge for, 64–5
Agencies, for recreation, 293–5
Agoraphobia, 190
Algophobia, 190
Ambivert, 21
American Association of Marriage Counselors, 258

American Social Hygiene Association, 221, 226, 258
Amnesia, 191, 193
Anastasi, A., 44, 47, 48
Anderson, J. E., 11, 12, 55, 56, 273
Anger, 115–17; sublimation of, 121–3
Anxiety states, 190–1
Aphasia, 193
Appetites, 56
Aptitude tests, 39–40
Armed Forces Qualification Test, 40
Army General Classification Tests (AGCT), 40, 272
Asher, E. J., 78, 79
Asthenic, 20
Astrology, 16
Attitudes: age levels and, 92–4; as directive forces, 98–9; and discipline, 106–7; effect of on us, 107–9; influence of unconscious, 94–5; toward life values, 99–103; mental qualities and, 91–2; nature of, 90–1; versus opinion, 97–8; personal emphasis, 90–9; physical constitution and, 92; projection of, 165–8; race, 107; in relation to conflict, 139–40; social emphasis in development of, 104–9; use of in emotions, 120–1; and values, 96–7; toward work, 102–3; of workers, 274–7
Athletic, 20
Attention-getting, devices of, 157–8; overemphasis upon, 158–60
Auterotism, 219–20
Autistic thinking, 77, 78–9

Behavior: arousal of emotional, 110–12; attention seeking, 157–60; compensatory, 155–7; criticism as form of, 160–2; daydreams and, 172–5; develop-

A NOTE ON THE TYPE

This book was set on the Linotype in Janson, a recutting made direct from the type cast from matrices made by Anton Janson some time between 1660 and 1687. Janson's original matrices were, at last report, in the possession of the Stempel foundry, Frankfurt am Main.

Of Janson's origin nothing is known. He may have been a relative of Justus Janson, a printer of Danish birth who practiced in Leipzig from 1614 to 1635. Some time between 1657 and 1668 Anton Janson, a punch-cutter and type-founder, bought from the Leipzig printer Johann Erich Hahn the type-foundry which had formerly been a part of the printing house of M. Friedrich Lankisch. Janson's types were first shown in a specimen sheet issued at Leipzig about 1675. Janson's successor, and perhaps his son-in-law, Johann Karl Edling, issued a specimen sheet of Janson types in 1689. His heirs sold the Janson matrices in Holland to Wolffgang Dietrich Erhardt, of Leipzig.

Composed, printed, and bound by The Plimpton Press, Norwood, Massachusetts. Paper manufactured by S. D. Warren Company, Boston, Massachusetts.